The
WHOLE
TRUTH
for Lawyers

The
WHOLE
TRUTH
for Lawyers

A Complete Guide to Flourishing in Your Life and Career

HON. STEPHEN PFAHLER

gatekeeper press

Columbus, Ohio

THE WHOLE TRUTH FOR LAWYERS

A Complete Guide to Flourishing in Your Life and Career

Published by **Gatekeeper Press**
2167 Stringtown Rd, Suite 109
Columbus, OH 43123-2989
www.GatekeeperPress.com

Library of Congress Control Number: 2022939883

ISBN (Hardcover): 9781662929496
ISBN (Paperback): 9781662928963
eISBN: 9781662928970

PRAISE FOR THE WHOLE TRUTHS FOR LAWYERS

"The Whole Truth for Lawyers provides a clear and comprehensive blueprint on how you can realize your full potential as a lawyer and a human being. We need more heroes in the legal profession, and this book will help you become one."

—BRIAN JOHNSON,
Creator of Optimize and Founder CEO of Heroic

"Judge Stephen Pfahler has written a book drawing on his deep experience as a lawyer and judge to offer a guide for flourishing professionally and personally. Judge Pfahler weaves together legal practice tips, philosophical reflection, psychology, and personal advice in a book that should find its way into the hands of every law student and lawyer seeking the good life."

—MICHAEL P. MORELAND,
University Professor of Law and Religion and Director, Eleanor H. McCullen Center for Law,
Religion and Public Policy, Villanova University Charles Widger School of Law

"Stephen's book is amazing and so inspiring. The strategies discussed in the book are applicable to anyone who wants to lead a meaningful, significant, and fulfilling life. It got me even further motivated to do and be my best every day. Thank you for sharing this wisdom."

—SYLVIA DSOUZA,
RAND Corporation, Executive Director of Development

"As a seasoned Judge, Stephen's wise and even funny insights will spark important epiphanies for lawyers at all stages of their career. Reading his book will undoubtedly increase your capacity for greater joy, success, and significance as a lawyer."

—MICHELLE HIEPLER,
Esq. Founding Partner, Law Offices of Hiepler & Hiepler

"Maya Angelou once said, 'I've learned that people will forget what you said, people will forget what you did, but people will never forget how you made them feel.' Stephen Pfahler has always had a gift that makes one feel seen, counted, and heard. In the thirty years I have known him, he has always been gracious to a fault, but that is not his superpower or what makes him and this book so special. It's that he operates with a gratefulness that can be felt whether an executive or a service worker. And despite his incredible success, he continues to strive to be better, do better, and bring others with him. This student of life is in the perfect position to become a teacher of others. Read and learn."

—SEAN JOELL JOHNSON,
Esq. Executive Director, Business Affairs, The Walt Disney Company'

"Super lawyer and Honorable Judge Stephen Pfahler weaves his mastery of law and life together to provide 'an education in real life.' His groundbreaking book is the perfect companion for every lawyer new and old to reach their full potential. Here is the 'whole truth' that makes for a complete happy, healthy, successful, and significant lawyer."

—KIM SHAPIRA, M.S., R.D.,
Author of This is What You're Really Hungry For, and Founder of Kim Shapira Method

"Judge Pfahler has written a book on thriving - not just surviving – that is essential for all law students and lawyers, and I look forward to sharing his wisdom with students for years to come."

—CHALAK RICHARDS,
Associate Dean, Student Life, Diversity, and Belonging,
Pepperdine University, Caruso School of Law

"Judge Pfahler lays out an extremely wise and practical approach for lawyers, law students, judges, and everyone else who wants to lead to a balanced and successful life — both personally and professionally."

—RICHARD LOPEZ,
Senior Counsel, Boeing Company

TABLE OF

CONTENTS

• • •

PART I: FLOURISH

Discover Your Ultimate Purpose

PART II: THE FOUNDATION FOR FLOURISHING

Build Your Life on a Solid Foundation

PART III: THE THREE PILLARS OF FLOURISHING

THE FIRST PILLAR—**Vision:** *Have Meaningful Goals*

THE SECOND PILLAR—**Action:** *Have a Process*

THE THIRD PILLAR—**Virtue:** *Have High Standards*

INTRODUCTION

• • •

THE DAY I FORGOT MY PANTS

I had been a lawyer for two years, working as a junior associate. Every day was identical: I was either buried in research or endlessly drafting tedious documents on my computer. My performance reviews were excellent, but at the same time, I felt stuck. I craved more responsibility. What I really wanted was to go to court. Then I got my wish.

A prominent partner in my firm called me into his office. "Steve, I want you to argue the motion to dismiss in the wrongful death case." *Finally.* I had lived with this case for a year and had written the motion to dismiss. Typically, however, the partners argued the case before the judge. Now, it was my turn. I was going to federal court.

I immediately went into full preparation mode for the hearing:

Review all relevant documents? *Check.*

Reread all key cases? *Check.*

Rehearse my main arguments? *Check.*

Repeat all the above? *Check.*

The night before the hearing, I worked late to get ready for court. I was home from work around 11:00 p.m. and in bed just before midnight. Best to be overly prepared. I woke at 4:45 a.m., my usual time, to go to the gym. I like a good workout in the morning, as it gets my endorphins going. I grabbed my suit and left for my thirty-minute commute to downtown Los Angeles.

I planned my morning to the minute and even gave myself some extra time just in case. My court appearance was at 8:30 a.m., so having finished my workout at 7:30 a.m.

meant that I was perfectly on schedule, especially with the court a mere five minutes from the gym.

At 7:45 a.m., I got out of the shower and started to get dressed. Then I realized—to my horror—that my pants were missing. *What?* I checked my gym bag and the locker again, frantically sweeping through their contents, but nothing. Could I have dropped the pants somewhere or left them in the car? I quickly put on the rest of my clothes and walked out of the gym as discretely as one possibly can while dressed in a coat, tie, and workout shorts.

The pants were not in my car. It was now 8:00 a.m., and I was in full panic mode. I couldn't go back home because I didn't have time. I tried to reach another lawyer in my firm, but no luck. I also didn't have the phone number for the court. (First practical tip: Always have the number of the court when you have an appearance.)

Although I was feeling lightheaded from stress, I quickly assessed my three options: First, I could miss the court appearance. Second, I could show up to court in my gym shorts, or third, I could throw a Hail Mary and try to find a clothing store that was open nearby.

The third option was my only realistic choice. The first would undoubtedly get me fired and the second would probably ruin my reputation for future jobs. I could just see the headline in the legal newspaper: "Lawyer who shows up to court without pants gets canned!"

I recalled that downtown Los Angeles has a garment district and prayed to myself as I drove around looking for anything open. Luckily, at about 8:15 a.m. I observed a man opening the doors to his store. I bolted into the store and asked the man to give me anything with a size 36 waist. He began to ask what color, style, and length I wanted, but before he could finish, I had already grabbed the first pair of pants in my size. I quickly pulled them on over my workout shorts and glimpsed at them in a mirror as I prepared to pay. Greenish-gray wool, they were hot, itchy, baggy, too long, and clashed with my red tie and Navy-blue coat. At least they covered me. I paid for them and sped off.

At 8:35 a.m., I parked my car in the courthouse parking lot and sprinted with briefcase in hand to the courthouse and up the escalator to the courtroom. Most civil courtrooms don't open their doors until a few minutes after 8:30 a.m., and thankfully, this court was no exception. It was 8:45 a.m. when I arrived. All the other lawyers had checked in for the morning calendar, and the judge had taken the bench. I was sweating profusely. I sat down and took a relaxing breath for the first time in an hour. I wasn't in my seat for thirty seconds before my case was called. I approached the counsel table with one hand on my briefcase and the other on my pants to make sure they didn't fall down.

After oral argument, the judge took the matter under submission and said he would issue a final decision next week. When I got back to my car, I almost passed out. Then, I started shaming myself in my own mind. *How could I have been so stupid as to forget to pack pants for one of the most important moments of my professional life?*

It was a life-altering experience. I had been spending way too many hours focused solely on my work and professional goals to realize that the rest of my life was out of whack. There was an underlying imbalance in my life. Things were so wonky, so heavily tipped toward professional perfectionism that I had forgotten an ordinary detail of daily living—pants—and had nearly bombed my career. I needed a new approach to life and law.

Fast forward some fifteen years to when I was sitting on the bench as a relatively new judge. I was presiding over a criminal prostitution trial with a defendant named Mi Suk. Yep, *Mi Suk;* I wouldn't make that up. During the trial, the defense lawyer was constantly late, unprepared, disheveled, and disorganized.

On the very day of trial, he was clueless as to how the court picked the jury and seemed very distracted. The next morning, his tardiness kept the jury waiting for close to twenty minutes. When he finally arrived, he explained that he couldn't call the court to let us know he was going to be late because he had no cellphone, having left his briefcase and phone in the court the previous day. On each day of the five-day trial, he made one misstep after another.

Although the lawyer provided "competent" legal representation to his client, he caused substantial delays, a great deal of unnecessary work for others, and considerable inconvenience. He seemed like a good guy, but he was a personal gaffe machine. He was hurting his case, his client, and himself through frustration, distraction, and wasted time. Outside the presence of the jury, he was regularly berating himself. He was a mess.

I specifically remember this situation sparking a flashback to my own transgression—forgetting my pants. Right then I wrote a note to myself on my yellow pad that read: "Which person is actually on trial—the defense lawyer, the defendant, or both?" The lawyer is the conduit for his or her client, so if the lawyer is out of sorts, the client will suffer, too. From that moment on I started paying closer attention to not only the parties but also the lawyers who were serving their clients, contemplating how I might help so many struggling lawyers.

I didn't know it at the time, but that was the genesis of the book you are now reading. I had a deep realization that I was put on this earth not just to become the best judge I can, but also to help lawyers and others reach their full potential personally and professionally.

It is well documented that many in the legal profession are living dysfunctional or dissatisfied lives. There is an alarming rate of depression, alcoholism, drug use, discontent, and burnout.[1] Approximately 50,000 students graduate from law school each year, so students are still flocking to law school. However, an incredible 78 percent of associates leave their first firm by their fifth year of practice.[2] There's an entire industry devoted to helping lawyers leave their jobs and finding new careers within a few years of graduating law school. "Law is the only career I know that has a sub-profession dedicated to helping people get out of it," says Liz Brown, author of *Life After Law*.

Some of this is endemic to modern society. We often fixate either on what we don't have (our lack) or what we want (our desires), which leads to dissatisfaction, discontentment, and envy. "We are the most in debt, obese, addicted, and medicated adult cohort in the U.S. history," says leading social scientist and author, Brené Brown.[3] Many individuals use food, drugs, alcohol, social media, shopping, and binge-watching to numb themselves from their maladjusted lives.

Lawyers are particularly susceptible to workaholism. This stems in part from the long hours, the nature of the adversary system, the cutthroat competition, the inflated and fragile egos, and the unwanted pressure from society, peers, and sometimes even parents.

I've met relatively few lawyers who will say they are genuinely fulfilled both professionally and personally. Fewer still who are truly thriving or living their best lives. I have concluded the legal field contains a vast wasteland of untapped potential. At the same time, I am more confident than ever that we are entering a new era where modern lawyers have vastly more opportunities to reach their highest potential for growth, happiness, and success. It is my hope that this book will help those in the legal field thrive both in and out of the courtroom, in a work-life balance that enables them to achieve the best for themselves and those they represent.

THE WHOLE TRUTH

For the past fifteen years, I have had the great honor of serving as a Los Angeles Superior Court Judge. Los Angeles is the largest court system in the country, if not the world. It's famously the same court system where O.J. Simpson was tried. Sitting on the bench, I'm essentially afforded box seats to life. People come into court from every walk of life, from the rich and famous to the downtrodden and disabled to everything in between. I see their ups and downs, triumphs and travails.

I have presided over several hundred trials. At trial, witnesses testify about the facts of the cases. Once the witness approaches the stand, the clerk asks them to raise his or her hand and then administers the oath: "Do you swear to tell the truth, the whole truth, and nothing but the truth, so help you God?"

Yes, many witnesses tell the whole truth. But unfortunately—and this will not come as a surprise—too many witnesses do not. Some relay partial truths but will not provide complete and full answers. Although they give testimony containing elements of truth, they withhold other key facts and details that would reveal the complete picture of it.

Likewise, I have found that most lawyers and others have not been provided the whole truth on what it means to be great in their career and live an extraordinary life. The information we are taught is often incomplete, inconsistent, or contradictory. We are merely provided bits and pieces here and there. We have been supplied with, at best, an incomplete education.

In law school, students are taught the law and how to think like a lawyer. But are we encouraged to consider how much law and life mirror each other? Both are governed by principles. In order to comply with the law, one must follow certain legal principles. Similarly, if one desires to live an optimal life, he or she must also live according to certain life principles. "Principles" are defined by author and entrepreneur Ray Dalio as "fundamental truths that serve as the foundations for behavior that gets you what you want out of life."[4] Without such principles, both society and a person's life would be in chaos.

French philosopher, Jean-Jacques Rousseau said that "man is born free but is everywhere in chains."[5] The point is that unrestrained freedom—freedom without rules or principles—leads to chaos and anarchy. Laws or principles actually *increase* our liberty and security. No society can properly function without laws. Likewise, no individual can fully function or reach their full potential without following certain life principles.

These principles benefit everyone. There is a famous legal maxim that says, "Ignorance of the law is no excuse." Whether you know the law or not, it still applies. The same is true for the principles of a good life. Whether we know or use them, they still apply to our lives. By choosing to live your life by these principles, you will experience greater satisfaction and fulfillment.

Importantly, there is no one single principle, no one magic bullet that ensures you'll live the good life. As we'll explore together in this book, there are several principles, or elements, necessary for humans to live well and thrive. However, if one or more of those essential principles or elements is missing in your life, you will be hard-pressed to reach your full potential. You will not be living the whole truth of what it means to flourish. To use one example, if you are having success at work, but your relationships with your family are failing, you are not thriving. Or, if you have meaningful relationships but your work life is meaningless or distressful, you will have a hard time flourishing. As Mahatma Gandhi wisely said: "One man cannot do right on one department of life whilst he is occupied in doing wrong in any other department. Life is one indivisible whole."[6]

EXAMINING THE WHOLE TRUTH:
My Approach to Writing this Book

As a judge, I make decisions based on evidence and the law. I might face a legal decision of whether somebody engaged in sexual harassment, breached a contract, or was responsible for a deadly car accident. When presented with such an important decision, I thoroughly research the law, hear from experts, and diligently review all the evidence.

I have approached writing this book in the same way I handle cases. I have thoroughly reviewed the evidence gifted to us from experts—classical to contemporary—to uncover and compile the whole truth of what it takes to thrive and live our best lives. I've synthesized all this information and distilled it into essential life principles—each of which I have lived, fallen short of, and grown with. I haven't written about anything I haven't practiced and strive daily to embody these principles in my own life. By my experience, I have validated that these principles work.

Fortunately, I had a head start, having had a deep interest in personal development for most of my life. My mother first exposed me to "success" literature when I was in my late teens. I started out reading the classics, such as Dale Carnegie's *How to Win Friends and Influence People* and Zig Ziglar's *See You at the Top*. These works taught me the importance of genuine interactions and a positive attitude. I was hooked.

Since then, I have read, studied, applied, and practiced the great wisdom literature along with the writing of current and cutting-edge thinkers.

I also formalized my study by becoming a certified life coach through an extraordinary program called Optimize, during which I learned from the program's head coach, Brian Johnson. A true kindred spirit, Brian also takes a very holistic approach to the good life. My formal study and practice of serving as a life coach has allowed me to teach and help others implement these life principles to great success. My studies and experience have revealed a beautiful alchemy, letting me see the big picture of what is essential to flourishing. I've been able to discern and test, not judge, the elusive truth.

In short, for over thirty years, I have been committed to intentionally and systematically studying, learning, and investigating the essential aspects of how to thrive in my personal and work life. All this knowledge has validated the critical import of living life according to the whole truth. This lengthy journey has led me to not only see the practice of law but also the practice of life from an interdisciplinary and holistic approach. I have realized that our life's journey can best be understood from a deeper understanding of how all things work together.

Everything in life is connected. Unfortunately, in my research, I've found no book to convey the "whole truth" about how to flourish in law and life—only ones that encompass a specific aspect of living, such as positive thinking or sleep or work. We have only been offered an obstructed view, not the full picture. No complete manual, only excerpts. This book fills the critical gap as it takes an evidence-based, interdisciplinary approach, including psychology, philosophy, neuroscience, biology, nutrition science, time management, financial planning, practice management, and more. In this book, I will not only explore my own experience but also show how to apply the practical gifts given to us by the great experts of past and present. I have drawn from the best wisdom on the planet—what has honestly worked for me and others—and my own lived experience to now present you with a holistic, tested roadmap to life. Use it to realize your full potential, to suffer less, and to flourish more.

ABOUT THIS BOOK: MY DREAM CLASS

I teach a college class called Public Policy and the Law at the University of Southern California. When I intersperse the content of the class with life lessons, the students really perk up. After class or during office hours, they are most interested in talking to me about life and their goals, aspirations, and challenges. It is clear there is a tremendous need for an education in real life.

Likewise, as a judge, I have had the great privilege of talking with hundreds of lawyers about the law, their legal practice, and their lives. We often talk about the latest trends or changes in the law, but they are more eager to talk about their lives, their goals, and their challenges than about anything on the docket that day.

Whether law students or lawyers, there exists a greater need than ever to learn how to live flourishing lives. Increasingly, I am asked by students, lawyers, and others for advice on various aspects of life. In response, this book is in essence my dream class.

Law students can benefit tremendously from such an education, so they can begin to form good habits early. At the same time, I picture a bar where lawyers are educated to better understand how their life matters, how to live a good, virtuous life, and how to deal with emotions and adversity as well as greed and success.

Sound interesting? Welcome to class.

Each chapter of this book is a single session of my dream class: It covers a particular principle or truth and shows how that truth interrelates to the others. These truths are timeless. They do not change over time. Now and later, they will serve as a bedrock for withstanding the difficulties of your own circumstances. They apply to your career and relationships. In short, my "class" will teach you how to truly thrive personally and professionally.

Again, this book is based on what ancient wisdom and modern science say about living a good life. Multiple studies have shown that students and adults who desire to thrive in their lives need to develop in the following ways:

1. Having a clear purpose,
2. Accepting personal responsibility,
3. Handling problems and managing emotions,
4. Being physically healthy,
5. Achieving competence in work,

6. Nurturing meaningful relationships,
7. Finding balance and renewal, and
8. Developing character.

At the same time, the principles herewith can and should be personalized to you and every individual. Everyone comes from different life circumstances. While the principles for thriving in life are well-established, they do not mandate a strict formula. Rather, they provide guidance and permit individuality. For instance, all people will benefit from some form of physical exercise, but the type of exercise is up to the individual and can vary widely, depending on one's own interests, health, environment, and so on. In other words, these principles are universally applicable but should be uniquely applied. Our lives can be principled yet personalized.

This class is also intended to be transformative, not additive. The goal is not to add more to your already full glass. To the contrary, it is to change what you put into the glass. Inner transformation always precedes outward success. My desire is to disrupt your status quo.

The stakes are high in this book. Law students, lawyers, judges, and others need and deserve the whole truth about living the good life while being great in their profession. I'm confident that this complete guide, if practiced consistently over time, will illuminate a holistic and enduring way of life. A way that will radically transform the path to becoming a flourishing lawyer.

I don't know about you, but I didn't get the memo on how to live a good life while practicing law. Nor was I ever made aware of any class that taught it. This book is that class. Not law school, but life school—a whole and complete philosophy for living well.

Let's now move to our first principle related to thriving, but before we do, let me caution you as any good lawyer would:

....

DISCLAIMER: What you are about to read, if properly applied, will profoundly change your life for the better. The change will be palpable. Both you and others around you will see the difference. You will find that you are significantly healthier, happier, and more successful in your life, work, and relationships. You have been forewarned!

....

1
PART ONE

FLOURISH

Discover Your Ultimate Purpose

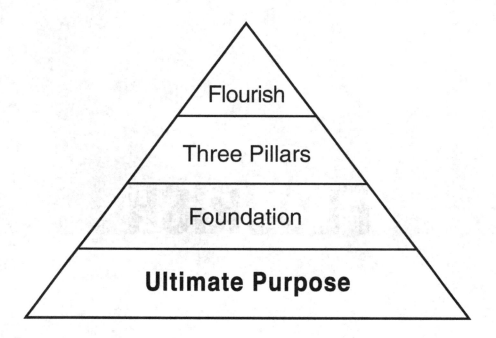

CHAPTER 1

THE ULTIMATE OBJECTIVE OF LIFE

• • •

*"The two most important days
in your life are the day you were born
and the day you discover why."*

— MARK TWAIN

For those new to the legal system, the first step toward understanding a trial is to know its purpose. You might ask yourself, "What is the objective? Why am I in court?" Seems simple enough, but these are such important and fundamental questions.

Briefly, the United States, like most civilized countries, has an established legal system. It is widely agreed that the object of our legal system is justice. In the U.S. Constitution, the Preamble lists that its first purpose is to "establish Justice." One of the founding fathers, Alexander Hamilton, echoed this purpose: "Justice is the end [goal] of government. It is the end [goal] of civil society. It ever has been and ever will be pursued until it be obtained, …."[1] Likewise, Alex de Tocqueville said in his famous book *Democracy in America*: "There is one universal law that has been formed, or at least adopted by the majority of mankind. That law is justice. Justice forms the cornerstone of each nation's law."[2]

As judges, we take an oath to follow the law as a "goal meant to serve justice."[3] Trials are designed to seek justice. At the end of trials, people desire to see that justice was done. If a trial were a game, the object would be justice.

Just like the legal system, as human beings, we also have an objective, or purpose, in the game of life. So, what is our ultimate purpose? Knowing this provides life-changing benefits. First and foremost, it gives meaning to our life. It allows us to each answer the question, "Why am I here?" In his book, *Start with Why*, Simon Sinek says that the first and most important question we ask is, "Why? Why do we exist? Why do we do anything?"[4]

Many people never seek to discover their purpose or meaning. They don't ask why. They just get by or worse, live lives of quiet desperation. Oh God, to have come to the end of your life, and not have lived.

We start with "Why?" because it empowers, inspires, and drives our actions. The answer to "Why?" provides the center of our being from which all other behaviors emanate. Do not worry or shame yourself if you have not found your answer yet. We will work on this throughout the book.

Knowing your purpose clarifies and simplifies your life. It guides the direction you take and the quality of the decisions you make. You will find yourself doing less, not more, when you're focused on what is most important. You will say "no" to things that are not consistent with your purpose.

Understanding your purpose instills great motivation for life. The author Ralph Marston said that greatness comes from living with purpose and passion. When you tap into your purpose, you have better energy and zest. You are ready to go and feel greater drive and passion.

Throughout law school, I learned the IRAC method, which has followed me through my legal career. IRAC, as most law students know, is an acronym for: Issue, Rule, Application, and Conclusion. Even today, I find the IRAC process to be alive and well for effective legal analysis, and lawyers can persuasively present their case using this format.

Interestingly, the IRAC method provides an equally excellent framework for analyzing our life and the ideas in this book. So, what is the Issue here? To identify your ultimate purpose. For those legal professionals who are familiar with this method, the Issue will become clear as you follow along. Even if you aren't familiar with this method, it should become simple for you to see that the Issue is the question of, "What is my ultimate purpose in life?" Just don't mistake *simple* for easy.

HOW IS THIS RELEVANT TO YOU?

When discussing life's big questions or critical issues, such as knowing your ultimate purpose or the meaning of life, some people find the topic too abstract or general to be useful. But let me be clear, knowing your ultimate purpose is particularly important. One of the ways I will encourage you to consider why it's so important is by using a hypothetical trial throughout this book. This hypothetical can serve as a tool to help you imagine your potential and transform your life for the better.

The hypothetical takes place in my courtroom on a regular Monday morning. The courtroom doors are open, and the parties are checked in.

"All rise!"

As I enter the courtroom, the bailiff states, "Come to order. In the presence of the flag of the United States of America, emblem of the Constitution, and of freedom and justice for all, the Superior Court is now in session. The Honorable Judge Stephen Pfahler presiding. You may be seated."

Like I have for the past fifteen years, I greet the audience with my standard, "Good morning" and proceed to call the cases on my docket, only today there is but one case on the docket. This time the courtroom looks different. There are just two parties sitting in the audience. Both of them are you. That's right, you are both the plaintiff and the defendant.

The plaintiff in this civil case is the aspirational version of you. It's you at your ideal best, perhaps even more ideal than you've imagined possible for yourself. The defendant is you right now, as you are reading this book, at this very place along your life's journey.

Simply imagine you are the lawyer representing yourself as the defendant in this lawsuit. (Yes, I am fully aware a person who represents himself or herself typically has a fool for a client, but for this exercise we'll make an exception.)

I call your case. The two versions of you walk up to the counsel table in front of the court. The defendant (current you) glances over at the plaintiff (optimal you), noticing something very distinct about them. Yes, the defendant is well-dressed, well-coiffed, and ready to make a good impression. Still, you notice a difference. Upon further reflection, what you see is startling. The plaintiff—the optimal you—is lively, radiant, full of energy, physically fit, healthy, confident, calm, and a dynamic lawyer. The defendant? We'll get to that.

In this case, the plaintiff is suing and seeking damages against the defendant for the losses suffered in health, happiness, career, and relationships. The difference between the life balance and fulfilment of your ideal and current selves is the damage. The discrepancy between who you currently are and who you could become is why we are in this court today.

I turn to the plaintiff and invite you to be heard. Prepared and eloquent, you stand and address the court: "Your Honor, for thousands of years, the great thinkers have consistently taught that the most important question one can ask is, 'What is my ultimate purpose in life?'"

Yes, that is the Issue.

FLOURISHING: THE UNIVERSAL PURPOSE OF LIFE

Fortunately, the question regarding the supreme purpose in life has been contemplated, studied, and researched for several thousand years.

Take Aristotle, one of the greatest and most prolific philosophers ever. He was born almost 2,500 years ago in 384 BC. He moved to Athens at the age of seventeen and studied under Plato at his Academy for about twenty years. He served as the tutor for Alexander the Great and founded his own school called the Lyceum. His influence on Western civilization has arguably never been surpassed.

In Aristotle's best-known book, the *Nicomachean Ethics* (named after the philosopher's son), he dives deeply into the question about life's purpose. He asks what is the chief or highest good in life? This is called the *summum bonum*, Latin for the "highest good."

In a vintage Aristotle passage, he says the highest good "must be... something that in itself is completely satisfying." He continues, "Everywhere we see people seeking pleasure, wealth, and a good reputation" and while "each of these has some value," none of these "can occupy the place of the chief good for which humanity should aim." Aristotle declares: "To be an ultimate end, an act must be self-sufficient and final, that which is always desirable in itself and never for the sake of something else."[5]

After analyzing all the possible objectives in life—such as pleasure, power, wealth, sex, fame, and so on—Aristotle comes to the well-supported conclusion that the highest good or the chief good in life is "happiness." We want money because it makes us happy; we want sex because it makes us happy; we want our family because it makes us happy, and so on.

When considering "happiness" as the highest good, it's worth closely examining the word's meaning. Importantly, the actual Greek word Aristotle used for happiness is *eudaimonia* (pronounced "you-de-moan-ee-ah"). It is commonly translated into English as "happiness," but I believe that perhaps a more accurate reading of the word *eudaimonia* is "flourishing."

To me, "happiness" isn't the best translation of the word eudaimonia (flourishing) because it (happiness) is commonly understood as an emotion or subjective state of mind. If I'm feeling good, I'm happy. If I'm kicking back with the latest TV show, I'm happy. But if I'm not having fun or enjoying myself, then I'm unhappy. Easily achieved, easily lost. The chief good can't be so fleeting as emotion.

Yes, positive emotions and pleasures are certainly good and important. But many pleasurable things are bad for us. We might have a positive emotion from an experience like eating lots of ice cream, but it certainly doesn't lead to flourishing. Or, what if somebody cheats on their taxes or steals from a client by overbilling on a task that makes them money? Maybe they're happy about the extra money they received. That person may find this pleasure-inducing, but is that really the standard they should use for living their best life?

Moreover, happiness is also tied to external circumstances. Indeed, the etymology of the word *happy* is "lucky" or "chance."[6] It means good fortune based on happenstance or circumstance. Do you want your happiness in life to be tied to your luck? To be subject to life's ups and downs?

The reason you see "happy" everywhere is because it sounds good, and who doesn't want to be happy? Happiness sells books and movies. It graces song titles like Bobby Mc-Ferrin's "Don't Worry, Be Happy" or Pharrell Williams's "Happy." The classic storybook ending is, "They lived happily ever after."

It's critical to understand that this modern emotion-centric or externally driven concept of happiness is vastly different from what Aristotle meant by "eudaimonia." Flourishing is not solely a personality disposition or an emotional feeling; it's a much more holistic concept.

Aristotle's conception of flourishing has been followed all the way to modern times. In the 1950s, famed psychologist Abraham Maslow examined this identical question about the highest good for humans, and he found the same as Aristotle. According to Maslow, our objective is to realize our true and fullest potential in service to something bigger than ourselves.

In *Motivation and Personality*, Maslow writes: "Musicians must make music, artists must paint, poets must write if they are to be ultimately at peace with themselves. What human beings can be, they must be ... to become everything one is capable of becoming."[7]

In our legal careers we experience flourishing by becoming the best lawyers we can be. Likewise, we do the same in other important aspects of our lives. If we are a parent, for example, then we want to become the best mom or dad we can be. That's what Maslow meant by saying what we can be, we must be. Striving to reach our full potential in order to love and serve others.

Spring ahead another fifty years to the early 2000s, when renowned psychologist Martin Seligman pioneered a revolution called "positive psychology." The goal of positive psychology is "exploring what makes life worth living ..."[8] Seligman originally postulated the highest good was happiness. Then, he argued that "happiness" is the ultimate aim in life. However, about a decade later, after thorough research, Seligman concluded "happiness" was not quite the right concept because it is too closely tied to pleasure and positive emotions. So, he revised his finding in his new book *Flourish,* in which he declares that "the gold standard for measuring well-being is flourishing."[9]

Following the lineage from Aristotle to Maslow to Seligman shows how each concluded that our highest aim—our ultimate purpose—is to *flourish*. You see, ancient philosophy has been empirically verified by modern science to help you become the best possible version of yourself!

This is the ultimate question in your life, the big Issue in your hypothetical case. Have you lived up to your full potential? Are you genuinely flourishing in your life? If not, what are the consequences of not flourishing?

Because the concept of flourishing as the ultimate purpose is so fundamental to the plaintiff's case (and to your life), I encourage you to really take your time to make sure it is fully ingrained in your heart and mind. You might reread this section, or, if you are so inclined, put the book down and take a walk alone—without your smartphone or other inputs—and ruminate on this idea—you are meant to flourish.

FLOURISHING IS GROUNDED IN REALITY

What I find particularly significant about flourishing is that life has meaning under any circumstance. Whereas positive emotions are a necessary condition for happiness, that is not true with Aristotelian flourishing.

Dr. Viktor Frankl, a survivor of the Nazi concentration camps, said in his transformative book *Man's Search for Meaning*: "Life holds potential meaning under any conditions, even the most miserable ones."[10] Dr. Frankl observed that the prisoners who lost their "inner hold" on meaning were the ones who failed to survive. But those who were anchored in a solid purpose survived, even if they didn't experience positive emotions.

In fact, study after study shows that those who have endured the most incredible difficulties in life have all had a strong purpose. Flourishing is realizing your own individual potential amidst your current reality. It's making the most of your life with what you have.

In *Life Without Limits*, Nick Vujicic describes how he was born without arms or legs. His family raised him as well as possible but growing up without limbs is unimaginably difficult. As a teenager, he struggled physically and was severely depressed and lonely. He tried to commit suicide. The turning point came when Nick found his purpose. This purpose inspired him to eventually become a pastor and a speaker. He founded and is the president of Life Without Limbs. He has spoken to over a million people, giving inspiration and a sense of purpose. He is also a musician, actor, and author, and he loves to fish, paint, and swim. He is married and has a family.[11] Nick is flourishing in every sense of the word.

Having your ultimate purpose as flourishing will stay with you throughout your entire life, even up to death. When a close family member was stricken with a terminal disease, she had a decision to make about how to respond. She chose to do the very best she could, given her circumstances. She still had a purpose, whether to handle the matter with dignity and courage or not. Suffering in all our lives is unavoidable—indeed, we will all die—but you can find purpose even on your deathbed. Dying with dignity is flourishing.

THE DEFENSE CASE

Let's return to our hypothetical case. It's the defendant's turn. You walk up to the podium, clear your throat, and quickly think how you will address the court. Before you do, I ask you to consider the following: Do you believe you are currently living your optimal life? Are you realizing your full potential—not just as a lawyer but as a human? In other words, are you flourishing? Take a moment or two now and close your eyes and think about what you would say.

In this hypothetical, your answer to each of the above questions is "No," and so you, the defendant, begin your defense.

"Your Honor, I am representing myself as the defendant in this case. Sure, I understand the plaintiff thinks he or she has been damaged because I have allegedly not yet achieved my full potential. Plaintiff asserts I am not flourishing."

The defendant turns to the plaintiff and states in a somewhat indignant manner, "How does the plaintiff know that I'm not living to my full potential? I believe I am living my optimal life."

The defendant then looks back at the court and matter-of-factly says, "My life is just great. I have a decent job making a respectable salary, pretty good relationships, and I work out when I have time." As the judge, I think to myself: *You say your life is "great," but your descriptions of "decent," "pretty good," and "when I have time" suggest mediocrity. Also, I hear what you are saying, but the tone of your voice and your body language say otherwise. Plus, having reviewed your case, this is not the whole truth. I also know because I've been where you are.*

Now, the defendant dives into more detail. You begin, "Your Honor, allow my story to refute the plaintiff's argument. I am a partner in a prestigious law firm because I have made the right moves in my career. I've billed a tremendous number of hours, including many twelve-hour days and weekends. When I'm not working, I'm networking, marketing, speaking, or writing. I sit on several boards and was the president of the Bar Association. I have a good reputation in the legal community and have made a name for myself.

"As a fairly new partner, I'm really committed to building my book of business. I've been doubling down on my legal expertise, keeping my cases and career at the forefront of my thoughts."

As I'm listening, I wonder whether the defendant's work is no longer an occupation but a preoccupation.

The defendant continues, "I have a supportive spouse who takes care of our two great kids and our home. Of course, I would love more time to enjoy with my family. Who wouldn't?"

"I love my family. It isn't ever my intention to be disconnected. Right now, I'm making a great future for us. I think I'm giving them everything they want! Everything I never had as a kid. A great home, private schooling, financial security, and the ability to travel, eat at nice restaurants, and have the finer things. Yes, I miss a fair number of the kids' games, recitals, and times just hanging out, but they're growing up, and what kids their age really want to play with their parents?"

"When it comes to my health, I'm healthy enough for now. I admit I could do with a little more exercise and a little less takeout. I might be a few pounds overweight. But I'm not that old, and I'm going to focus on my health for sure once things quiet down."

"I have one of the biggest trials of my career coming up and know I will never be outworked by my adversary. Certainly, things will become calmer after that four-week trial. If I prevail at trial, it could mean a multi-million-dollar verdict for the firm, and my reputation will really be cemented. A trial victory would also be huge for my family and me financially, and that will mean I can spend a lot more time with them."

"Currently, I have never been busier. On top of my caseload, the managing partner asked me to head up the firm's overhaul of IT. I have so many ideas on how to revamp our firm's technology to be cutting edge and am especially keen on technological advances that would allow lawyers to be connected to all our cases twenty-four hours a day. The future looks bright, and my family and I will soon be reaping the benefits of the sacrifices being made right now. Our lives will be set and secure."

"Yep, that's who I am. I have everything I always wanted right in front of me. I can almost touch it. I'm a happy and a successful lawyer. Nothing further, Your Honor. The defense rests."

As you walk back to counsel table to take your seat, you feel in the pit of your stomach that something was missing in the perfect tale you just presented. Yes, you stated your case, but it felt so empty. You wonder, *Do I really have everything I wanted in my life? I mean, does anybody even really knows me? I have devoted the last twenty years of my life almost exclusively to doing one thing: to become a great lawyer.* But then you snap out of it; you have work to do.

THE VERDICT

Let me offer you a break from playing our defendant in this case while I take the matter under submission to deliberate on the evidence. As a judge, I consider all the facts carefully. As it happens, I have been studying the topic of the ultimate purpose in life for a very long time.

To look closely at the life as described above, virtually nobody would say this hypothetical defendant is thriving. While the defendant has professional success, everything else is middling to poor, or even failing. His or her low priority of health objectively raises the risk for a heart attack. And, although the defendant did not intentionally plan to neglect his or her spouse and kids to pursue career success at all costs, he or she is simply too busy to notice.

Yes, the defendant is dedicated, but to the wrong ultimate aim. They are playing the wrong game with the wrong priorities—material success, reputation, and control. It's important to understand that these things are not bad. They are not. To the contrary, success is good. Making money and pursuing achievement are essential parts of living a flourishing life. But if material success is your highest good, well, then, Houston, we have a problem.

We are all committed to or driven by something. The question is, to whom or to what? We are all willing to pay the price for something, whether it's pleasure, peace, love, success, happiness, or God. Where does your own heart lie?

While we may enjoy food, if it becomes our obsession, we end up overweight or unhealthy. If pleasure is our ultimate goal, we typically end up addicted to that pleasure and craving more. People whose endgame is money often find themselves as workaholics, burned out, and never satisfied.

Based on the totality of the evidence in this case and the well-established principle that flourishing is the highest good, I find in favor of the plaintiff and against the defendant. Notice I did not say succeeding is the highest good but *flourishing*. At first blush and from society's perspective, the defendant may seem to have it all. He or she is hardworking, perhaps a workaholic, and financially successful, with a good work reputation. But it is equally clear he or she is not living a flourishing life. That life is built on a castle made of sand. As Jiddu Krishnamurti said, "It is no measure of health to be well adjusted to a profoundly sick society."

Since this trial is hypothetical, I award no monetary damages—that's not what's on the line here. Instead, I order the defendant (and invite you) to really learn and apply the principles in this book, starting with knowing your purpose. In the coming chapters, I will discuss tried-and-true methods for thriving in all aspects of your life. I make this promise to you: If you spend the time truly mastering the concepts in this book, you will progressively become the best version of yourself as well as better able to love and serve others along the way. Isn't that what life is all about?

....

Chapter Summary:

- What is the ultimate "Issue" in life?
- The most important question is: What is the highest good?
- The answer to that question is flourishing, which is our universal purpose.
- Our highest aim in life and the object of the game we are playing is flourishing.

SIDEBAR _____

A sidebar is an area in the courtroom next to the judge's bench where the lawyers may be asked to speak to the judge outside the jurors' presence. At the end of each chapter, I will offer a key sidebar tip of what I believe is the most practical wisdom to help lawyers succeed in their practice. My tips come from observing countless hours of lawyers in court during thousands of court hearings and hundreds of trials.

So, here is my first sidebar tip: Use sidebars sparingly and appropriately. Only ask the judge for a sidebar when it is a true emergency that can't wait for a break. Remember, sidebars interrupt the flow of trial and waste the jurors' time. If it's a true emergency, always make a formal request by asking, "Your Honor, may we please approach the bench?" Then, wait for the judge to grant your request before approaching.

CHAPTER 2

THE RULES FOR ACHIEVING YOUR ULTIMATE PURPOSE

• • •

"You have to learn the rules of the game."
—ALBERT EINSTEIN

person who does not have a lawyer in a lawsuit but instead represents him or herself is called a *"pro per."* That term is short for "in propria persona," which basically means "for one's own person." One of the biggest challenges facing an individual appearing *"pro per"* is that he or she often doesn't understand the law or the procedures. They don't understand how the legal system works. In short, they don't understand the rules.

While judges work hard to ensure access to justice for all parties, self-represented litigants often find themselves at a disadvantage. Indeed, I have found that *pro per* litigants struggle mightily with preparing proper legal documents, meeting procedural requirements, following deadlines, and explaining their case to the judge.

In contrast, lawyers spend three years in law school immersing themselves in the language, the law, and the justice system. After graduation, they embark on a career where they expand their knowledge and learn the skills necessary to succeed. In brief, lawyers know the rules to effectively practice their profession.

Let's again turn to the IRAC method. The Issue—the answer to the question, "What is the ultimate purpose in life?"—is *flourishing*. Now, let's look at the "R"—the Rules—for achieving that ultimate purpose.

EVERY GAME HAS RULES

Professor Bernard Suits wrote an article in 1967 called, "Is Life a Game We Are Playing?"[1] Suits asserted that life is indeed like a game. He generally defined a game as an activity designed toward some objective and which follows some type of rules. Dictionaries similarly define a "game" as engaging in an activity typically involving a challenge or contest toward some goal, which has a set of rules for the game.

As the definitions above provide, there are two parts to every game. One is knowing the object; the second is knowing the rules.

In Chapter 1, we identified the object, or purpose, of that game as "flourishing." It's not a board game, a sport, or whatever your game of choice is. No, the ultimate game, the most important one you'll ever play, is about how to live your life to its fullest, how to give yourself wholly to others, and how to leave the world better than you found it.

Some of the "games" we play, such as law school, a trial, or a sports contest, have a distinct ending. Most games, however, are "infinite games," because there is often no endpoint. In marriage, friendship, and health, for example, there is no specified finish line. There may be a marital ideal or health goal but no clear-cut conclusion. The same is true for life: We are always playing until the final act, death.

Notwithstanding the serious nature of life at times, I think viewing life as a game is both a playful and helpful metaphor. Most of us, however, don't realize we are playing a game or that there are rules to follow. Rather, we haphazardly go through life and make up our own rules.

As there are for all other games, there are rules to flourishing. For our purposes, the terms "rules" and "principles" will be used interchangeably. Both are meant to convey a basic truth or guideline for our conduct. Principles are often defined as "rules of conduct." And rules are commonly defined as "principles governing conduct." So, they are essentially synonymous.

I find it utterly fascinating we spend so much time learning the rules of law as a lawyer but virtually no time learning the rules to live a successful life. We haven't properly educated ourselves on the rules for thriving in our physical health, mental well-being, relationships, or time management or how they work together to create one holistic and flourishing life.

If you want to learn a hobby such as playing music, you undoubtedly study and practice your instrument. If you want to master becoming a gourmet cook or auto mechanic, you acquire the required knowledge and skills through studying, attending classes, and practicing. You don't become a skilled surgeon, an exceptional trial lawyer, or a professional athlete without study and deliberate work.

Shouldn't it therefore be evident that if you want to have a flourishing life, you should also put time and effort into studying and practicing its essential principles? Yes, study life like you're learning the law or mastering a musical instrument and then practice what you've learned.

There is little chance you will realize your best life by random chance. A great life is not just going to happen. Rather, a flourishing life requires specific knowledge and deliberate effort. The process of learning to live a good life can be divided into two parts: The first is mastering the rules, and the second is mastering the practice. This is the approach we will take through this book, first exploring knowledge (or principles) and then application (or practice).

THE RULES DERIVE FROM THE THREE PILLARS OF FLOURISHING

In a trial, every case has a unique set of facts. The facts are as varied as life itself. The case could involve a crime, a business dispute, a car accident, or a family matter. The diversity of cases is truly endless.

However, the decision-making process is always the same. The objective is justice. The court instructs the jury on the law, and the jury takes the facts that it found, and applies them to the law and comes up with a decision. This is how the justice system works.

In this process, the judge or jury may not make up the law. Rather, they must obey the law based on the United States Constitution, statutes, or case law. In other words, the rules of law serve as the foundation of our justice system.

Using the game metaphor for the legal system, the rules of the game are the laws. The laws not only provide the rules for a fair process but also rules for the specific case itself, such as the elements for a crime. But no doubt there are rules. As John Adams famously said, our system is based on "a government of laws, not of men."

The same is true for life. Having now firmly established that our universal purpose is to flourish, what are the principles or rules for achieving that objective? Both classical and contemporary wisdom have bestowed us with great guidance for determining the rules to achieving a flourishing life.

The place to start for learning the rules is by examining the word *flourishing*. In the most general sense, flourishing is defined as "thriving and having vigorous and healthy growth."

I find it helpful to think of flourishing through a botanical metaphor. A plant that is flourishing is healthy, radiantly alive, and giving back to the world, whether by providing food, shade, beauty, or carbon sequestration.[2] In contrast, a plant that is not flourishing is floundering, struggling, weak, unhealthy, or retreating.

Flourishing is also closely related to another ancient Greek concept of life force or soul force which was called *entelechy*. It's what brings a seed to a fully blossoming plant. It essentially means moving from one's actual self to one's full potential. We all possess this life force as living beings to grow and become the best versions of ourselves. It is fulfilling what is the highest and best of our potential.

Flourishing means living "within an optimal range of human functioning."[3] It includes experiencing positive emotions, positive contribution, and positive relationships. Almost all wisdom traditions have found that the ultimate purpose is for humans to realize our full potential in order to give back in some constructive way.

More specifically, Aristotle provided a distinctive and instructive definition for flourishing. He said eudaimonia (flourishing) is "an activity of the soul in accordance with virtue."[4] I find it helpful to break this definition down into its three essential elements: Flourishing is an "activity" of the "soul" "in accordance with virtue." These three elements have inspired what I call the Three Pillars of Flourishing, which are Vision, Action, and Virtue.

Notice that the Pillars I've identified, based on Aristotle's definition, have been renamed and rearranged in a logical order. Here's why: I believe we should first start with our life targets. Thus, the first Pillar of Flourishing is to have meaningful goals—*Vision*. Our goals are what we want life to look like, what we pursue. I call these goals "soul goals," to honor Aristotle, as the word *daimon* in "eudaimonia" means "soul." We want to pursue noble, worthwhile, soul goals that are deeply personal to us. Our priorities, our destinations. We pick what mountains we want to climb. Our goals are *where* we want to go with our lives. Our goals make up the Vision Pillar.

After we have set our goals, we then want to act toward them. So, the second Pillar of Flourishing is Action. To flourish is not merely based in thought or emotion, like feeling happy, but it also encompasses physical activity. *Flourish* is meant to be a verb— to act, to love, to work, to serve, to care, to help, to pursue, and so on. It's what we do.

Finally, the third Pillar is Virtue. We should act with virtue and character, hold ourselves to high standards, and strive for excellence, not mediocrity. The Greeks had a great word for this—*arête*—which essentially means expressing the best version of ourselves in each moment. It's how we do things.

The concept of the Three Pillars of Flourishing—Vision, Action, and Virtue—is the magic formula for optimizing your life. It's the Flourishing Formula. All the rules in this book will flow from the Three Pillars. But, in short, flourishing is *goals pursued virtuously.*[5]

The beauty of the Three Pillars is they can be implemented uniquely to each person. Like the countless varieties of plants in our botanical metaphor, where each will have its own unique combination of sun, soil, and water to flourish, you, too, can choose your own unique application of the Pillars. What's good for a cactus plant is not the same for a giant sequoia tree. The same is undoubtedly true for each of us. The Three Pillars provide both guidance and adaptability. To paraphrase author Dr. Jordan Peterson, the beauty of rules in our lives is that it allows us to strike a balance between order and freedom. We will each uniquely determine our goals, our actions, and our virtues.

I liken the principles and rules in this book to the law. Yes, the law provides us guidance. But as any law student and lawyer knows, the laws are both pliable and dynamic. The laws are designed to be flexible to apply to the countless variety of situations. Just think of the "reasonable person" standard in torts. Also, the laws are subject to change— sometimes radically—to allow for progress and new circumstances.

I encourage you to learn, memorize, and practice the Three Pillars along with their related principles. They are designed to always be available to you whenever you need them. The ancients said to keep your rules or tools ready at hand.[6] Students throughout the ages wrote them down, repeated them, and kept them close, as if they were wearing a toolbelt. Humans are forgetful, so we need to meditate on and consistently repeat the rules until they become deeply embedded.

THE RULES PROVIDE A TARGET FOR OUR ACTIONS

When I was a young boy, I loved the game Risk. It's a board game where you try to capture all the world's territories. Some of my neighbor friends introduced the game to me, and they were ruthless. Not in a mean-spirited way; they just knew how to play the game better. They beat me every time.

Then, one day my cousin, who also loved the game, came over and explained how to play properly. We played several times, and I learned the rules. It was a lightbulb moment. The next time I played my friends, I almost beat them. Soon enough, victory was mine.

The advantage of knowing the rules or principles of how to do anything seems obvious. It guides us in our actions. If we want to flourish in our lives, it makes common sense that we should have a target for our behaviors. That's what the rules do. They provide optimal standards for our behavior. How else would we know how to act? The rules provide specific guidance for our actions.

Each rule or principle in this book is designed to move you toward the ultimate objective of flourishing (the Issue). The principles point us in the direction of flourishing. They do this by serving as the bridge for our actions. They are the link between our actions and flourishing.

When we are not sure how to act or when we are pulled in different directions, the rules serve as a guidepost. Around 400 BC, the philosopher, Plato, wrote the *Allegory of the Chariot*. In that story, a chariot driver is trying to get to what is essentially a virtuous heaven where wisdom, goodness, justice, and beauty reside. (Think of a flourishing paradise.) The chariot is being pulled by two winged horses. One of the horses is a "crooked lumbering animal," bred of "insolence and pride," and does whatever it wants. The other horse is noble and disciplined, "a lover of honor and modesty and good," and is guided by the wise words of the chariot driver.

The two horses typically pull in different directions, but the chariot driver takes decisive action to move the chariot into a single direction toward the virtuous heaven. Not surprisingly, the ride is turbulent and challenging, but the charioteer keeps his eye on the target and ultimately persists in reaching his or her destination.[7]

This abbreviated version of this allegory offers many different interpretations, but one is that, notwithstanding our own personal desires and foibles, we can choose to keep moving in the right direction. Instead of fighting an internal civil war, we can choose to stay the course by following the principled path. In short, Plato argues that we must ultimately decide whether to move toward our noble purpose of flourishing. Science has corroborated the truth in Plato's allegory that knowing we are headed in the right direction is one of the keys to happiness.

This is what the rules in this book accomplish. They are firmly grounded in the here and now, so they can be applied daily. For example, if one of your goals is to have meaningful relationships, one action you can take is to be present (not distracted) with your loved ones. As you can see from the diagram below, flourishing moves us in a linear progression toward meaningful relationships, which points us toward being present.

As a quick side note, I intentionally used the phrase "increased flourishing" above. It is worth remembering that flourishing is a holistic concept, and one rule alone does not lead to a flourishing life.

In the subsequent chapters of this book, I will provide a simple set of principles for flourishing every day or, as I like to say, from moment to moment to moment. The next few chapters provide the broad foundational rules, and then we will drill down into the specifics. At the beginning of a trial, I instruct the jury that the evidence can only be presented one piece at a time. The same is true here, and each principle builds on the next in a systematic way toward achieving flourishing.

Having a universal purpose of flourishing and knowing that each of the rules to achieving it moves you in the direction of that purpose will become a driving force for virtually all aspects of your life. You will begin to treat life like you are on a heroic quest to flourish, to become the best version of yourself. It guides you to live vertically rather than horizontally. All your actions exist on this worldly plain. But they can all point up toward flourishing.

Each of the rules or principles in this book provides a pathway to both moving toward a better future and enjoying the present moment. By acting in accordance with the rules, you will make progress toward your optimal self and appreciate and delight in the journey along the way. So, yes, you will be striving but also enjoying the striving. These are the ideal conditions for flourishing.

This is described beautifully by Tal Ben-Shahar in *Happier*, in which he playfully depicts this approach to life as the "Hamburger Model." Since I'm a sucker for In-N-Out Burger, this really resonated with me. In his book, Ben-Shahar presents four types of burgers: the Junk Burger (delicious and unhealthy), the Veggie/Soy Burger (healthy but not tasty), the Worst Burger (unhealthy and nasty tasting), and the Ideal Burger (both tasty and healthy).

These burgers each represent a different happiness archetype or approach to life. The Junk Burger represents the hedonist, somebody who is exclusively interested in the pleasure of the present moment, ignoring potential future negative consequences. The hedonist is not interested in future benefits; instead, he or she seeks being entertained over becoming optimized. The Veggie/Soy Burger represents the rat-racer, by analogy, the healthy but completely tasteless burger. Here, the person gains lots of future benefits, but he or she does not enjoy the present while constantly striving toward the next goal. No need to taste the burger; too busy working toward what's ahead. (Sounds like a lot of lawyers.) The Worst Burger is represented by the nihilist, someone who has lost the love and meaning of life. This person's burger and life are tasteless, and he or she has no hope for a better future. What's the point? The Ideal Burger (Double-Double, anybody?) is illustrative of the happiness or flourishing archetype. There is both a present reward and a future benefit.[8] Which one of these burgers represents your life?

This is why the rules contained in the three-pillar flourishing model are so important: They provide you with guidelines for both identifying future targets and future benefits as well as being fully engaged in and enjoying the present. You are heading toward the mountain top and savoring the views along the way. You get to have your hamburger and eat it too.

So, commit to flourishing in your life by learning the rules in this book. These rules will help you flourish. Your health, work, and relationships will all dramatically improve. Commit to living these principles, and a balanced, beautiful life will follow—a purpose-driven life based on rock-solid principles.

Chapter Summary:

- Now that we know the ultimate object of life, we need to know the rules, or principles, to achieve that object.
- The Three Pillars of Flourishing in life are Vision + Action + Virtue.
- All the rules for flourishing emanate from the Three Pillars.
- The rules all guide us in the direction of flourishing and allow us to all at once strive for a better future and enjoy the present moment.

SIDEBAR

Just like you need to know the rules of life, you must also know the procedural rules of the specific court in which you are practicing. In addition, make sure you read and understand the local or general court rules that keep the courts running smoothly and efficiently. It's amazing how many gems can be found within the local rules.

CHAPTER 3

APPLYING THE RULES TO LIVE OUT YOUR PURPOSE

• • •

"Life's a game, all you have to do is know how to play it."

—UNKNOWN

It was my very first day of law school. I nervously walked into the classroom and took a seat. Shortly thereafter, the bow-tied and bespectacled professor walked in, put his materials down, and without so much as a greeting, said, "Mr. Pfahler, can you please recite the facts from the case of *Palsgraf v. Long Island Railroad Co*?"[1] With a lump in my throat, I stumbled through the facts. He continued, "What is the rule in that case?" I barely mumbled a response. Then it happened.

"Mr. Pfahler, let's assume the facts in that case are different." He then presented facts materially distinct from the *Palsgraf* case. "What would be the outcome under the new facts?" I was completely befuddled. Frozen. "I'm sorry, I don't know." I thought he was going to ask me to leave or fail me on the spot, but instead, he moved to the next victim, I mean, student. "Mr. Rutherford, what do you have to say about this hypothetical?"

The professor employed what is called the Socratic method. It's a pedagogical technique to develop critical thinking skills and learn how to apply the law to different factual scenarios. The Socratic method is implemented by using the IRAC method we have previously discussed.

As a law student and lawyer, knowing the Issue and the Rule of law is never enough. It's merely the starting point. We also need to know how to apply the law. This is the "A" in the IRAC method, the "Application," and it is a lawyer's bread and butter.

The same is true in life. In this chapter, we will focus on applying the rules from the previous chapter. Yes, we must know the rules of flourishing, but ultimately it comes down to application. Knowledge is important but application is essential. We must actually play the game. So, that begs the question: How do we play the game well?

CLOSING THE GAP

The best way I know how to actually "apply" the principles or to live out a flourishing a life is through a concept called "closing the gap." You can succeed in the game of life by using the principles you learn in this book and "closing the gap" between how the ideal version of you would apply the principle and how the current version of you would live out that principle. Otherwise stated, your aim is to close the gap between your current and your optimal self.

There is no single way to play the game; each of us will have to figure out what works for us individually. For me, I originally learned about closing the gap in college when reading Viktor Frankl's *Man's Search for Meaning*. It was the first time I really understood at a deep level the need for the intersection between our actions and our beliefs. In his book, Dr. Frankl pinpoints a "tension between what one has already achieved and what one still ought to accomplish, or the gap between what one is and what one should become."[2]

The mission is to narrow the gap between who you currently are and who you can become. It's closing the gap between who you are *capable* of being and who you are *actually* being.

Another way to describe closing the gap is self-congruency. As the diagram below illustrates, your aim is to move the circles closer together until they are eventually overlapping or congruous with one another.

Brian Johnson, the founder of Heroic, says "the gap" is where stress and disappointment live. Thus, you can reduce those negative feelings by narrowing the distance between the two circles.

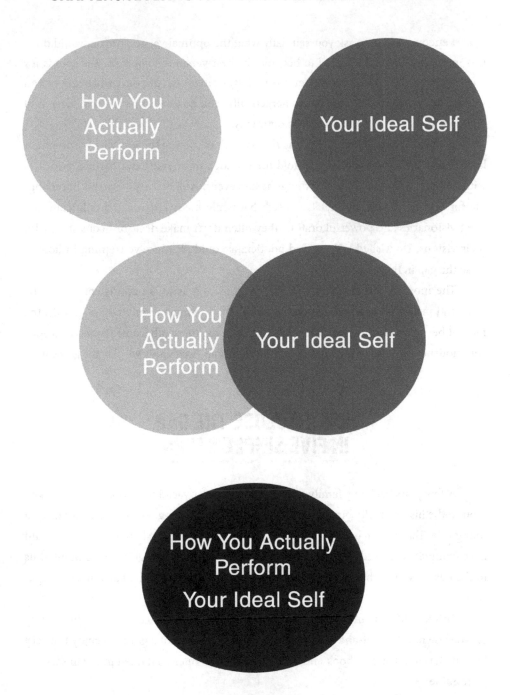

I encourage you to ask yourself daily what the optimal version of you would do at this moment? Then, get excited to become the best version of yourself. The goal is for your optimal self to become your new normal. By doing this, your days will begin by you waking up refreshed and exercising energetically. You go to work as the best version of yourself. You get home and show love optimally.

A few years ago, I was discussing the concept of closing the gap with a prominent lawyer and U.S. Congressman. He told me the idea of merging our highest priorities with our actions is one of the best things he had ever heard. Not only was this life changing for him personally, but he also noted that while many lawyers and politicians are great visionaries and powerful orators, they often don't make decisions consistent with their visions. He wished lawyers and politicians could also receive training in how to close the gap in their professions.

The most important thing you can do every day is to act consistently with the rules and principles that lead to your optimal self. The more regularly you do this, the more it becomes a habit. The more you practice it, the more it becomes baked into your consciousness. So, today and always, let's close the gap. That's how we play the game well.

HOW TO CLOSE THE GAP
IN FIVE SIMPLE STEPS

A few years back, my family and I took a summer vacation to Boston. We walked around the historical city but felt there was something missing. The next day, we hired a tour guide. That person brought the history of the city alive and shared stories we would have completely missed by going about our trip ourselves. The guide even pointed us to the best tavern in the city. Because we had our tour guide, we had an amazing experience.

Think of life like my family's trip to Boston. You can either choose to just get by on your own, with a hit-and-miss approach or use the help of a guide to enjoy the very best life has to offer. This book and the principles and rules contained in it will serve as your guide.

The Five Steps to Close the Gap Between
Your Current and Ideal Life

Sure, you can understand that closing the gap is important, but do you know the specific steps to achieve this? In particular, there are five simple steps. Yes, simple, but not *easy*. These steps are simple to understand, but the key is doing them consistently.

1. Be aware of your need to change. Closing the gap begins with an awareness of the need to change. To ensure self-awareness, we must be radically honest with ourselves. We cannot engage in self-deception or justify our actions, no matter how bad our circumstances might currently be. Instead, it is crucial we see our life as it really is and to recognize our strengths and weaknesses, for better or worse. Even if we are doing something that is unbecoming, it is critical we are aware of our actions and never lie to ourselves. Period.

The problem often is we essentially know what to do, but we don't do it. We fail to heed the call or act on our self-awareness. As a judge, for example, I try to be aware of my role at all times. I have a constant mindfulness that I'm a judge. As I focus on this throughout the day, I increase my awareness of the responsibilities of being a judge. Self-awareness involves "slowing down one's mental processes enough to allow one to notice as much as possible about a given moment or situation, and then act thoughtfully based on what one has noticed."[3] My awareness allows me to better close the gap between who I am currently as a judge and who I aspire to be as a judge.

2. Get clear on what is most important now. Hopefully, you have identified your most important priority at this time. Maybe it's doing a work project, helping a child with homework, talking with a friend about a problem, or exercising. If you are unsure of your highest priorities, you will be prompted toward clarity on those priorities in the following chapters.

It will be up to you to determine what's most important to you in your own life at any given moment. I encourage you to take the time to figure this out before anything else. It's a critical step. And realize that this will change over time as your life and circumstances change.

For now, how about asking yourself what one area of focus would most improve your life today. For example, it could be exercise, sleep, eating, work, time with others, or time for yourself. Getting clarity on your one thing may be the most important part of this book.

3. Focus solely on your one important thing. Fully concentrate on your one thing in the present moment, eliminating distractions or interruptions. So, for instance, when you are working on a legal brief, helping your child with homework, or talking with a friend, put away your phone and don't check texts or emails. I have a friend who goes to the gym and spends more time texting than exercising. The fingers get a great workout, but the body, not so much. I advise you to shine that uninterrupted spotlight of attention on whatever you are doing to make the most impact.

4. Act on the one thing you identified. You are writing, helping, talking, or exercising. You are acting on one thing to the exclusion of all others, aiming the whole time to close the gap with your actions.

Many times, I have seen lawyers who have great ideas for their career, firm, or a particular case, but just as often, I see those same lawyers fail to act and implement their ideas. Many entrepreneurs do the same thing with a great idea. Ideas are a dime a dozen, but the implementation of those ideas is where success lies.

Another example is my former colleague, who regularly states he needs to lose weight. He knows he needs to eat differently. But he is simply unwilling to align his actions with his desire. He understands he should eat more salads but routinely chooses the fish and chips. Or, when he orders a salad, he drenches it in unhealthy dressing.

5. Repeat. Multiple scientific studies have established we thrive from the routines we follow daily. For instance, the quality of our sleep increases significantly when we go to bed at the same time each night. If we change our routine for a day, that's perfectly fine. But doing so for several consecutive days makes some things harder as we lose the benefit from doing something regularly.

Based on my research and experience, I believe that establishing a daily routine is what really makes the difference. Today, you may not feel like doing something, but by establishing a routine, you become committed to doing it. On the other hand, things might be going so well in your life you rationalize that you don't need to do something. Those times when you say to yourself you can skip doing that thing are exactly when you should double down and stick with it. It's during those good periods of your life you are baking in your habits and routines for the inevitable challenging times.

One of the major obstacles to closing the gap is rationalizing. Often, when we know that something is important in our lives but don't do it, we rationalize our actions. Rationalization is when we try to justify not living consistently with our values or priorities. It's when we try to explain away—whether to ourselves or others—why we are living in contradiction with our priorities. Because not one of us is perfect and never will be, we will always have some inconsistencies between our actions and our priorities. There will always be times when we are not closing the gap. When this occurs, we want to avoid rationalizing.

I have been advocating the concept of closing the gap for the better part of twenty years. It's my experience that closing the gap is the single most significant principle for flourishing. When you achieve consistency between your actions and your priorities, you will experience amazing satisfaction, success, and meaning in both your personal and professional lives like never before. Closing the gap is the way to transform your life.

Are you ready to make a commitment to being the best version of yourself? Remember: Be honest with yourself, define your priorities, focus on one thing that will put you in closer alignment with them, act on that one thing, and repeat. Your life is no longer a dress rehearsal. We all have just one life, however long or short. Today is your Super Bowl. There is no do-over in life. So let's close the gap starting now.

FLOURISHING IS A BY-PRODUCT OF LIVING THE RULES WELL

Yes, the rules and your actions aim you in the direction of flourishing, but at the same time, flourishing is fundamentally a by-product of life lived by consistently applying the rules for flourishing. In other words, when you act consistently with the rules, the result is that you will experience a flourishing life.

Your best life comes from identifying what is most important to you in each moment and acting on that priority. When your priorities and your performance are in alignment, you will then enjoy flourishing. Flourishing is the subsequent reward of closing the gap. As Eleanor Roosevelt said: "Happiness ... is a by-product of a life well lived."

The by-product is the "C" in our IRAC rubric. If we apply the rules through our actions and thereby close the gap, the "Conclusion" is that we will be living a flourishing life.

Don't think that closing the gap will lead to a life of ease or unending pleasure. The path that is easiest or filled with the most pleasure is often disguised as the right way. But don't be fooled by beauty, ease, and pleasure.

The philosopher Socrates told a mythological story called "The Choice of Hercules" that is instructive of the allure of pleasure. In the story, Hercules is unfulfilled and discontented with life. He sits alone one day contemplating his dissatisfaction and was confused about the life he should live.

He then sees two goddesses approaching him from different paths. The first goddess is dressed in fine clothes and wearing fancy jewelry and heavy makeup, like she is heading to a night club. Her life appears to be one of luxury, ease, and excess. She tells Hercules to follow her on her path, and his life, too, will be easy and filled with much material and sensual pleasure.

The second goddess is also equally beautiful but in a more natural way. She has a confident but noble air about her. Strong and kind. The second goddess tells Hercules if he chooses to follow her path, his life will be challenging, but it will also be meaningful and filled with much good.

As you can guess, Hercules chooses the second path. He chooses a eudaimonic over a hedonic life. He chooses a life in which he faces continual danger and persecution. Hercules lives an extraordinary life, undertaking the fabled Twelve Labors, slaying the Hydra, and ultimately entering Hades, the Underworld itself. These dangers and challenges are what make Hercules into the great man he is and the legend he becomes. His incredible strength and character are a result of the life he chooses to live.

"The Choice of Hercules" is a powerful allegory that a flourishing life is a consequence of living a life consistent with our highest calling. The closer we align the two circles, the greater the flourishing we will experience. As we narrow the gap, we get closer to becoming the best versions of ourselves and we experience higher levels of flourishing. It's how we become the heroic versions of ourselves.

Flourishing Is the Ultimate Aim	Rules for Flourishing	We Act Consistently with Those Rules (Close the Gap)	A Flourishing Life Results

There will be times when you don't feel like closing the gap. It's hard. But I encourage you to stay committed even when you don't feel like it. Almost anything that is worthwhile is a result of great effort. Yet it's not just any effort. It's effort specifically directed to closing the gap.

So, paradoxically, flourishing is not only the aim of our actions or a by-product; it's *both*. Flourishing is both pursued (as it directs our actions) and also ensues from our self-congruent actions. It's the beginning and the end. This paradox of flourishing can be graphically illustrated as follows:

We know we are flourishing because we are realizing our full potential, becoming the best versions of ourselves, and making progress toward our most vital priorities. In short, flourishing results when we know the game we are playing, the rules of the game, and how to apply them to play the game well. We've got this!

....

Chapter Summary:

- **Once we know the rules, we must apply them to our lives.**
- **We apply the rules for life by closing the gap between our current reality and our optimal self.**
- **As we close the gap, we will experience an increased flourishing in our lives.**

SIDEBAR _____

In court, keep your oral argument concise and to the point. When arguing a motion, don't repeat what you already said in your papers. If the court's tentative is not in your favor, be respectful of that tentative and then civilly and persuasively show the court how the decision can better comport to the law and facts. If the tentative is in your favor, respond to any material arguments by opposing counsel and remind the court why its well-reasoned tentative is correct.

PART
TWO

THE FOUNDATION FOR FLOURISHING

Build Your Life on a Solid Foundation

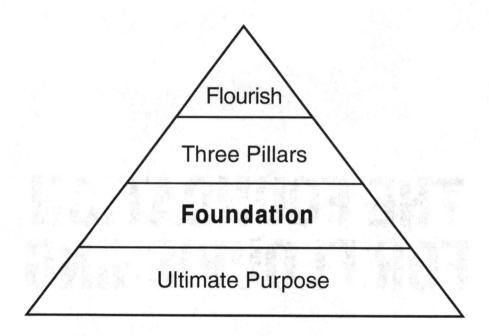

CHAPTER 4

THE RIGHT FOUNDATION

• • •

*"You can't build a great building
on a weak foundation."*

—GORDON B. HINKLEY

In the middle of my career, my firm moved to a beautiful new building in down-town Los Angeles. It was obvious that great thought and planning had gone into its design. It was truly inspiring.

As I walked each morning from the parking lot to the new building, I noticed that construction was starting on the vacant lot next door. Each day, I observed the same construction worker standing outside the gate entrance to let the busy dump trucks safely enter and exit the site. I asked the worker what they were constructing, and he replied they were building an identical version of my new building.

Since construction had just begun, I was anxious to watch it unfold as I walked by each morning. However, for the next six months, all they did was dig a deep hole. It was remarkable how deep they went.

By then, I had formed a nice acquaintance with the construction worker at the entrance, and I inquired how much longer they were going to dig the hole. He replied they still had a few more months to dig the foundation. "Why?" I asked. He responded that the taller the building, the deeper the foundation must be. A big, tall building requires a deep, sturdy foundation. In contrast, a tent merely takes a few stakes in the ground.

The same is true for our life. If you want your life to be strong and sturdy and able to withstand the inevitable storms, you need to build it on a solid foundation. If you have big goals and want to truly flourish, you need to ground your life on deep, fundamental principles. The bigger your life, the deeper and stronger your foundation needs to be.

So, are you building a tower or a tent for your life? If you want a tower, then how is your foundation? If you want a tent, I offer no judgment, but rest assured it will blow over.

The quote at the beginning this chapter is derived from the Sermon on the Mount in which Jesus told the story of the wise and foolish builders. The wise builder built his or her house on a solid rock foundation. The Book of Matthew says, "And the rain fell, and the floods came, and the winds blew and beat on that house, but it did not fall, because it had been founded on the rock."[1] The inevitable storm came, but the house on solid ground was not shaken or damaged. However, the foolish builder did not build the house on a solid foundation, and when the same storm came, the house collapsed.

Let the construction story and the Sermon on the Mount serve as reminders: A life built on the Three Pillars of Flourishing needs a deep, strong, unshakeable foundation. In the next three chapters, we will examine the underlying foundation—a key life rule or principle—that coincides with each of the Three Pillars of Flourishing, which we'll cover in Part III.

These foundational principles will apply to all the different aspects and circumstances of your life. Let them serve as your bedrock foundation for building a flourishing life. I strongly encourage you to return to these foundational pillars again and again. They will provide you the strength you need to reach your full potential along with the stability to keep you going when you inevitably encounter a storm.

Chapter Summary:

- The bigger your life goals, the stronger the foundation upon which your life must be built.
- The biblical Sermon on the Mount illustrates the importance of laying the right foundation for your life, one that supports you through life's obstacles.
- The foundational principles within the Three Pillars of Flourishing encompass proven truths for building a solid foundation for your life.

SIDEBAR

Speaking of foundations, honesty and civility are the two cornerstones for a long-term successful practice. Always, always tell the truth. Show respect to all persons involved in the case, especially opposing counsel. Pick up the phone and speak to the other side. Good relations will only help your client's case.

CHAPTER 5

A PURPOSE-DRIVEN LIFE

• • •

*"The average man does not know what
to do with his life yet wants another
one which will last forever."*

— ANATOLE FRENCH

I t was my first day of work as a brand-new lawyer. After the perfunctory introductions, the other first-year associates and I gathered for our first training session. The senior partner entered the room and turned on the PowerPoint presentation entitled, "Litigating the AD&H Way." (AD&H were the initials of the law firm.) The senior partner immediately began: "For every case, we start with the closing."

As I tried to take notes on everything he said, my mind kept returning to "We start with the closing." *Huh?* The closing argument is the last thing done in trial. I knew that years of case preparation ensued before even getting to trial. Lawsuits start when a complaint is filed. After that, the parties conduct discovery, and if the case isn't settled, it may go to trial in a few years. At trial, a jury is picked, opening statements are done, and witnesses are called—all before closing. How could you possibly do the closing first? At this point I wondered whether this partner even knew what he was talking about and if I'd chosen the right firm.

As the partner went on, his advice would ensure our ability to navigate cases for optimal outcomes. You see, the trial is the central event in litigation, looming over the rest of the case. Everything done from the beginning of the case is in anticipation of a trial, with the closing argument being the final culminating act. It's the one and only chance to tell the jury how you want them to decide and why.

During that initial training session, the partner told us that when we get a case, the first thing we do is look at the verdict form, which includes the final questions for the jury. These outline the elements of the law that the jury needs to determine. For example, in a murder trial, the verdict form asks:

1. Did the defendant commit an act that caused the death of another person?
2. When the defendant acted, did he or she have a state of mind called "malice aforethought"?
3. Did the defendant kill without lawful excuse or justification?

Starting with the verdict form gives a purpose for everything else done in a case. It provides a clear focus. With this target, you can gather the relevant facts, perform the necessary research, and create a case plan. Everything flows from where you want to finish.

For the murder trial, you know that most of your investigation and research are going to center around the three questions in the verdict form.

I can honestly say that by the end of the hourlong presentation I was stunned and convinced. I remember sitting there thinking I had just been given the "secret" to successfully litigating a case, but little did I know that this foundational principle is also how to live life.

It's like when you're constructing a building, you don't start with the actual physical work, but a vision of what the building will look like. Then come the blueprint drawings. There are always two creations. The first is in the mind and the second is in reality. First, you need a clear picture of what you are trying to build. You begin with the end product.

The same is true for your life. Part I of this book established that flourishing is our universal aim or objective in life. But flourishing, without a clear vision of what we hope to achieve, will be much less likely to occur. That's why the first Pillar of Flourishing is Vision; it provides more clarity and specificity on how we aim to flourish.

Pursuing a purpose-driven life is part of having meaningful goals (Vision) for our life. Even the ancient Greeks showed that humans are "teleological," meaning that we need to have an end purpose for our actions. We need to make progress toward worthwhile targets to flourish. In the *How of* Happiness, Sonja Lyubomirsky said that happy people have projects. Vision allows you to set clear targets and to know the direction of your life.

In his best-selling book, *The 7 Habits of Highly Effective People*, Stephen Covey echoes this idea by saying we should "begin with the end in mind." He asserts: "To begin with the end in mind means to start with a clear understanding of your destination. It means to know where you're going to better understand where you are now and so the steps you take are always in the right direction."[1]

Clearly knowing your goals is vital to closing the gap between who you are currently and the best version of yourself. How to get that clarity is what we are going to explore in this chapter. This does not necessarily mean you will already have a clear target on the specifics of your career or other aspects of your life. At this stage, your goal could be more general, such as you want to help people, or you want to raise your children while they are home.

However, the greater your clarity about your targets, the more effective you can act toward meeting those targets. Also, making progress toward your specific goals will add more meaning to your life, boost your hope for the future, and inspire you to arise each morning with enthusiasm. This also helps in dealing with setbacks and challenges. After all, as Viktor Frankl noted, "Nothing is more important to help a person overcome difficulties than having a purpose in life."

We could be doing all the right things but heading in the wrong direction. It doesn't matter if you have a great attitude and work ethic if you're on the wrong bus heading to the wrong destination; you aren't going to get where you want to go. As the baseball legend Yogi Berra said: "If you don't know where you are going, you might wind up somewhere else."

Now that we understand the importance of gaining clarity on what we want in life, what are the specific steps for achieving Vision? We will now examine two key elements to creating your own personal vision—missions and identities.

ONE PURPOSE, MANY MISSIONS

Tesla is one of the wealthiest companies in the world. In identifying its purpose, however, Tesla never mentions anything about making money. Rather, the CEO of Tesla, Elon Musk has remarked that Tesla's purpose is "to accelerate the world's transition to sustainable transport." Its purpose answers its own question of "Why?" Tesla's mission flows from that purpose and answers the question of *what* they exist to do, which is manufacture super innovative and cool electric cars.[2]

Both purpose and mission are critical because the purpose provides the motivation behind the mission. As Musk stated in the interview mentioned above: "Putting in long hours for a corporation is hard. Putting in long hours for a cause is easy." With a clear purpose, the mission of building its amazing electric vehicles becomes equally compelling.

As individuals, while we all share the same universal purpose of flourishing, our missions are personal and unique to each of us. We all have one purpose (flourishing) but many missions—a mission being an objective or task that we aim to accomplish within a specific role.

There are two broad categories of missions in life: (1) missions that are self-directed—those which help us realize our own individual potential and (2) missions that are directed towards others, those which enable us to love, serve, and contribute to the world. The psychologist Abraham Maslow famously called the two types of life missions as missions toward "self-actualization" and "self-transcendence."

When on a self-directed mission of "self-actualization," you strive to become the best version of yourself. Before giving yourself away to others, you first need to flourish individually. You can't give away what you don't have. How can you serve your clients as a lawyer if you don't first possess the requisite skills?

However, self-actualization is only part of the equation. Ancient wisdom and modern science tell us to give our greatest gifts away to a cause bigger than ourselves. This is self-transcendence, which essentially means "beyond the self." It places the focus on others. You become others oriented. "We" becomes greater than "me." It is ultimately in giving of our best to others that we achieve more than we can by flourishing in and for ourselves. In short, flourishing is becoming the best version of ourselves in service to something bigger than ourselves.

Ray Dalio affirms the two aspects of our mission: "It's now clear to me that my purpose, your purpose, and the purpose of everything is to evolve and to contribute to evolution in some small way."[3] Be shaped and help shape others. Find your own voice and then help others find theirs. Be the change, so you can change the world.

The amazing result of this two-part, purpose-driven mission is that you are helping make the world a better place. Think about this. If you commit to becoming the best person you can be, and to deeply loving and serving others, how can the world not be improved? For example, as a lawyer, if you improve your physical energy, your mental focus, and dedicate yourself to mastering the law to better serve your clients, how can you not be more effective in your career? We all have a role to play in improving our world.

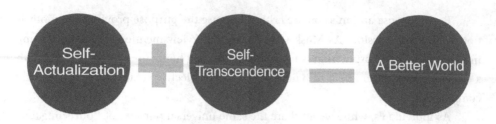

Now that we've broadly considered the concepts of self-directed and others-directed mission types, let's get a little more specific in our own lives. You might find yourself on a mission to be a great lawyer, spouse, parent, son, daughter, friend, coach, community leader, or student, and sometimes these may overlap. At times, managing your missions can be a bit overwhelming. Remember to allow yourself to simplify. Think of it this way: Ray Dalio says life is essentially boiled down to meaningful relationships and meaningful work. Our missions in love and work are two of the cornerstones for being human.

While I agree that these two missions are fundamental, I strongly believe we need to add a third mission: our personal well-being. This is similar to "the Big 3" life mission model of energy, love, and work by Brian Johnson. Too often, our own well-being takes a backburner to other things, but I believe that personal well-being is crucial to flourishing in our other missions. I encourage you to prioritize your missions by reducing them to only the most important at a given season in your life. You will have many seasons in which you may find yourself devoting much of yourself to one or more of these missions while trying to balance all three. For example, when your children are young and most dependent, you might allow yourself to make being the best parent you can be one of your main missions in that season. Of course, your well-being and work still require your attention, but perhaps for a time your core focus is your children.

As you think about defining your own personalized missions, one of the best practical tools to help you identify your priorities is Stephen Covey's Eulogy Exercise, in which you write your own eulogy. In this exercise, you imagine walking into a funeral. You take a seat, look at the program, and see that it's your own funeral. What would the speakers say about you? Who would the speakers be?[4]

You might think it's a bit morbid to imagine your own funeral, but I have tried it and it offered me great insight into my own life and missions. In doing so, I had to consider how well I was prioritizing my life by asking myself what those at my funeral would say about me, my accomplishments, and my relationships, and whether or not their comments aligned with what I would have hoped to hear. My answers helped me identify what is most important to me and what I find to be the most important personal values and qualities. This helped me crystalize my vision for my most vital missions in life. I encourage you to give it a try!

YOUR OPTIMAL IDENTITY

As does Covey's Eulogy Exercise, confronting who we are presents an excellent opportunity to tap into the power of our own sense of identity. Are we who we want to be, or do we have work to do? How can knowing who we want to be help us achieve our vision for life? Before we can harness its potential impact for our lives, we must examine how we think about identity itself.

In order to determine and fulfill the right missions in our lives, we need a clear sense of identity. Yet, identity is not always easy to nail down. Interestingly, in his book *The Alter Ego Effect*, Tom Herman recalls a survey that posed the questions of whether Superman or Clark Kent is the alter ego. Ninety percent of the people he surveyed said the alter ego is Superman, but the correct answer is Clark Kent. Superman is the true, authentic identity who only takes on the persona of Clark Kent to better understand human beings.[5]

I find it useful to know that the term "identity" derives from Latin meaning "repeated beingness." Identity is *who* you are. It's the distinguishing character of an individual. It's different from what you do. Identity is not doing, it's being.

Herman also tells the true story of Bo Jackson, who assumed another identity to transform his behavior. Jackson is the only professional athlete to be an All-Star in both professional football and baseball. Jackson was a mild-mannered gentleman off the field, but he struggled on the field with anger and emotional outbursts. It hurt his performance and caused unnecessary penalties and stupid mistakes.

One day, Jackson was watching the movie *Friday the 13th*, when he noticed the hockey-mask wearing killer, Jason, was always emotionless during his crimes. Jackson decided to take on the identity of "Jason" on the football field. Herman writes, "Suddenly the hotheaded, penalty-prone, easy-to-provoke Bo Jackson transformed into a relentless, cold, and disciplined destroyer on the field. Channeling a different 'identity' helped him focus every ounce of his talent and skill, and enabled him to show up on the field, without any emotional issues interfering with his performance."[6] Granted, there are more lovable archetypes than what Jackson used. But whether your mission is to optimally perform on the football field, in the courtroom, or as a friend or partner, harnessing identity shows tangible impact.

Clearly, your identity provides a crucial link between your missions and your behaviors. James Clear offers further helpful insight: In *Atomic Habits,* Clear writes: "Are you becoming the type of person you want to become? The first step is not what or how, but who. You need to know who you want to be. Otherwise, your quest for change is like a boat without a rudder."[7]

A word of caution at this point. When you imagine an identity for yourself, it's important to do so while being truly self-aware and honest. Often, identity and actions aren't self-congruent. By way of example, I had planned to have dinner with a colleague. I arrived on time, but after forty minutes had passed, the colleague hadn't shown up. I texted and called him to no avail. The owner of the restaurant, who knew my friend quite well, finally came over and assured me not to worry because he is always late. He never did show up, and I eventually ate without him. The next day he texted me and apologized for falling asleep. I told him not to worry about it and then said that the owner had jokingly commented he was always late. He responded by saying that was strange because he was never late. It appears my colleague's identity and behaviors were not yet aligned.

It would serve us extremely well to take on an identity that is both unique to, and the ideal version, of the person we want to become. For instance, one identity I think many of us would love to aspire to is a "hero." The word *hero* does not mean a type of tough guy or girl or a killer of bad guys. We too often have the image of a hero being a soldier in battle or firefighter pulling a child out of a burning building. Of course, those are heroes. But the term is much broader than that.

The etymology of the word *hero* comes from the Greek word *hēros,* which means "protector" or "defender." Hero means having the strength for two to help others. What's more, a hero's secret strength is rooted in love. So, imagine yourself as protector having the strength for two powered by love.

If you thought of yourself as a hero, how might you approach your own self-care, work, and relationships differently? What does the heroic version of you look like on each of these missions? Is the heroic version of your health a strong, energetic protector? Is the heroic version of you professionally one who helps and serves others? As a hero in love do you provide kindness and encouragement? Try coming up with your own identity. Or consider looking for role models who inspire you.

Personally, I believe our legal system would be better if lawyers saw themselves as humble heroes. By definition, a lawyer should be a hero. Her or his primary role is to protect or advocate for another's rights. We need more heroes in today's world than ever before.

For your own life, let's start by creating an identity for your three main missions of well-being, work, and love. Yes, you can have three different identities as you take on different missions in your life. You simply make a mental transition from one mission to another as needed.

For instance, when I go to work, I typically bring my gym clothes with me. For work in the morning, I wear my judicial robe and assume the identity of an ethical, exemplary judge. As soon as the lunch hour arrives, my mission is well-being, so I quickly change from my work clothes into my gym clothes and head to the gym. Along with that change of clothes comes a change of identity from exemplary judge to elite athlete. I personally love making this mental switch in identities and find it energizing. When I get home from work, I'm on a mission of love, and I very purposefully switch my identity again to being a "BFF" for my family.

In creating your own unique identities, be creative and use your imagination. It should be personal to you. This is not about "what" you want to accomplish, but about "who" you are committed to becoming. Visualize your ideal self—one, two, or five years from now—in each of the three missions of personal well-being, work, and love. Let's get really specific.

For personal well-being, let's start with your health. How do you envision yourself and your well-being? Are you radiantly alive and healthy? Strong, fit, energetic, athletic? Are you a nature-lover, a runner, a skier, a cyclist, a dancer, a basketball player, or a swimmer? Keep it healthy and positive. In fact, I have one judicial colleague who says her identity is "healthy person." Everything she does—from eating to exercising to sleeping—is done as a healthy person, and it works great for her.

When I participated in a Spartan Race, I met a fellow runner, and we ran together for a part of the course. She was in great shape and pushed herself. She lives in the California High Sierras, which has snow about nine months of the year, and she loves being active in nature. She told me with a smile that she calls herself an "outdoor warrior goddess." As our conversation continued, it became clear her actions were consistent with her fun, yet meaningful identity.

For work, what identity gives you a sense of a calling? How do you want to give back to the world? Who are you at your professional or career best? Are you an elite trial lawyer or a world-class litigator? A preeminent transactional lawyer? A professional paralegal? Sensational secretary? Master mediator?

Imagine a lawyer whose mission is to fight for victim's rights. She sees herself as the knight or dame in shining armor. Her work identity is that of a champion of justice for victim's rights or a heroic victim's advocate. When she is making decisions throughout her day, she asks whether her actions are consistent with her powerful identity. It emboldens her to stand up for her clients and causes. Operating from a sense of such a strong identity, how is this "champion" likely to approach her day?

For stay-at-home parents, you can be super creative in how you see yourself. Your identity as a mom or dad can certainly be your calling. If you are a stay-at-home parent, then who are you at your optimal best? It's not about getting a paycheck. It's about your gifts, service, sacrifice, and love. One of my friends is a stay-at-home mom and great at what she does. This mom declares "professional mom" to be her identity, which is amazing.

In your relationships, who are you at your loving best? When you step back and see the most loving example of who you are, whom do you see? Are you an excellent mom, dad, wife, husband, or friend? One friend of mine wants to be a "radiant exemplar" to his family, and another told me that her mission of love is to be an "extraordinary wife, parent, and friend." Both are excellent identities.

If you are having trouble identifying your ideal identity in any of the three missions, consider asking yourself these questions: What if I were absolutely guaranteed to succeed—in terms of well-being, love, and work? What would that best version of me look like?

Also remember that your missions and identities will continually change over time. That's a good thing. Just write down your identity now, and as you flourish, it will evolve. You will not remain static. This is especially true as we mature and attain wisdom. As the psychiatrist Carl Jung said in describing the two halves of life: "One cannot live the afternoon of life according to the program of life's morning; for what was great in the morning will be of little importance in the evening, and what in the morning was true will at evening become a lie." [8]

Wherever you are in your life, commit to knowing who you are at your optimal best. Before you leave this section, can you say what your identity is? Even one word will do. Does it represent an ideal vision of yourself? Your actions will flow from that identity. You will become the self that you created in your own mind's eye. "We are," said Amy Cuddy in *Presence*, "at our best and most powerful when we affirm our identity." Enjoy and embrace your new identity, your optimal you!

....

Chapter Summary:

- **Start by creating a great vision for your life.**
- **Have one purpose, but many missions.**
- **Develop your ideal identity for each of your missions.**

SIDEBAR _____

Make sure you know the judge's preferences for your ability to move around the courtroom during jury selection, opening statement, examining witnesses, and closing argument. Ask the judge for permission before approaching a witness by inquiring, "Your Honor, may I please approach the witness?"

CHAPTER 6

THE FREEDOM TO CHOOSE

• • •

"The strongest principle of growth lies
in the human choice."

—GEORGE ELIOT

I
t was a blustery winter day in Eastern Europe during World War II. The Nazis had decided to hold their battle lines at the Danube River until the bitter end. After several devastating artillery strikes, the governor of Hungary ordered his citizens to evacuate immediately. Leaving their homes and belongings behind, people flocked to the train stations.

One of those fleeing citizens was my father, just a young boy. His family packed their suitcases, waited in line, and eventually crammed into the train. The train would not be cleared to leave for some time, so my father went to get coffee and bread for his family. Suddenly and without warning, the train pulled away while he was still in the food line. His mother (my grandmother) screamed for him to come. Seeing the train leaving, my dad started sprinting but couldn't catch up. With one final burst of adrenaline, he drew near and leapt onto the train's stairwell as it sped away from the station.

My dad and his family eventually arrived in America as penniless immigrants after World War II. They had lost their home, their savings, their jobs, their friends, everything. As a first generation American, I grew up hearing about my dad's stirring travails. He told the story of how he and other boys were playing in a field when a Nazi landmine exploded right next to them, severing the leg of his boyhood friend.

Although these stories were often heartbreaking, my father typically ended them by saying he was grateful for being able to come to America, where he had a chance to be free. My dad is a rock, stoic from his upbringing but thankful for his freedom. When I was growing up, he repeatedly told me as if it were his mantra, "I'm not going to tell you what to do; I didn't have a choice growing up. You choose." For instance, when I asked him where to go to college, he quickly said, "It's your decision. You choose." Those two words— "you choose"—have become one of my mantras.

The second foundational principle is that you have the power to choose. Thus, the freedom to choose aligns with the Action Pillar of the Three Pillars of Flourishing. As Aristotle said, flourishing is "an activity." We want to become deeply aware we have the absolute freedom to act, think, and respond. By exercising that incredible power of freedom, you can begin to make choices and take actions that move you in the direction of flourishing.

Let's now explore the key aspects of our freedom to choose.

YOU HAVE THE ABSOLUTE POWER TO CHOOSE THINGS WITHIN YOUR CONTROL

Perhaps not surprisingly, one of the books that has most influenced my life is Frankl's *Man's Search for Meaning*. In it, Dr. Frankl describes the horrors of his imprisonment in Nazi concentration camps during WWII. His parents, wife, and brother all died in those camps. During his imprisonment, Frankl endured indescribable pain, torture, and hunger. Stripped naked, shaved completely, and fed only water and small rations of bread, he described himself and other prisoners as tattered skeletons. They performed hard labor in the freezing outdoors, such as building rail lines. Anyone unable to work was sent to the camps where they were exterminated.

In surviving this unspeakable experience, Frankl made an incredible discovery: *Every person has the ultimate power to choose his or her response to any given situation or challenge.* In one of his most powerful quotes, Dr. Frankl states: "Everything can be taken from a man but one thing; the last of the human freedoms—to choose one's attitude in any given set of circumstances, to choose one's own way."[1] Never forget this.

Frankl's experience provides one of the most poignant examples of our power to choose how we will respond to any given situation. Frankl had essentially lost everything that mattered to him in the Nazi concentration camps, except one thing—his power to choose his thoughts and attitudes.

Frankl had drawn his wisdom from the sage Epictetus, who said: "We cannot choose our external circumstances, but we can always choose how to respond to them." In contrast, when you have no control over something, there is no reason to spend any time trying to change it. You can't argue with the weather, an accident, or the latest social media post. Any time spent on those matters will simply be a waste of your time. As Marcus Aurelius wisely stated, "Nothing is worth doing pointlessly."[2]

When you are litigating a case, you want to prevail. The outcome, however, is an external goal, not within your control. What *is* in your control are your actions, thoughts, and attitudes that you direct toward your goal. Thus, your goal becomes to litigate a case to the absolute best of your ability (which is internal to you and within your control).

It should come as no surprise to you that setting and focusing on your internal goals has a causal connection to whether you achieve an external goal. Is there a better way to prevail in a case than litigating it as excellently as you can? You have done your best and exercised as much influence over the outcome as ethically possible, but you can't control how a judge or jury will decide.

When things don't go your way, how do you respond? How do you react when something bad happens? How do you feel when you get criticized? Dr. Frankl gave us wise, practical advice. "Between stimulus and response, there is a space. In that space lies our freedom and our power to choose our response." The stimulus usually takes the form of a challenge, a criticism, or setback. After the stimulus, there is a "s-p-a-c-e." A gap of time. This gap is where your freedom lives. This space is where you have the freedom to choose your response, hopefully a more optimal, less reactive response.

I use this advice regularly. When I get triggered, sure, I have an immediate re-action. But, almost simultaneously, I remind myself to enter that space where I have time to respond appropriately. This space is where we have the power to choose how to respond.

As we become more aware of this space, we gain a calm ability to respond to trigger-ing situations. I encourage you to practice widening the gap to allow for response-ability. Do this in your daily routine where it matters most: first with yourself, next at work, and then the more challenging relationships.

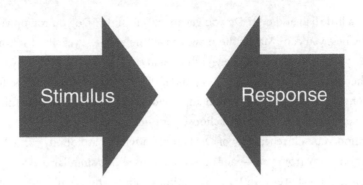

You have the amazing capacity of being responsible. The word *responsible* seems like a duty or a burden. But look at it as just the opposite. If you divide the word into two parts— "response" and "able" you see that you are "able" to "respond" how you choose. You are "response-able."[3]

I liken this power to choose our response to arguably the single most important Supreme Court case in United States history, *Marbury v. Madison*. In that case, the Supreme Court declared that an act of Congress was unconstitutional. More importantly, however, it established that the Supreme Court is the ultimate and final interpreter of the Constitution. In a vintage opinion, Chief Justice John Marshall stated it "is emphatically the duty of the Judicial Department to say what the law is."[4]

We have that same power. We are the Supreme Court of our mind. We get to say what our thoughts are. To decide how we perceive an event or input from someone. To form our beliefs. To respond to situations. To choose our attitudes. To act.

You possess this amazing power over your perceptions. You are constantly interpreting what you are doing, seeing, hearing, tasting, and feeling. You are always making perception choices. You can look at the same circumstance—your boss or spouse giving you constructive criticism, for example—through whatever lens you choose. The bottom line is that you are invariably choosing.

Objection, Your Honor, some of you might think. *What about real tragedy, the kind that judges see every day on the bench, involving death, murder, injury, illness, divorce, or bankruptcy?* Every day, the dark side of humanity and the deep despair of life rear their ugly heads. The child who has cancer, the family that lost its father in a car accident. There is almost nothing I haven't seen.

These horrible events don't change the truth that you are still responsible for your thoughts, feelings, and responses. Ultimately, life still empowers you to respond. Do you curl up in a little ball and quit? Do you get angry and fight? Do you roll up your sleeves and do the best you can? Maybe the answer to all the above is yes. But these actions are all choices you get to make. Maybe you first realize the common humanity of suffering that is inherent in life, and it's okay to cry and pull the sheets over your head for a while. Then you may get mad at the situation and cry out, "Why me?" But hopefully, you will eventually exercise your freedom to choose your best response.

Remind yourself repeatedly of Dr. Frankl's advice that nobody can take the ultimate freedom away from you—your power to choose. This singular realization that you have absolute control over your thoughts, attitudes, and actions will have greater impact to empower and help you thrive than any other aspect of your life.

THE MOST IMPORTANT QUESTION: WHAT IS WITHIN OUR CONTROL?

We have the freedom to choose things within our control. But what is within our control?

About 2,000 years ago, the philosopher and former Roman slave Epictetus, mentioned previously, observed the critical importance of determining what is within our control and what is not. He said: "The chief task in life is simply this: to identify and separate matters so that I can say clearly to myself which are externals not under my control, and which have to do with the choices I actually control."[5] I believe we should direct our energy toward what we can control, with an awareness that, because we're also faced with what we can't control, we can't always ensure our desired outcomes.

As a judge, I see this play out daily. A lawyer's job is to serve as a zealous advocate for his or her client. Lawyers argue the law and facts to the best of their ability. They can control how they present the law and marshal the evidence. At the end of the hearing or trial, however, it is the judge or jury who will ultimately decide the case.

In a recent trial, the plaintiff's lawyer controlled everything within her ability. Her attitudes, actions, and preparation. But, in the end, she couldn't control how the witnesses came across to the jury, what laws were in effect, or what the other lawyer did. The defense lawyer also did an exceptional job. The defense prevailed, and the plaintiff lost.

Even though disappointment is difficult, keeping your eye on what you can impact and doing your best are key to thriving and being resilient. A super practical way to identify what we can control is by classifying or sorting. We can place everything in life into one of two zones: the Control Zone or the No Control Zone.

In your Control Zone, there are only three things: your thoughts, your attitudes, and your actions. All three are within your complete control. That's all. Only with these do you possess 100 percent freedom. You can control what you believe in, how you think, and how you behave. Within the Control Zone, you are your own sovereign king or queen. You have complete control.

What type of matters and things are in the No Control Zone? Regarding what Epictetus referred to as "the externals"—such as our parents, friends, reputation, boss, co-workers, the weather, the economy, our past, our future, our body, and the time of our death—we can have some influence, but ultimately, they are not within our control.

Stephen Covey talks about two similar levels of control. One he calls the Circle of Influence, which includes things such as your family, your health, and your job. The other is the Circle of Concern—including environmental disasters, overpopulation, or the president's actions over which we have no real control (unless that is your job).[6]

Covey is essentially saying your thoughts, attitudes, and actions can influence (but not ultimately control) certain externals, such as your family, your health, and your job. On other things, such as what a politician does, you may be concerned, but ultimately, their actions are not within your ultimate control. Of course, we can and ought to do what is in our control regarding our leadership by voting, volunteering, and so on.

Importantly, the benefit of exerting control over the things you can control—your thoughts, attitudes, and actions—is increased flourishing and decreased negative emotions. If a co-worker is having a bad day or criticizes you, you can't control this. A driver who cuts you off or won't let you merge on the freeway is not within your control. You shouldn't ride the emotional roller coaster based on the actions of others. Nobody has permission to hurt you unless you let them. But you can control your responses to those events. This is key in responding to setbacks and challenges.

A fellow judge approached me after one of his decisions was reversed by the court of appeal. He had thoroughly researched the law, applied the facts appropriately, and written a sound opinion that appeared correct. The appellate court disagreed and came to the opposite conclusion. The case was a matter of public significance, so there were several newspaper articles identifying the judge. We discussed the importance of understanding the fundamental difference in what he can and can't control. I reiterated to him that he did everything to the best of his abilities and within his control, but he couldn't control how the court of appeal interpreted the law or how the press reacted.

You just played the best game of tennis in your life but still lost. How can that be? Your serves were amazing; you hit the ball consistently within the lines and had an excellent strategy. You nailed it. But the other player just played better. You can control how well you play, but you don't ultimately control whether you win or lose the match.

Everyone has some modicum of control in their lives. Remind yourself every day about what is and what isn't within your control and focus on the former.

TAKE INITIATIVE

Working tirelessly to realize the dream of becoming a partner is one of the most time-honored stories in the legal profession. Many of us start out in law school dreaming of changing the world, but by the time we start our first jobs, we dream of becoming a partner for the prestige, the security, and the money.

In my own life, I realized that dream when I made partner. I had interesting cases, a great book of business, and was making good money. At the same time, I felt I was living a nightmare. The job never left me alone. I saw I couldn't keep up with my current lifestyle. Work was good, but I was certainly not thriving at home, with friends, or with my health. I was seriously out of balance but felt I had no choice. I know what it's like to feel trapped and not see a way out. I needed to be brutally honest with myself and remember I had a choice.

We can change by taking initiative. The word *initiative* means "taking the first step or proactive action toward some objective." You set your own goal and take action toward that goal. You decide what you want to do with your career, your health, your relationships, your day, and then you act on those decisions.

Back to my story, I had choices. But at some point in time, I stopped examining my life from a higher level to make sure being a partner was what I truly wanted. I just got sucked into the vortex of becoming a partner and never really looked back. Sure, partnership is a worthy goal, but there were many other paths I could have chosen: in-house counsel, public agencies, or smaller firms with less billable hours.

I remember "that day" like it was yesterday. I had just gotten to my car after another late night at the office. It was about 11:00 p.m. on a Friday. I had three young children, and my wife was home taking care of them. I thought to myself, *What am I doing? This is crazy*. I started my car and began to circle out of the multi-level parking structure. I turned on my radio, hit the search button, and immediately heard this line from the song, "Homesick" by MercyMe: "If home's where my heart is then I'm out of place." I pulled my car into an empty parking space, and my eyes started to tear up. I decided right then. It was time to make a change.

The next day, Saturday, I did not to go in to work as was my typical weekend routine. Instead, I stayed home to think about my options. I took out a blank pad and started to brainstorm my choices. I came up with a good game plan to explore several alternatives and an exit strategy within six months. I was finally taking initiative.

Returning to work, I felt a new sense of hope. At lunchtime, when I had planned to do some more thinking about my choices, the phone rang. It was Terry, one of my former mentors. We were both college football fans, and he wanted to know if I was interested in some extra tickets to the upcoming game. Terry was also a judge, and he remarked that the new governor was looking for excellent judicial candidates, and he thought I would make an excellent judge. Ding, ding, ding!

Terry and I only talked for a few minutes, but when we hung up, I knew that was it. My Plan A was to try and become a judge. I flipped the page on my pad and wrote "JUDGE!" I then set off on a very deliberate plan to become a judge. The more I learned about it, the more I realized how the odds are seriously stacked against a candidate. Nevertheless, I absolutely became proactive to the core. I researched all the steps necessary; I talked to many judges about the subject and then deliberately executed my plan.

Was becoming a judge out of my control? Yes, but the process for applying was clearly within my control. The steps for becoming a judge in California are painstaking, and you can be eliminated through any of the multiple levels of the process. I told myself that I was going to go for it with my very best effort, and if I didn't get appointed by the governor, then I'd go back to Plan B.

After a six-month process, including multiple interviews and background checks, I eventually received a phone call from the assistant to the State's Judicial Appointments Secretary to set up a personal interview. I was excited and flew to the State Capitol about three weeks later. I prepared thoroughly for the interview and rehearsed how I would answer the myriad difficult questions, such as those regarding death penalty cases. The interview with Judicial Appointments Secretary John Davies lasted ninety minutes, and it seemed to go well.

After the meeting, it was still a crapshoot. You never know when or if you will get "the call." They never tell you, "No." You just don't get a call. In fact, a friend of mine who was about six months ahead of me in the process also had an interview and never got called.

About two weeks later, as I was getting ready for work, it happened. "Hello, Steve, John Davies here. How are you?" My heart leapt out of my body. "Fine, Mr. Davies, thank you. And you?" Davies replied, "Well, I have good news and bad news for you. What do you want to hear first?" *Okay, that was interesting.* Normally, I prefer to deal with the bad news first but wanted to know whether I was appointed, so I asked for the good news first. "Well, congratulations, the governor would like to appoint you as a judge of the Superior Court!" I thanked him sincerely and felt this incredible, but temporary, sense of joy.

"And what's the bad news, may I ask?" He answered, "Well, the governor is appointing you to an open seat, but you already have a challenger who will be running for your position." I got a little wobbly. He told me that if I accepted this appointment, I would be up for an election in a few months. I would have to run for my seat but under the title of "Judge." Running in an election in California is time consuming, very expensive, and stressful. I got answers to a few questions, including that I would have to wind up my legal practice, serve as a judge for a few months, and immediately start running for office while attending judicial college.

Davies asked, "So, what do you think? Do you want the appointment?" I had one internal voice fearfully saying, *seriously? You want me to give up my lucrative partnership so I can run for judicial office in an election as a novice Judge?* But the other voice was courageous and reminded me this is what I wanted, and I could do this. I also immediately remembered a judge telling me that if you are fortunate enough to get the call from the Judicial Appointments Secretary, you better accept the offer, or you won't ever get the call again. There were other outstanding candidates who would eagerly take the position if I hesitated or turned it down. So I accepted the appointment. He replied that I would be contacted shortly to get sworn in as a judge.

Shortly thereafter, I was sworn in and began my training as a judge. Long story short, once I was appointed and the seat no longer vacant, the person decided to run for a different judicial opening where there was no sitting judge. My seat was safe.

Throughout this process, I was very proactive in my approach to becoming a judge.

Stephen Covey identifies being proactive as "the first and most basic habit of a highly effective person."[7] It is the habit upon which all others are built. He's right. By proactively exercising my power to choose, I etched out and sealed a new course for my professional future.

In my opinion, the number one trait for a young lawyer and/or associate is to be proactive: continually take the initiative in your work. Often the difference between those who succeed and those who don't is initiative. Don't wait to be asked to do something. Rather, after you have finished an assignment, approach the partner in charge and ask what's next? This is the first and most basic level of being proactive, asking "What's next" or "How else can I assist?"

With more experience, you can ascend to the second level of being proactive by making specific suggestions for the next action. For example, you could say: "I just finished summarizing the responses to interrogatories, and I would like to follow up with speaking to the witness, or I suggest we serve a follow-up set of interrogatories." At this second level of initiative, you have done the task requested and then made a specific proactive suggestion of what you think should be done next.

As you gain further confidence, you can then take it to the third and highest level of proactivity. After you complete a task, inform the partner of what you plan to do next and then, with her or his approval, do it. For instance, you could say: "I just finished researching the statute of limitations and believe we have a good argument for a motion to dismiss. If it's okay with you, I'll have a draft of that motion to you by next week, which is seven days before the deadline to file the motion." At this level, you are proactively taking one step after another.

In my own experience as a partner and in my many conversations with other partners, one of the most challenging tasks in running a practice is finding associates who are proactive. More often, they are reactive. They wait for the partner to ask them to do an assignment. This requires a great deal more work by the partner to monitor and babysit an associate. Those who can consistently and competently work at the third level typically have a bright future.

This applies to every aspect of your life, not just your work. You are the captain who steers your own ship. You are the author of your own story.

If you want to start becoming more proactive, I recommend you think of the one thing—just one—that would have the biggest, most positive impact in your life, then make a commitment to do that one thing and follow through with your action. As you begin to consistently take initiative in your life through Action, the other principles of Vision and Virtue will be empowered.

TAKE RESPONSIBILITY FOR YOUR ACTIONS

Now that we have firmly established our power to choose things within our control, let's take this principle to a higher level. If you want to master this principle in your life, start to take full responsibility for everything within your control.

I have always admired the Navy SEALs. Not just because of their extraordinary bravery and skills, but also for their dedication, training, and commitment to becoming the most elite warriors on the planet. In their excellent book *Extreme Ownership*, former Navy SEALs Jocko Willink and Leif Babin discuss the SEALs' secret to success: Absolutely own everything in your life. In other words, take 100 percent responsibility for the success and failure of your missions. The authors write:

"In virtually every case, the SEAL troops and platoons that didn't perform well had leaders who blamed everyone and everything else—their troops, their subordinate leaders, or the scenario. They blamed the SEAL training instructor staff; they blamed inadequate equipment, or the experience level of their men. They refused to accept responsibility. Poor performance and mission failure were the result.

"The best performing SEAL units had leaders who accepted responsibility for everything. Every mistake, every failure or shortfall—those leaders would own it. During the debrief after a training mission, those good SEAL leaders took ownership of failures, sought guidance on how to improve, and figured out a way to overcome challenges on the next iteration. The best leaders check their egos, accepted blame, sought out constructive criticism, and took detailed notes for improvement. They exhibited EXTREME OWNERSHIP, and as a result, their SEAL platoons and task units dominated."[8]

The principle that you own everything within your control will set you free and empower you to your fullest potential. It's your choice and responsibility. Even if you choose not to accept responsibility, you are choosing. You make choices every moment of your life. You accept responsibility to get out of bed or not. You accept responsibility for when you go to bed or choose not to care. You accept responsibility for how you interact with people. You accept responsibility for how you spend your time.

I understand that lawyers feel like they don't have much control over their work life. I vividly recall when I was an associate and being excited to go away for the upcoming, three-day weekend. It was a late Friday afternoon, and I was packing my briefcase when an email with a large attachment arrived. It was a dreaded summary judgment motion. A trial on paper. Seriously! My due date to oppose the motion was just fourteen days away. I needed all fourteen days to work on an opposition. How was I going to go away for three days? How was I going to enjoy myself and relax during that time?

Realistically, lawyers can recognize they do not have control over what other lawyers or judges do. You are not in control in those respects. But that is not the most important aspect of control you have. Not even close. Within your control are still many critical choices. And many people in other occupations and businesses have told me this advice applies equally to them.

First and foremost, you can choose to go on your three-day weekend and enjoy it. You still have plenty of time to work on drafting an opposition to the motion. The ability to compartmentalize your life, to understand that recreation and balance are good for your health, and that your work must not control your life are all within your control.

Second, if you are going on a pre-planned vacation, consider serving ahead of time a standard notice of unavailability on your cases. That way, you give a heads up to opposing counsel and make a clear, written record.

Third, if you get a motion right before a trip, immediately contact the other side (hopefully you have a good relationship) and tell them you are in receipt of the motion and that you are leaving on a pre-planned, prepaid vacation for three days, so would they please continue the hearing for three additional days. You are not asking for more time than you would normally get and are not trying to get an advantage. You are just asking for the courtesy of a short extension. If they won't extend that common courtesy (which they should), then make a written record of their refusal and go before the judge upon your return and request three additional days. I can tell you from experience that most judges would grant that request and not be happy with opposing counsel. If the judge denies your request, then you roll up your sleeves and draft the very best opposition you can. You are now accepting responsibility and ownership over each of your choices.

Starting today, let's pay attention to the language we use. Consider words where we are accepting responsibility for more things in our life. People commonly speak as though they must do something. We hear ourselves or others saying, "I have to," as if there is no choice. But we do have choices. When we see that all our "have tos" are actually "choose tos," we will make better decisions and thrive more. We just need to look for alternatives and then choose how to respond. And when we start using phrases like, "I want to" and "I choose to" and "I'm going to," then we'll hear ourselves accepting personal responsibility for our lives.

The opposite of taking responsibility is blaming others, making excuses, or being a victim. This negative behavior cuts across all facets of our life—our health, our work, and our relationships. We are all good at making excuses as to why some aspect of our life is not flourishing.

I know a hardworking couple with two young children. Both are lawyers. The husband puts in long hours at his firm, and the wife works as both a part-time lawyer and part-time stay-at-home mom, raising their toddler and new baby. When the family's newest addition was just a few months old and having problems sleeping at night, he would cry for long stretches of time, night after night.

The husband would lie awake in bed thinking, *Why doesn't my wife get up and take care of the baby? I'm the one who must wake up early and work all day. I'm the primary breadwinner. Doesn't she realize that I need my sleep? How could she be so uncaring?* He would stew all night, blaming his wife. She, on the other hand, was able to sleep through the night because of sheer exhaustion from both working and taking care of the kids. When he awoke in the morning, the husband was typically mad at his wife, and it showed. He was unsupportive, uncaring, and uncommunicative. But what did the wife really do that was so bad? She slept. By blaming his wife, however, he saw her in a negative light and treated her accordingly.

The worst thing about blaming is you disempower yourself from exercising your own freedom. You are taking your greatest power—the power to choose your response—and giving it to someone else. Be aware of when you blame others. Any time you find yourself being a victim, stop and redirect yourself to controlling what you can control.

I'm not talking about the person who has been a true victim of such things as a crime, domestic violence, a terrible accident, a health crisis, or post-traumatic stress disorder (PTSD) after a long tour of military duty. Unfortunately, I've seen too many real victims in my court. Such victims may benefit from professional help. There are victims in this world, and I'm not in any way trying to minimize this.

Blaming or being a victim focuses on the past, which is something you have no control to change. In contrast, your power to choose focuses on the present, which you can control. Best-selling author Dr. Jordan Peterson says there are essentially two types of people—those who blame the world or others for their problems, and those who choose to respond to their problems by asking what they can do differently. Dr. Peterson believes that it is the second type of person who can truly improve his or her own life.[9]

Have you ever noticed when you point a finger at someone else, there are three fingers pointing back at you? If you want to grow as a person, start by accepting "response-ability" for your own choices. You can't thrive in life if you are constantly blaming others for your problems.

If you were to write your own story, would you write it as a victim or a hero? By accepting responsibility, you begin to create that story for yourself. You move from victim to hero. Accepting responsibility for those things within our control is an incredibly empowering action. And whether or not you do so is ultimately your choice. I encourage you to start flourishing by taking action and by realizing your foundational freedom to choose.

··

Chapter Summary:

- **A key question to ask yourself every day is, "What is within my control?"**
- **You have the absolute power to choose those things within your control.**
- **Take initiative.**
- **Take full responsibility for all your thoughts, attitudes, and actions.**

SIDEBAR _____

Don't be afraid to apologize to the court if you made a mistake. Courts are typically much more forgiving when counsel or a party accepts responsibility, rather than making excuses or blaming others.

CHAPTER 7

HAPPINESS IS A PURSUIT

• • •

*"My aim in life isn't so much the pursuit
of happiness as the happiness of pursuit."*
—CHARLES SAATCHI

The Preamble to the Declaration of Independence famously proclaims: "We hold these truths to be self-evident, that all men are created equal, that they are endowed, by their Creator, with certain unalienable Rights, that among these are Life, Liberty, and the pursuit of Happiness." These three fundamental rights of life, liberty, and the pursuit of happiness fortify the principles of flourishing in this book.

Regarding "life," we've established the game of life to have the objective of flourishing and our ability to create a clear Vision—the first Pillar of Flourishing—for our life.

When it comes to "liberty," we understand we have the freedom to choose and be responsible for the things within our control. This is the truth supporting our second Pillar—Action.

Now let's consider "the pursuit of happiness." On this pursuit, we must act virtuously and with antifragile confidence, even when things don't go our way. This is the third Pillar of Flourishing, Virtue.

The great movie, *The Pursuit of Happyness* (yes, the producers misspelled "happiness" intentionally), tells the true-life story of Chris Gardener, who is played by Will Smith. Chris is married with a child and working as a struggling salesman. He wanted to pursue his dream of becoming a stockbroker. However, he had to compete against many other high-achieving candidates for the lone, coveted position. At the same time, his wife left him and moved to another state; he got evicted, became homeless, and tried to be a loving, single father to his five-year-old son. The movie powerfully portrays Chris's attempt to make the most of his opportunity as an unpaid stockbroker intern while also caring for his son.

During a poignant point in the movie, Chris tells himself: "It was right then that I started thinking about Thomas Jefferson on the Declaration of Independence and the part about our right to life, liberty, and the pursuit of happiness. And I remember thinking, how did he know to put the 'pursuit' part in there? That maybe happiness is something that we can only pursue and maybe we can actually never have it. No matter what. How did he know that?"

We have the right to life and liberty. But we only have the right to pursue happiness. Yes, happiness is not a right but, as a byproduct of flourishing, it is attainable as we apply Vision, Action, and Virtue in our lives. Let's examine the four key characteristics that underlie the foundational principle for the Pillar of Virtue.

CHALLENGES AND PROBLEMS ARE GUARANTEED

Yes, life is often good. Much of life is filled with joy and happiness—until the cell-phone breaks; your internet crashes; your spouse criticizes you again; your boss throws a new assignment at you when you're already overwhelmed; and your back pain is throbbing. Or, worse, you or someone one you know loses their job; your marriage winds up on the rocks; and your doctor tells you your health isn't what it should be. Much worse could be that one of your parents is dying; you lose your home; some tragedy strikes. That's right: We interrupt this broadcast to give you breaking news: Your pursuit of happiness will encounter a never-ending cascade of challenges and problems along the way. This is a fact.

Consider this, the opening from the classic book, *The Road Less Traveled* by Dr. M. Scott Peck: "Life is difficult. This is a great truth, one of the greatest truths. It is a great truth because once we truly see this truth, we transcend it."

It is an absolute guarantee your life will be filled with challenges, problems, and even suffering. I am not saying life only involves challenges, problems, and suffering.

To the contrary, I'm an unapologetic optimist who thinks life is amazing, beautiful, and joyous. But I'm also a realist. And having problems and having a great life are not mutually exclusive. In fact, as we will discuss later in this chapter, challenges serve as our primary fuel for our growth and evolution as humans.

You are guaranteed to face adversity, and most problems and challenges fall into three general categories:

1. Those challenges you intentionally set or create for yourself—your goals and dreams,
2. Those challenges thrown at you that you didn't ask for, and
3. Society and other people's challenges, problems, and suffering.

Regarding the first category, it is difficult to live up to the standards we set. Undoubtedly, we will miss the mark. Sometimes, we will stumble, trip, and fall embarrassingly short along the way. If we are completely successful every single time, with every one of our goals, then we are not aiming high enough. Simply put, nobody is perfect.

Lawyers often face enormous stress, anxiety, and burnout in attempting to reach their lofty goals, including billable hours, pleasing the partner, marketing, servicing clients, or getting the work done on time. During my own legal career, many times I felt out of balance, overworked, or unsuccessful—sometimes all three simultaneously.

The founding father of positive psychology, Martin Seligman, concluded in his research that there is a "pervasive disenchantment" among lawyers. This disenchantment often leads to all types of emotional problems, including depression, alcoholism, drug abuse, and even suicide.[1]

As for the second category of problems, those that are thrown at us, we are constantly bombarded with unforeseen challenges. A difficult co-worker or boss. A marital dispute. A problem friendship. One of the most difficult types of challenges we face stems from interpersonal conflict. Indeed, such perpetual conflict occurs with and among our families, friends, workplace, communities, and nations. The primary reason interpersonal conflict is so difficult is because it isn't just about us. There is another person or persons on the other end of that disagreement. And she or he will have their equally strong thoughts, opinions, and emotions.

For lawyers, they make a living off life's never-ending problems, accidents, and transgressions. Society is honey-combed with disputes. Lawyers exist because of people's conflicts. If there were no disputes, there would be no need for lawyers. Imagine a world completely free from disputes—what would lawyers do?

For the third category of problems dealing with the world at large, where do we even start? The constant divisiveness among the political parties, the important societal issues of our day, such as immigration, healthcare, gun control, taxes, and much more. And the existential threats due to the climate, the pandemic, and war.

While it seems like problems may be worse in today's complex world, each generation since the dawn of human time has faced its own unique challenges. All the religious texts written thousands of years ago concur. The Bible says: "We all stumble in many ways."[2] The first Noble Truth of Buddhism is that life involves unavoidable suffering. Hindus view suffering as a part of living. The Jewish Talmud is replete with tragedy. Islam says it is God's design for people to face tests from their suffering.

So, yes, in your pursuit of happiness and flourishing, it is beyond any doubt that you will regularly face problems, challenges, and even suffering. That is the truth. I promise. But, as we will discuss next, that is not necessarily a bad thing.

EVERY CHALLENGE PRESENTS AN OPPORTUNITY

It was my very first day as a judge. I was ready. I had been a lawyer for a long time. I knew what I was doing. I was prepared. In fact, I had reviewed each of my files twice that morning before calling my calendar.

Never mind that my first judicial assignment was presiding over criminal cases, and that my background was primarily in civil law. I had been reading, studying, and training in criminal law for the past several months and had even observed criminal judges calling their calendars for the past week.

So I confidently took the bench, greeted the lawyers, and called my first case. The prosecution and the defense lawyer both stated their appearances, and before I could utter another word, the defense lawyer said, "Your Honor, I would like to make an Arbuckle Waiver."

A what? I had never even heard of an Arbuckle Waiver. (An Arbuckle Waiver is essentially a request by the defendant to be sentenced by a different judge when the original judge who took the plea is unavailable.) I was mentally knocked down with the first punch. But outwardly, I needed to keep my composure, so I calmly said, "You may proceed." After hearing from both sides, I asked counsel to approach at sidebar. I sincerely confessed my ignorance about Arbuckle Waivers. Fortunately, both the prosecutor and the defense lawyer were seasoned. They both were very respectful and appreciative of my candor. This gave both lawyers an opportunity to educate the judge.

It was an immediate and eye-opening experience right off the bat to realize judges don't know everything, nor should they. Most judges certainly know a fair amount, but typically the lawyers know more about their case than the judge, at least initially.

So, yes, I got knocked off my feet as a judge in my very first case. It certainly wasn't the first or last time I faced setbacks, challenges, and failures. Likewise, for many of you, you may have a goal and know what needs to be done but get tripped up or side-tracked. For others, you don't have a goal but are just trying to get through the day or not feeling perpetually lost. In either situation, the first step in the pursuit of happiness is understanding that *every problem is an opportunity*. The word *opportunity* means "a good chance for advancement or progress."

I learned this truth early in my own legal career. After one particularly stinging criticism about a legal brief I drafted for a partner, I came to this deep realization: Everything is an opportunity. I could either get dejected after being criticized, or I could get better. I chose the latter. Because challenges and problems are inevitable, I now saw that *life is a series of one opportunity after another*. In each moment, I get to choose how to respond to that opportunity. It was only when I realized all challenges were simply opportunities to grow that I started to really improve as a lawyer and person.

Problems equal opportunities.

Realize deeply that you can choose to use your challenges as opportunities for growth. The author Nassim Taleb, in his book *Antifragile*, calls this powerful concept "antifragile confidence."[3] He asks us to imagine three types of boxes. The first box is fragile. If it gets dropped or kicked, the thing inside the box breaks. The second box is sturdy. When it gets dropped or banged around, the thing inside doesn't break. It may get bruised or dented, but it essentially stays intact. The third box is "antifragile." When it gets dropped or kicked around, it *actually gets stronger*. It thrives from challenges. That's our goal: to be antifragile. We use our challenges as fuel for growth.

As Taleb writes: "Antifragility is beyond resilience or robustness. The resilient resists shock and stays the same; the antifragile gets better." Each time we get kicked, challenged, or fail, it's an opportunity to get better, an opportunity to grow.

Competition helps spur that growth. It is a biological fact that life involves competition. Evolution stems from survival of the fittest. There will always be competition for resources, jobs, mates, money, etc. However, as Charles Darwin noted: It is not the strongest of the species that survive, nor the most intelligent, it is the one that proves itself most responsive to change.[4]

Do you think your industry is going to stay static? For those who refuse to change or understand that technology is driving changes, you may face serious disadvantages in your practice. But if you embrace and learn from change and its associated technological progress, the future has never looked brighter.

Indeed, the American economy in general, and the U.S. legal system in particular, are undergoing major changes in the way they do business. You must change and grow with it. Every time you hear the word *change*, think *opportunity*. Rarely does life stand still. Are you moving forward in growth or going backwards because life is passing you by?

Your job as a lawyer or in any career provides an opportunity to serve others. Why are lawyers necessary in a civilized society? Because they are presented with a problem or a conflict and have an opportunity to resolve that problem or conflict for their client. Isn't that the purpose of our justice system? To resolve conflicts.

Just like sick and injured people need physicians, society needs a legal system to resolve disputes. A world without a legal system would lead to chaos, tyranny, and violence. In a civilization riddled with disputes and governed by laws, lawyers play a critical and important role. Remember you graduated from law school with a Juris Doctor, a Doctor of Laws. People see their Juris Doctor when they have a legal ailment. This is your opportunity to help them.

Look at your own health challenges. I'm sure you have at least one. At a younger age, many of you could eat whatever you wanted and look fit and trim. When I was seventeen, I remember regularly consuming an entire carton of ice cream after dinner and remained as skinny. I couldn't put on weight no matter how hard I tried. Fast forward fifteen years, and I started to notice love handles, while my waistline and other areas of my body were increasing in size. Hopefully, we come to the realization we can't keep doing the same things we used to do with our health. Problems equal opportunities.

Even injuries can present an opportunity to grow. When I turned forty, my friends and I planned on living out our lifelong dream of attending the Los Angeles Dodgers Adult Baseball Camp. It's a place where grown-ups can live out their childhood dreams of playing baseball with the pros. We planned our trip, and I started training for the camp.

At that same time, I was also in the process of moving to a new home. I was awkwardly moving a large, heavy object when I tripped on a box. I immediately felt an extremely sharp pain in my foot. It felt like I had been shot. I fell to the ground and took off my tennis shoe. My foot was bleeding. I assumed I had stepped on a nail, so I went to the ER where the x-ray confirmed I had a puncture wound in the fifth metatarsal bone of my toe. The nurse gave me a tetanus shot and sent me home. Several months and several doctors later, my foot was in more pain than ever. Needless to say, I couldn't play at baseball camp, and the trip was rescheduled.

Almost a year after my accident, my foot had gotten worse. I finally saw a renowned foot surgeon who informed me I had a major foot infection and if I did not have surgery immediately, I would likely have to have my toe amputated. I had surgery the following week, followed by a month of IV antibiotics administered by a pic-line. I was finally hopeful again about my health and attending baseball camp.

A month after my surgery, my foot was just as painful and swollen as ever. I went back to the surprised surgeon, who took a CT scan and said, "I see it." "What?" I asked. "I'm not exactly sure," said the surgeon, "but there is an object right inside your bone." The surgeon scheduled a second surgery a few days later. When I awoke after the surgery, the doctor said, "You won't believe it, but I found an intact, wooden golf tee inside your foot." (One hundred percent a true story!)

When I tripped while carrying the heavy object, the golf tee was thrust into my foot, but because it was made of wood, it did not show up in the initial x-ray or earlier CT scan. After the first surgery and the bone was cleaned, the golf tee just popped to the surface of my foot, and it was easily removed during the second surgery.

The entire injury and episode took almost a year and a half to resolve. Although I couldn't do normal physical or baseball training, I nevertheless used it as an opportunity to do things I had never done before like strengthen my throwing arm by focusing on rotator cuff exercises. I also read every book I could get my hands on about the art and science of hitting a baseball.

When I was finally able to attend the Dodgers baseball fantasy camp, I performed much better and was much stronger than I would have been without the injury. I stayed committed to doing things even with my injury. I was able to "make lemonade out of a lemon."

The Chinese symbol for the word *crisis* actually means "a dangerous opportunity." When Dr. Peck wisely observed that "life is difficult," he also showed us that we have the opportunity to take the path less traveled. It is the path marked "dangerous opportunity."[5] Each time you are confronted with a difficulty, challenge, or problem, you will have a fork in the road. You can take the path of being a victim/defeated or seeing it as an opportunity.

This became a true paradigm shift in my life, and I hope it does for you as well. I now look at problems completely opposite from the way I used to—even those that are thrown at me unprovoked. When I was young, I often loathed problems. "Oh, not again," I would say to myself. Now, I no longer see them as bad things; instead, they present me with opportunities. They are problems to solve in order to get better and grow in virtue.

The more difficult type of challenge is when you didn't specifically ask for that challenge, but it just arose from your spouse, family member, child, friend, boss, health, etc. These are typically more complicated because they involve another person or something not entirely within your control. Yet, they also present an opportunity to practice this truth. No matter what happens, you can look at the challenge as an opportunity.

When one of my children faced a life-threatening illness, it was the scariest time in my life. When the doctor first told us the news, I almost fainted. My wife and I were in tears. There was immediate denial, but almost as quickly, I turned that around to viewing this as the most important opportunity for me to show up at my very best, an opportunity to love and support my child, as well as an opportunity to get the best medical treatment possible. You see, it was a fact: my child had a life-threatening and incredibly serious medical condition. I could have argued with reality all I wanted, but I would have lost that argument every time. Seeing that this incredible problem also presented an incredible opportunity was empowering. While I certainly do not wish this on anyone, I became more committed to being the best father than I ever had before.

If flourishing is the ultimate purpose in life and if we are constantly faced with challenges, then our golden opportunity is to solve problems, to overcome challenges. Every time we do, we learn and grow in virtue.

EMBRACE THE SUCK

Linda Brown was a nine-year-old girl living in Topeka, Kansas, in the 1950s. She lived just a few blocks from the nearest public school. However, because she was Black, Linda and her two younger sisters had to walk one mile through a railroad switchyard and then take a bus several more miles to an all-Black school.

Can you imagine being their parents? Having your children walk right past a perfectly good school solely because of their skin color? Well, enter Mama and Papa Bear—Mrs. and Mr. Brown—who attempted to enroll their children in the "White" school right next to their home. They were denied, so they filed suit in a case called *Brown v. Board of Education*.[6]

The case eventually wound up before the U.S. Supreme Court. There, in a unanimous decision, the Supreme Court overturned the so-called "separate but equal" laws for public schools, finding that they violated the Constitution. Chief Justice Earl Warren wrote the opinion: "We conclude that, in the field of public education, the doctrine of 'separate but equal' has no place. Separate educational facilities are inherently unequal."

I think about all the people who endured the challenge of trying to achieve the noble goal of racial equality in education: How their school applications were rejected, how they were tormented and ridiculed for their efforts, how they lost in trial courts, and how they hoped for the courageous Supreme Court to do the right thing.

I think of Elizabeth Eckford, just fifteen years old, who was captured in the dramatic Pulitzer Prize photograph showing her bravely walking into her high school after the *Brown* decision while being screamed at by an angry White mob. I think of all the Black children who came before and after her.

I think of lawyers like Thurgood Marshall, who argued the *Brown* case before the Supreme Court. Marshall endured segregation his entire life. When he wanted to attend law school at the University of Maryland, he was denied because they did not accept Black people. Those obstacles continued to make Marshall stronger. Just two years after graduating from law school, Marshall pursued and won his case against the University of Maryland, ordering it to integrate the school. Marshall was eventually appointed to the U.S. Supreme Court.

Years later, a speaker at an event commemorating Justice Marshall recalled a story about him as the lawyer handling the *Brown v. Board of Education* case. When Marshall faced incredible pressure from the case, he would think of Justice John Marshall Harlan, who in 1896 had written the lone dissent in *Plessy v. Ferguson*. The speaker noted: "Marshall admired the courage of Harlan more than any justice who has ever sat on the Supreme Court. Even Chief Justice Earl Warren's forthright and moving decision for the court in *Brown* did not affect Marshall in the same way. Earl Warren was writing for a unanimous Supreme Court. Harlan was a solitary figure writing for posterity."[7]

Challenges are not just opportunities. When properly understood, problems and challenges can actually serve as fuel for growth and positive change. As wood is to fire, challenges serve as your propellent for getting stronger.

The U.S. Navy SEALs have a motto for this truth. It's called "Embrace the Suck." The SEALs know the "suck" is what actually gives them their strength. They don't just deal with challenges, they embrace them. They love challenges. They become their energy bars.

Could you imagine Superman, Wonder Woman, the Black Panther, or any of the Avengers without obstacles to overcome? What if Harry Potter had no Voldemort? Luke Skywalker had no Darth Vader? Their nemesis provided them with opportunities for greatness. The Roman emperor Marcus Aurelius said swallow your challenges as if they were a pill to make you stronger. What you swallow becomes your power.

Here's a great exercise that will help you identify your own power to overcome and achieve. Take a moment to write down three accomplishments for which you are most proud. (Cue the music from *Jeopardy*.) Next, consider the challenges associated with them. In fact, for virtually all great achievements in life, there exists a direct correlation with the degree of difficulty.

When you go on your own personal hero's journey, you will find the greater the challenge, the greater the reward. The great heroes all descend into what Joseph Campbell calls the abyss, some metaphorical deep pit. It's through those travails the hero comes out stronger and better. Campbell calls this the "boon," which is where the hero learns how to effectively handle the suffering, challenge, or failure. The hero now possesses a new, special skill.

One of Campbell's most famous lines is: "Follow your bliss." In other words, follow the path that makes you flourish. But that advice is better understood in its more complete context of the hero's journey, which is to first "follow your blisters" and then you can achieve your bliss. You are not pursuing a hedonic life but a challenging life. Eudaimonic, not hedonic.

One of my favorite practical tools to remind myself of the principle that challenges are our power is: "OMMS." I don't mean "ohms," which are often repeated during meditation. I mean "OMMS" as an acronym for "Obstacles Make Me Stronger." Literally see that every time you face an obstacle or challenge of some type, whether it is physical, mental, emotional, or spiritual, it actually gives you an opportunity to get stronger and to do so virtuously.

I first learned of OMMS from one of my own coaches, Michael Balchan, as he was discussing our training for the Spartan Race. The Spartan Race is an obstacle course race where you must overcome one obstacle after another. You train for the Spartan Race by running, jumping, climbing, and pulling yourself over obstacles and undoubtedly get stronger in the process.

This is obvious in the physical sense. You can't get stronger by lifting Styrofoam weights. You must lift heavier weights. You get stronger, faster, and have more endurance by challenging yourself physically. Challenges are *necessary* to grow. Yes, they are uncomfortable, but they are transformational.

There are several versions of a great poem called "Choose Your Hard."[8] Here is my own version:

Life is hard. But that's not a bad thing. In fact, every person who has accomplished greatness has done so only through his or her own challenges.

Yes, life is hard.

At the same time, life is also good. There is much joy in life.

Life is both hard and good.

As we go through life, we will have numerous opportunities to choose our hard, and those hard choices will often dictate the type of good life we will experience.

Marriage is hard but so is divorce.

Being healthy is hard but so is obesity.

Saying no to the things you really want to buy is hard but so is being in debt.

Choose your hard.

Genuine communication with a close friend or family member is hard. It's also hard not communicating and letting the problem fester and the relationship erode.

It's hard to go to work or study. It's especially hard when your friends want to go out, or there is a fun show to watch. It's also hard to not do well in school or to not get a good job. To not fulfill your potential.

It's hard dealing with an addiction. It's also hard to be imprisoned by one.

Yes, life is hard.

Choose your hard wisely.

Choose noble, uplifting goals.

Choose to work hard.

Choose to do the right thing.

For every challenge or adversity, there are at least two choices—often two hard choices.

Which hard will you choose?

At every moment of your life, you will have an opportunity to choose!

THE PURSUIT IS A NEVER-ENDING PROCESS

He is not a lawyer, a judge, or even in the legal profession. You may have never heard of him before I mentioned him earlier in this book. But Ray Dalio was one of the seventy wealthiest people on the planet as of 2020. Once considered one of the fifty most influential people in the world, according to Bloomberg publications, he founded and ran a company, Bridgewater Associates, which was said to be one of the top five most impactful private companies in America.

Dalio was certainly not born with a silver spoon or set up so that such achievement would be easier. He was a poor student in New York and didn't like school. His initial work life had more failures than fortune. He started his own investment company but floundered. Early in his career, he made a widely publicized prediction and bet everything he had that the U.S. would plunge into a depression in the early 1980s. He ended up being, in his own words, "dead wrong." He lost almost everything, had to borrow $4,000 from his dad just to pay his bills, and downsized to just one employee—himself.

But Dalio repeatedly realized the pursuit of happiness and success, if done right, follows an established process. He articulated five-steps for success in which you (1) set a goal, (2) fail, face an obstacle, or confront a challenge, (3) diagnose the problem, (4) learn and grow, and (5) set a new, higher goal based on the new information you learned.

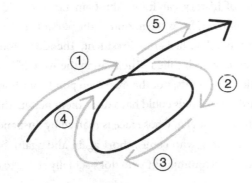

What I love about this process is that instead of giving up or scaling back when we experience failure, we instead analyze our failure, learn from it, and use what we learn to take an even bigger leap. Dalio says, "I believe that the key to success lies in knowing how to both strive for a lot and fail well. By failing well, I mean to be able to experience painful failures that provide big learnings without failing badly enough to get knocked out of the game."[9]

This advice has profoundly impacted my own life. By following such a process, I can keep striving and continually spiral upward and grow in all my endeavors—even my failures. As long as I reflect on and learn from my pain, challenges, and failures, I will progressively evolve.

Growth is a process, a true pursuit in all aspects of life, from health to work to relationships. For instance, if I eat something that doesn't agree with me or do something that causes me not to sleep well, I learn from those events and spiral upward in improving my health. As a young lawyer, I had an opportunity to take the deposition of an important witness in a big civil rights case. The lawyer defending the witness was a seasoned lawyer. Throughout the deposition, he asserted numerous objections and badgered me. When the deposition ended, I was frustrated and felt like he had prevented me from getting the testimony I needed. The next day, I thought about what I learned and how I could do better the next time by not being so rattled by opposing counsel and by focusing on getting the answers to my questions. I had the opportunity to take another deposition in that same case with the same opposing lawyer, and while I was far from perfect, I definitely improved.

We can all share in that same transformative process. Just like Chris Gardner in the *Pursuit of Happyness*, we can intentionally undergo a metamorphosis "if" we understand the spiraling up process. As author Sarah Young puts it, "When you reframe setbacks as opportunities, you find that you gain much more than you lost."[10]

Study the lessons of history carefully, Abraham Lincoln said, otherwise you're doomed to repeat past failures. This is the notion of the pursuit. To learn from your mistakes and continue striving. Another great President, Theodore Roosevelt, said something similar in his famous speech called "The Man in the Arena:"

"It is not the critic who counts; not the man who points out how the strong m a n stumbles, or where the doer of deeds could have done them better. The credit belongs to the man who is actually in the arena, whose face is marred by dust and sweat and blood; who strives valiantly; who errs, who comes short again and again, because there is no effort without error and shortcoming; but who does actually strive to do the deeds; who knows great enthusiasms, the great devotions; who spends himself in a worthy cause; who at the best knows in the end the triumph of high achievement, and who at the worst, if he fails, at least fails while daring greatly, so that his place shall never be with those cold and timid souls who neither know victory nor defeat."

In your own life, enter the arena, set bold goals, and learn to fail well. Know you will inevitably face adversity, problems, or even failure. Each of these challenges will present an opportunity—an opportunity to learn, grow, and become a wiser and stronger person. Now equipped with that new knowledge and strength, set out on your new goal and adventure. This is the process of pursuing happiness. Repeat and enjoy!

As we finish Part II of the book, we have now covered the principles embedded in the Three Pillars of Flourishing—Vision, Action, and Virtue—and how they apply to every aspect of your life. To recap, no matter what you are doing and where you are in your life, I believe it is possible for you to:

- Be purpose-driven by gaining clarity on the missions, roles, and ideal identities in your life (Chapter 5),
- Use your freedom to choose your thoughts and actions (Chapter 6), and
- Face your inevitable challenges, not only as opportunities but also with confidence, causing you to grow and evolve (Chapter 7).

Together, these three principles constitute the great evolutionary process of life. They will allow you to continually progress toward achieving your most important goals. Now let's move to the specifics of the first Pillar, Vision, and how exactly it contributes to your professional and personal flourishing.

Chapter Summary:

- You are guaranteed to face challenges and problems in life.
- View every challenge and problem as an opportunity.
- Understand deeply that challenges and problems are your fuel for growth.
- The pursuit of happiness is a never-ending journey of evolving and improving.

SIDEBAR _____

Don't speak directly to opposing counsel in court, and never interrupt opposing counsel when they are speaking to the judge. Let them finish, and then you can address the court.

PART
THREE

THE THREE PILLARS OF FLOURISHING

The First Pillar of Flourishing

VISION: Have Meaningful Goals

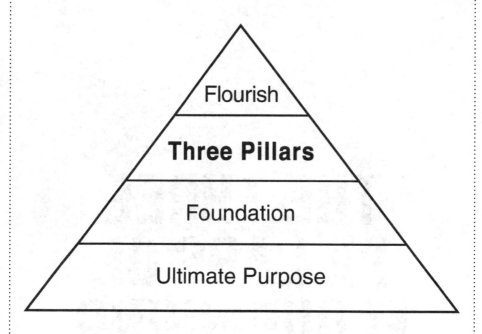

CHAPTER 8

PERSONAL WELL-BEING

• • •

"To optimize potential, we must train ourselves in a whole person, balanced manner."

—MARK DIVINE

It was about 2:00 a.m. when I crawled into bed. Exhausted, I had just fallen asleep when flashing lights and loud bangs startled me awake. Somebody was in our room, hitting what appeared to be a trash can lid with a stick. "Get up, get dressed, and be out in one minute—or else!" I threw on my clothes and ran outside, where I was blasted with cold water from a hose. "Thirty burpees. Now!" barked the leader.

After finishing the burpees, we were off for a run. We ran several miles soaking wet until we arrived at the beach. We were told to lock arms with our teammates and slowly walk backwards into the dark, cold Pacific Ocean. When we were about knee-deep in water, we were told to lie down but under no circumstances could we break the arm locks we had with our team. The cold waves crashed on us continuously. Our straight line soon zigzagged. We tried to stay in line, but it was nearly impossible. The ocean current was strong, and we were pulled backward and forward. It seemed like we were in the water for hours. We were cold, wet, and battered, but we never let go.

Upon exiting the water, we headed to the middle of the sand, where we were ordered to cover our swim buddy with the white sand from head to toe. "Make sure you make a great sugar cookie," the leader said, laughing. "If I see any clothing, you're going back into that cold ocean." Naturally, I covered my swim buddy from head to toe with sand. Then, I lay down and closed my eyes as he coated me in sand.

We next performed numerous exercises—squats, push-ups, sit-ups, sprints, and more—all while blanketed in sand. We then ran back to our camp, where we were hosed off again with frigid water and ordered back to bed. About two hours later, we began our next training.

The time I spent at the Navy SEALs training camp was quite a memorable and impactful experience. This was a civilian camp run by Navy SEAL Commander Mark Divine and his fellow SEAL trainers, who provide the attendees a weeklong experience of what it's like to be a member of that elite tribe.

The penultimate goal of the Navy SEALs training is essentially to push you past your normal limits physically, mentally, and emotionally. I got a taste of this during the training camp, because for most of my time there I was wet and sandy. I mean, sand was literally everywhere.

The supreme aim of the SEALs is to create physically, mentally, and emotionally strong individuals who can handle unbelievable challenges. That's why at camp they teach you to be comfortable with being uncomfortable. I believe it's true that growth is right outside your comfort zone—it's going to feel uncomfortable.

Although I'm not equating working in the legal profession to being a Navy SEAL, our profession is incredibly stressful and pressure packed. The physical, mental, emotional, and spiritual dimensions in our life are each important to our personal well-being. As we develop and strengthen in each of these dimensions, we'll not only thrive more in our lives, but we'll also be better able to handle the daily pressures and challenges thrown our way.

Personal well-being should be an essential part of our Vision (the First Pillar of Flourishing) for the future. Without it, how can we thrive while achieving our goals? Our aim should be to optimize our complete personal wellness and be as psychologically fit as we are physically fit. In this chapter, we will examine the four key aspects of personal well-being, which are to (1) develop the whole person, (2) pursue excellent health, (3) have mental and emotional intelligence, and (4) cultivate spirituality.

DEVELOP THE WHOLE PERSON

The Navy SEALs are elite athletes, no doubt, but they are also true warriors of the mind. They cultivate and practice mental control and emotional resilience as much as physical training. They understand the symbiotic relationship between their body and mind. Make no mistake about it, the Navy SEALs are elite because they train and develop all aspects of their person. This is called "whole person" development.

True well-being consists primarily of four qualities—physical, mental, emotional, and spiritual. People too often treat each of these areas as separate silos, saying, "I'm working so hard at my job; I don't have time to exercise or eat well." Or "Yes, I'm stressed, but it is just part of the job."

Ancient wisdom has long taught the connection between the body, mind, and spirt. They understood that each was one part of the whole. Likewise, modern science, including integrative medicine and positive psychology, have overwhelmingly established that your health and well-being have to do with much more than just your physical body. It is now simply beyond dispute that your physical health is significantly impacted by the mental, emotional, and spiritual aspects, and vice versa. All four aspects are interdependent.

For example, modern medicine has shown that your emotions, such as stress, have profound influences on your physical body. Stress can increase your risk of heart attack, weaken your immune system, cause high blood pressure, decrease sexual libido, and cause insomnia. That's not even including all the resultant behaviors from stress, such as exercising less, withdrawing socially, becoming more prone to anger, overeating, and ingesting alcohol, caffeine, tobacco, marijuana, or other drugs more often.

The opposite is also true. If you want to have a great mental and emotional state, you need to take care of your body. Numerous studies conclude that psychology is substantially impacted by physiology. A person who is physically well resourced through good sleep, good nutrition, and proper exercise is much more likely to have stronger mental clarity and emotional resilience. It's an amazing positive feedback loop. Better health, then better mental and emotional state of mind. Bad health, worse mental and emotional health.

By the same token, if you want to be physically healthy, your mind is the key to taking proper actions. To paraphrase the great Yogi Berra, life is 90 percent mental, and the other half is physical. If you have appropriate mental control, you are much more likely to eat healthier, exercise more, and sleep better. That's why one of my favorite mantras is "strong mind, strong body." A healthy body starts with a strong mind.

Think of your health and well-being like the Pixar movie *UP*. Carl, the elderly protagonist, sets out on an adventure by attaching a multitude of balloons to his home, which floats away. Afterward, Carl encounters several obstacles—some of the balloons start to pop, and his house begins to fall to the ground. That's the way your health and well-being work. Each of the balloons represents a different facet of your whole self. Let a few of them pop or go flat, and you will start sinking. Keep the balloons inflated, and your life will soar!

PURSUE EXCELLENT PHYSICAL HEALTH

Our physical health provides the energy and vitality necessary to flourish. Think of your physical health as a vehicle. Your body needs to have energy to take you where you want to go. In fact, the etymology of the word *energy* means "the capacity to do work." Your energy is your engine.

In Maslow's original hierarchy of needs, the base of his pyramid is physical. If you get yourself physiologically healthy, you will naturally move up to the next level. You are not going to actualize your potential if you don't have good physical health and energy.

What constitutes a solid foundation of health? In his best-selling book, *Eat, Move, Sleep*, Tom Rath discussed the three necessities for health—nutrition, exercise, and rest. As Rath said, "I am a more active parent, a better spouse, and more engaged in my work when I eat, move, and sleep well." All three work together. Improvement in one area will make it easier to improve in the others. Rath continues: "Starting your day with a healthy breakfast increases your odds of being active in the hours that follow. This helps you eat well throughout your day. Consuming the right food and adding activity makes for a much better night's sleep. This sound night of sleep will make it even easier to eat well and move more tomorrow. See the synergistic circle here."

"In contrast, a lousy night of sleep immediately threatens the other two areas. That bad night of sleep gives you less willpower to eat a healthy breakfast and decreases your odds of being active. In the worst-case scenario, all three elements start to work against you, creating a downward spiral that makes each day progressively worse."[1]

Let's get these three fundamentals—eating, moving, and sleeping—dialed in and make daily healthy choices. Small decisions will pay huge health dividends now and in the future. So let's energize to optimize our lives.

One word of caution: I'm not a medical doctor. If you have any significant health or medical issues, please consult with a health care provider. Everybody is different and has his or her own issues, genetics, hormones, and so on, so find what works for you. There is no "one-size-fits-all" for health. The principles I'm highlighting are based on the best and most trusted scientific research currently available.

Eating

If our body is the engine, then eating is the fuel. Eating is the propellent our body needs to go. Optimize with the right fuel, and we're on our way to improving our energy, health, and vitality. By eating poorly, we do just the opposite. We have less energy, less vitality, and we are more likely to gain weight and have medical issues.

Moreover, most people don't understand that eating plays a significant role in our mood, mental functioning, and overall well-being. In their book, *The Happiness Diet*, Tyler Graham and Drew Ramsey show "your personal pursuit of happiness is at the end of your fork." The hormone serotonin is considered the feel-good hormone. Surprisingly, however, 90 percent of the body's serotonin is produced in our gut, not our brain. Fortunately, there is a pathway that connects the gut to the brain. What we eat impacts our serotonin levels and, thus, our mood.[2]

My life-coaching client, Patricia (not her real name), was a typical lawyer, spending ten to twelve hours a day chained to her desk. She was twenty-five pounds overweight with little muscle tone, no energy, and she was certainly not healthy. After I met with her, Patricia decided to take health into her own hands. We decided to break her health into smaller goals, starting with eating.

To help her regain control over her eating and overall health, I shared with Patricia the four key guidelines below for healthy eating, which I uncovered through extensive research and experience.

1—Maintain Healthy Weight by Eating Right

Societal obesity is an epidemic. According to research, 75 percent of men and 60 percent of women are overweight. Further, the number one predictor of illness is being overweight. So, the very first step toward optimal nutritional is to aim for a healthy weight.

The chief measure of morbidity is your waist circumference. Specifically, your height-to-waist ratio is the best predictor for your health, better than just how much you weigh. If your height-to-waist ratio is good, chances are your weight will be good.

Based on a plethora of scientific data, the ideal height-to-weight ratio is 0.5.[3] Start with your height. For example, if you are six feet tall (72 inches), then you would divide your height in half or by 0.5. A person who is six feet tall would have an ideal waist size of 36 inches or smaller (72/0.5 = 36). If you are five feet tall (60 inches), your ideal waist size would be 30 inches (60 inches divided in half = 30 inches).

When Patricia first measured her waist-to-height ratio, she was a 0.6. She called to tell me lightheartedly, "Darn, it looks like I need to grow three inches taller." Her ratio placed her above the healthy range for abdominal obesity.

The reason we put weight management under eating is because your weight and waist circumference are dictated primarily by your eating. Evidence shows weight loss is essentially 80 percent eating. If you want to lose weight, you should primarily focus on your eating. You can lose weight without exercising. But you can't lose weight if your caloric intake through eating exceeds your calorie burn through exercise. You must have a caloric deficit to lose weight, and you can't out-exercise a bad diet.

It is very important to note that any discussion of weight should never be construed as shaming. Instead, focus on optimal health, more energy, and preventing health problems by being intentional about what you choose to consume. In fact, it's exciting to consider all the immediate positive impacts in your life getting into a healthy weight range.

2—Eat Real Food

Next, Patricia and I discussed different nutritional plans and principles, and she realized that picking and sticking to a simple, doable nutritional plan would be the key. I'm intentionally not using the word *diet*. Look for a nutrition plan you can stick to in the long run. It's a lifetime eating plan.

While there are literally hundreds of different plans, virtually all the proven ones agree on one thing—eat real food. The father of modern medicine, Hippocrates, said, "Let your food be your medicine, and your medicine be your food." In their best-selling book *It Starts with Food*, the authors Dallas and Melissa Hartwig echo the same thought: "The food you eat either makes you more healthy or not. Those are your options." There's no food neutrality; there's no food Switzerland.

Whatever nutritional plan you choose, it should consist mostly of real food. Real food heals your body (and the planet). It comes mostly from plants but is not made in manufacturing plants. You know what real food is. For me, it's simply what was available to our ancestors because we know they didn't have access to food in the industrial modern era. Look for your food to be in its natural (unprocessed) state and as close to the source as possible. From the farm to your fork is best.

Vegetables, fruits, meats, oats, whole grains, brown rice, yogurt, cheese, eggs, nuts, and legumes are good examples. If you eat meat, your protein sources should be high quality such as organic, grass-fed, and free-range. Your fruits and vegetables should be fresh and include an assortment of varieties and colors. Fats should come from healthy, natural sources such as whole nuts, seeds, avocados, olive oils, and the like. Choose organic whenever possible.

What are you putting in your mouth? Is it mostly real food? Are you getting more or less healthy with your eating? Fruits—healthy! Captain Crunch—unhealthy. Vegetables—healthy! Donuts—unhealthy. Water—healthy! Soda—unhealthy. You get the picture. Don't look at eating as a negative. Look at is as gift of energy, health, and vitality.

3—Eliminate the Negative Foods

One of the biggest steps you can take toward eating right is simply eliminating some of the bad or unhealthy foods from your diet. Just removing the dietary "kryptonite" will make you feel like a new person. There are numerous foods to eliminate from the American diet, which can wreak havoc on our health.

Michael Pollan, one of my favorite authors on nutrition, discusses the serious consequences of the Modern American Diet and the Standard American Diet—MAD and SAD, respectively. Pollan writes that individuals who follow the MAD and SAD way of eating "invariably suffer from high rates of the so-called Western diseases: obesity, type 2 diabetes, cardiovascular disease, and cancer. Virtually all the obesity and type 2 diabetes, 80 percent of the cardiovascular disease, and more than a third of all cancers can be linked to this diet. Four of the top ten killers in America are chronic diseases linked to this diet."[4]

What can you get rid of if you currently follow the typical American way of eating? I would argue that the two most important eliminations you can make for the biggest impact are sugar and white flour. The science is overwhelming: Sugar and white flour are simply bad for you.

Sugar has the same effect on the brain as a drug and is addictive. In fact, sugar lights up the same response in the brain as do nicotine, cocaine, and alcohol. It's the fundamental cause of obesity and the explosion of diabetes. When you eat sugar, your body will continually crave it and be hungrier more often. Not a winning combination for weight management.

Like sugar, white flour is also a fast-acting carbohydrate that causes the same erratic blood-sugar levels. It also lights up similar parts of the brain for addictions. By eliminating the white flour from your diet, you can avoid the regular highs and lows of feeling full and then famished. If that is not enough, white flour adds to your belly fat, is bad for your liver, impedes proper digestion, damages your teeth, and may contribute to depression.

I call the process of eliminating sugar and white flour as "slaying the white dragon." For Patricia, the elimination of processed sugar was her ticket to better health. When she first tried eliminating sugar, the "white dragon" raised its ugly head, almost crushing her determination. But, after several weeks, the cravings decreased, and eventually she slayed that dragon. For the first time in her life, Patricia was genuinely starting to get control of her eating. Her food was no longer controlling her. By simply eliminating these two food kryptonites, she felt better, looked better, and had more energy.

Step 4—Eat in Moderate Quantities

In his book, *Food Rules*, Michael Pollan summarized his simple food philosophy in eight words: Eat real food, not too much, mostly plants. Let's focus on the second of his guidelines—not eating too much. I'm talking about portion control.

You can have too much of a good thing. A healthy dinner with chicken, roasted vegetables, and a salad with oil and vinegar dressing can still be too much if your portion is too large. Then there's my good friend who loves chocolate chip cookies. Of course, enjoying soft, warm, mouth-watering cookies on occasion is one of life's great pleasures. The problem for my friend is that if he eats one, he'll eat a half-dozen.

We need to eat in moderation. This is mostly being conscious of not taking too large a portion. If you want to apply this very specifically, I recommend you learn the healthy serving size for your body type and stature. The authors of *It Starts with Food* recommend your protein portion should be about the size of the palm of your hand, two-thirds of your plate consist of vegetables, and a small portion can be fruits and/or good fats. For those who are better off with clear-cut rules, numerous diets offer specific measurements, such as in the *Bright Line Diet* or the *21-Day-Fix*, which uses portion control dishware.

A Few Practical Eating Tools to Consider

Create bright lines. Eating is often tied to emotions and willpower. One of the most effective tools is to mentally create a bright line in your eating. That means you pre-commit to sticking to your plan. When you play in the grey areas, you are constantly having to decide whether you should or shouldn't have that cookie. If you create a bright-line—say, sugar—then you have decided in advance you will not eat something with added sugar. Decision made.

Play offense. Rather than reacting to the unhealthy stimuli in your cupboard, refrigerator, or office, make your kryptonites invisible. Go on the offensive and purge your pantry or office of those items. Either throw it out or give it to somebody. Same for when you're shopping. Author Tom Rath says "the most influential choices you make for your health occur in a grocery store. Once you put something in your cart, good or bad, it's likely to end up in your stomach."

Replace. It's difficult to just eliminate things without replacing them with something else good. You can't just get rid of everything delicious in life. I love blueberry muffins and regularly ate them for breakfast. If I had just gotten rid of them, I would have felt feel deprived. Fortunately, when I was young, my father created mouthwatering desserts out of fresh fruit. Whatever the season, he would find the best ripe, fruit and cut it up in a delectable way. As a result, I grew up associating fruit with dessert. So, when I dropped the blueberry muffins, I replaced them with amazing berries—ripe, delicious strawberries, blueberries, and blackberries. It was a great trade and much healthier.

Make incremental progress. I love the story I heard from a friend about a woman named Maxine, who when sharing her own progress, proudly proclaimed that she's overweight and loving it. Maxine said, "Today, I am celebrating being overweight. I have been obese for so long. Now I am just overweight, but no longer obese." She celebrated her progress and acknowledged she still had a way to go.

Maxine's happiness with her progress reminds me how eating healthier contributes to much more improvement than what occurs on a scale. Happier, more energetic, and enjoying life better than before; in short, healthier eating increases our flourishing.

Moving

The modern lifestyle is sedentary by nature. We sit for a large part of our day, working on some form of phone, monitor, or screen. Most of us sit for breakfast, sit during our commute, sit at work, sit for lunch, sit to drive home, sit for dinner, and then finally sit to watch a show, sit to read a book, or sit to look at our phone. That's a lot of sitting!

As the comic above illustrates, our screens were heavier in the past, but we didn't spend as much time on them and were healthier. Today, our screens keep getting lighter, but we are more obese and less active than ever.

Back to Patricia: After her nutrition plan was established, she took the initiative to start exercising regularly. She wasn't the gym type but liked working out at home. After doing some investigation, she decided to invest in a stationary bike along with a reasonably priced, streaming class. She started slowly and struggled at the beginning. Many times, Patricia couldn't finish the class or had to scale way back. She persisted, and then one day it hit her. She was in the middle of a spinning class and looked outside her bedroom window during a beautiful morning. The teacher was full of enthusiasm, and Patricia felt great. She was doing well and feeling energetic. She was no longer paying the price for working out; she was enjoying the benefits.

Patricia is now able to finish the intermediate workouts; her strength and stamina have increased substantially. Her waistline has shrunk, and her muscle tone has improved. Now Patricia looks forward to her morning workouts. You couldn't pay Patricia to miss a workout.

The Three Key Aspects of Exercise

Most experts agree that a combination of cardio, strength training, and stretching are a winning combination for physical health. Ideally, your exercise throughout the week will contain all three aspects.

I recommend planning your exercise over a weekly basis. You may not be able to train your cardio, strength, and flexibility each day. So, divide them up over the course of the week. All three are important, and they work together in a synergistic manner. Pick exercises and routines that you will enjoy and stick to over the long term.

1—Cardio

Of the three different aspects of exercise, let's start with aerobic exercise because it's the most foundational and easiest to perform. I could say just walk every day and be done with this entire section. But let's go a little deeper. "Cardio" is short for the term "cardiovascular exercise" which is designed to increase the ability of the heart to pump blood and distribute oxygen to the body. Cardio also strengthens your heart muscles, burns calories, controls appetite, lowers your blood pressure, boosts your mood, reduces arthritis and joint stiffness, and aids in sleep.

For those new to cardio, just start walking or engage in some other regular from of movement. This could be swimming, bicycling, jogging, or playing a game, such as basketball, tennis, or golf. Start slowly, perhaps just five minutes in the morning and five minutes in the evening. Over time, you can increase the duration. Leading author Dr. Mark Hyman says twenty-five minutes of continual movement six days per week is ideal. This gets to the Center for Disease Control's recommendation of 150 minutes of moderate exercise per week.[5] Other experts suggest a target of 10,000 steps, as it approximates five miles and burns up to 3,500 calories per week, which is one pound of body fat.

For those who want to continue to progress, consider doing some high-intensity training. This includes exercises like sprinting, plyometrics, spin cycling, aerobics classes, or stairs. High intensity workouts raise your natural testosterone levels (good for both men and women), burn more calories, improve your overall athleticism, and increase your capacity for work. At the same time, be careful not to overtrain. It's important that you allow for days off and recovery.

2—Strength Training

The second component of exercise is strength training. Many individuals are not just over-fat; they are under-muscled. One of the best ways to stay vital and live longer is to maintain your muscle tone. Studies show that starting in our thirties, we begin losing muscle every year. This, in turn, decreases our balance, posture, and ability to perform daily tasks. It's one of the main reasons you often see the elderly hunched over and moving slowly. I want to have vitality, strength, and energy for as long as possible. If you agree, you need to do strength training.

Traditionally, people think of strength training as lifting weights or going to the gym. But that's not necessary. Some of the best fit athletes use their own bodyweight to increase their strength—think gymnasts and martial artists. They do push-ups, pull-ups, handstands, air squats, lunges, and different core exercises, such as planks.

For a beginner, many experts recommend doing strength training three days per week for twenty minutes each day. Train the major muscles such as your legs, back, chest, and shoulders. Do two to three sets for each body part. If you want to continue to progress, you can either increase the duration of your workout (for example, Monday-Wednesday-Friday for one hour) or start training four days per week (for instance, Monday-Tuesday-Thursday-Friday for forty-five minutes).[6]

Another great way to get excellent resistance training is to partake in whole-body exercises such as swimming, martial arts, tai chi, or yoga. Some of these exercises offer classes from beginning to the highest level of fitness as well as incorporate functionality, mindfulness, and breathing.

If you sit for long periods of time, it's particularly important to train your core. The core consists of your abdominals, lower back, hips, and pelvis. A weak core leads to low back pain. Two things health care professionals recommend for preventing low back pain are not sitting for too long (more on that later) and strengthening your core. Having a strong core is like a having a strong foundation.

There is no one perfect type of exercise, so engage in a variety of movements you enjoy. Not only will this be better for improved muscle stimulation but will also keep you mentally fresh. Changing routines also helps avoid overuse and overtraining injuries.

3—Stretching

....

The third aspect of exercise is stretching, which gives you durability and flexibility. If you stretch, you are less likely to get injured. Stretching elongates your muscles and improves your range of motion as well as your performance in physical activities. It keeps you in the game longer. For those who regularly sit, stretching also improves your posture and proper body alignment.

Stretch all the major muscle and tendon groups. Start by rotating each ankle in circles or pointing the foot up and then down. Then, stretch the calves, quadriceps, hamstrings, hip flexors, and glutes. Next, move to the torso, and do a few trunk twists and low back stretches. Finally, stretch the upper body, including chest, shoulders, upper back, and neck. Ideally, stretch two to three times per week with each body part for about sixty seconds.

Whether doing cardio, strength training, or stretching, I recommend two rules. First, do no harm. Don't do anything that causes physical pain. I'm not talking about muscle soreness the next day. I'm talking about things that will actually hurt or injure you. Second, strive for consistency, not perfection. Try to exercise regularly and on a schedule.

You can look at exercise as a chore or as a gift. I choose to look at it as giving a gift to myself. You get to enjoy the amazing return on your investment.

Regular Movement

The Director of the Mayo Clinic, Dr. James Levine, said that "sitting is the new smoking." He has extensively studied the negative effects of the modern, sedentary lifestyle, concluding: "Sitting is more dangerous than smoking, kills more people than HIV and is more treacherous than parachuting. We are sitting ourselves to death."

Although exercising is necessary for optimal health, it is not sufficient by itself. You must also move throughout the day. We need both. Dr. Joan Vernikos was the former NASA Director of Life Sciences and responsible for making sure the astronauts remained healthy during their flights in space. She says we must move regularly throughout the day or suffer the physical consequences.[7] Simply exercising daily will not cure the problem for being sedentary the rest of the day. As you can see from the diagram below, exercise is one component of movement.

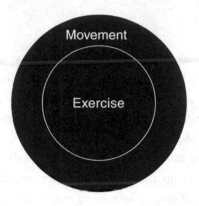

When I'm sitting at the office or home, I set my timer for every thirty minutes and take a few moments to stand up, stretch, walk, and move my body a little bit. Dr. Michelle Seager calls these "Opportunities to Move" or "OTMs." Look for these OTMs throughout the day. Maybe you take the stairs instead of the elevator, walk to lunch instead of drive, or stand every time you text. Whenever my family goes to the airport, we make it a game to take the stairs instead of the never-ending escalators. I am fully convinced that being intentional about regular movement and not skipping chances to move helps me maintain energy and health.

Lastly, when it comes to your health and eating, moving, and sleeping, have fun doing this. Yes, your health is fundamental, but you can't spell fundamental without "fun." You should not only enjoy the process but also the great benefits resulting from your improved health.

Sleeping

When most people think they need to lose weight or get healthier, they automatically think diet or exercise. But science shows sleep is actually the best and most important place to start. When I mentioned sleeping, Patricia, like most lawyers, demurred. You see, lawyers really believe either they can get away with four or five hours a night or that they don't have enough time to sleep more.

Sleeping seemed the least important to Patricia. "I mean, it is so unproductive to sleep seven or eight hours every night. You are just lying there, doing nothing." Patricia explained she had a busy life, too much work, too many things to do around the house, and too many people to see—plus a few shows to watch and social media to check before she went to bed. She couldn't do what needed to be done if she slept seven or eight hours. "There just aren't enough hours in the day," she said. So, she "hoped" to get six hours a night, but it was closer to five.

I recommended that Patricia read the book, *Why We Sleep*, by renowned sleep expert, Dr. Matthew Walker. "In fact, if there's just one book you read about your health, it would be this one," I said.

What Patricia and most of us don't realize is science has unequivocally proven how important—no, how critical—sleep is to our health and ability to optimize our lives. In fact, *sleep is so crucial that it is no longer considered just one of the necessary factors for good health, it is now considered to be the foundation on which all the other factors of well-being rest.* You will eat and exercise better if you get a good night's sleep. To quote Dr. Walker: "A balanced diet and exercise are of vital importance, yes. But we now see sleep as the preeminent force in this health trinity ... The physical and mental impairments caused by one night of bad sleep dwarf those caused by an equivalent absence of food or exercise."

Not only will you be more likely to succeed in changing your eating and exercise routines with better sleep, but it's one of the easiest things to control. Sometimes people find eating well and exercising right to be challenging—more on that shortly—but sleeping is not as difficult. I believe it's the easiest of the three health pillars to control. Let's get a win by adding a little more sleep to our lives.

Why is sleep so important? In one sentence: Sleep powerfully restores your brain and body. Did you know your brain has a glymphatic system? Not to be confused with the lymphatic system, which is part of your circulatory system, the glymphatic system essentially serves as a cleaning and renewing function for your brain. By flushing out the toxins, it supports optimal brain function, mental clarity, enhanced memory, and better concentration. In fact, recent research has shown that an impaired glymphatic system can lead to Alzheimer's disease. Studies indicate the glymphatic system needs about eight hours of sleep to properly clean the brain and restore brain health.[8]

If that's not enough, Dr. Walker also tells us: "Scientists have discovered a revolutionary new treatment that makes you live longer. It enhances your memory and makes you more creative. It makes you more attractive. It keeps you slim and lowers food cravings. It protects you from cancer and dementia. It wards off colds and the flu. It lowers your risk of heart attacks and strokes, not to mention diabetes. You'll even feel happier, less depressed, and less anxious." What is this magic treatment? Sleep!

As author Shawn Stephenson in *Sleep Smarter* says, "Sleep is the secret sauce. There isn't one facet of your mental, emotional, or physical performance that's not affected by the quality of your sleep." If you want an advantage at work, at school, in your health, in dealing with difficult people, then start with getting the right amount of sleep.

The opposite is also true. If you don't get adequate sleep, you will substantially impair your physical and mental functioning. In fact, studies show even moderate sleep deprivation produces impairments equivalent to those of alcohol intoxication.

According to Dr. Walker, the odds of being able to function effectively, let alone optimally, when you get less than seven hours of sleep a night are about 1 in 12,000. This means you are more likely to be struck by lightning than to live effectively on less than seven hours of sleep per night. And, as Dr. Walker points out, if you round those odds down to the nearest whole number, your chance of functioning well on less than seven hours is essentially zero.

By now, I hope you are convinced of the importance of getting eight hours of sleep nightly.

I wrote this book during the coronavirus pandemic. Although I used to sleep fewer than seven hours pre-pandemic, while sheltered in place I began getting eight hours of sleep daily. My energy, well-being, and mental clarity skyrocketed. Knowing myself and not having changed much else, I attribute my significant boost to my extra sleep. In fact, I can now say that sleep is unequivocally my most important self-care habit.

Seven hours of sleep to survive and eight hours to thrive. Most lawyers and professionals get far less than that. Let me ask you: If you were a defendant in a criminal trial, would you want your lawyer to be well rested, mentally sharp, and fully energized? How about the medical doctor performing your surgery? The pilot who is flying your plane? I rest my case.

Three Tips to Improve Your Sleep

If we are ideally spending a third of our day sleeping, we should be proactive to do it well. The quality of your sleep is as important as the quantity. Numerous studies show how to maximize your chances for getting a great night of sleep. Here are three key tips:

1. *Try not to eat a few hours before bed.* Your glymphatic system can't function at its most efficient levels when your body is using its energy to digest food or rid itself of caffeine or alcohol.

2. *Have a regular bedtime.* Your body and sleep thrive on routine. The more consistent you can be in going to bed, the more likely you are to sleep well. This is Matthew Walker's number one tip—try to go to bed at the same time every night.

3. *Cooler, darker, quieter.* Improve your sleep environment. For most people, the optimal room temperature is sixty-seven degrees. Also, light is not your friend when it comes to sleep, as it tells your body that it's time to be awake. For quiet, some people like ear plugs or white noise, but the aim is to have a steady quiet, with no startling or loud noises.

Even if you implement the above steps, you don't have perfect control over whether you get a good night sleep. Sometimes, we simply don't sleep well or get up in the middle of the night. If that happens, don't sweat it. Continue to follow your healthy sleep routine. If you are really tired from inadequate sleep, consider taking a nap. The Romans used to take a nap in the sixth hour of the day, which is how the word *siesta* originated.

Sleep is the gift that gives all day long. You are going to have a hard time reaching your potential if you lack sufficient sleep.

HAVE MENTAL & EMOTIONAL INTELLIGENCE

The first part of this chapter discussed the importance of the body. Now let's move to the mind. The mind is the control tower for our lives. If the body is the engine, the mind is the computer that operates it. It tells us where we are going, what is working, and what's not working. It governs our thoughts, feelings, and actions.

When working well, the brain allows us to make decisions, to think rationally, to feel positive emotions, to manage negative ones, and to stay motivated to do the things we want to do. Science confirms what most high performers already know—that winning and mastering any skill is predominantly mental. Navy SEAL Commander Mark Divine states unequivocally that the key to completing Navy SEALs training is mental.

When not working well, our thoughts are distracted and negative; our emotions are angry or sad, and our motivation and willpower are low. In fact, lawyers have a much higher percentage of depression and stress than those in almost any other occupation. And those percentages are rising at alarming rates.

So if we know our mind is so critical to flourishing, why are we not putting more effort into developing the mental and emotional intelligence necessary to thrive? We put time into keeping our bodies healthy, learning about our work, and spending time with our loved ones, but it is rare to find a person who intentionally takes the time to develop and train his or her mind. We must start with our own inner life if we also want to achieve outer success. True transformation is an inside job.

Although there are numerous traits that comprise our mental and emotional well-being, I'm going to highlight what I believe to be the three most important. These traits are variations first developed over 2,000 years ago by the Roman Emperor, Marcus Aurelius, what he called the three disciplines. Borrowing from Aurelius, I propose three unique traits to fit our contemporary life (with the disciplines from Aurelius listed in parenthesis): (1) mental control (the discipline of perception), (2) emotional resilience (the discipline of acceptance), and (3) positive attitude toward others (the discipline of action). While each of the three traits (or disciplines) promotes well-being, when combined they "constitute a comprehensive approach to life."[9]

After we explore these three disciplines, I'll share with you a little-known, but powerful, ancient idea that is more needed today than ever. It can serve as your go-to and default state of mind that harmonizes perfectly with flourishing.

Mental Control

A defendant convicted of murder and sentenced to death invariably appeals. Those death row appeals create huge backlogs on the court's docket. Because those cases often sit idle for years, the courts began requesting law firms to submit proposals to handle the appeals. The firm I worked for as a lawyer was one of the firms selected, and I was tasked to serve as the junior associate on the case.

Our new client had been convicted of a horrible murder and given the death penalty. I'll spare the gory details, but suffice to say, the murder was so heinous he was placed on "walk-alone" status at San Quentin prison, so other death row inmates wouldn't harm him. As I pored over the evidence, it was hard to read and even harder to want to defend him. The documents contained graphic details of this man's unspeakable deeds. The more I learned, the more he appeared to be a monster.

I spoke to a partner about my reluctance in handling the case, as he was a former prosecutor of high-profile crimes. He said the best thing for our criminal justice system is to have a great lawyer representing the defendant. He knew the prosecution would be well prepared. If the defendant also had excellent representation, he had confidence that justice would be served. Two equal adversaries both zealously representing their clients is the cornerstone of our legal system.

Of course, he was right. A good lawyer knows you need to separate the facts of the case from your personal thoughts about the client. Once you are able to truly separate the two, you can then rationally analyze the case and more effectively represent your client. I went on to successfully represent him, and he ultimately died of natural causes in prison rather than be executed.

Let's face it. We all make judgments. But rather than making objective judgments, we mostly make value-laden judgments. We add our own personal interpretation to the judgment, just like I did for my client on death row. When I learned to take control of my thoughts, to shift my perceptions, it completely changed everything. I no longer jumped to judgmental conclusions but instead looked at facts more objectively for what they truly were and became more curious. How you choose to see things is the key to mental well-being and mental control.

The first discipline of mental well-being is mental control. We exert our mental control by becoming aware of our perceptions and taking control over them. Perception is the act of how we view or see things. Two people can see the same thing very differently based on their perception. So, we want to control our perception and thoughts. We do this by seeing things as they actually are. Epictetus said: "Men are disturbed not by the things which happen, but by the view they take of those things."

We are rational human beings and attempt to make sense of the world and our lives. This requires us to continually think and interpret. We can actually think about our thinking. This is exercising our metacognition, which means to be aware of our own thought processes. We respond to the world not necessarily the way it is, but by how we think about it and interpret what is happening in our world. Our mind is always looking at reality through our own interpretive lens and that lens helps us make sense of our lives.

We take control over our thoughts without letting subjective values or opinions override our thoughts. We use our rationale thinking to see things objectively. I believe we cannot flourish unless we learn to control our thoughts, to think rationally, to recognize our value judgments, and to see things as they truly are. Mental control requires objectivity of thought.

As discussed in Chapter 6, we don't always get to choose what happens to us, but we can always choose how we think about it. That is the essence of mental control. So, for example, when we are challenged at work, criticized by our spouse, or have suffered a health setback, we usually have an immediate negative reaction. What we don't realize, however, is that in between the challenge, criticism, or setback and our reaction is our interpretation.

In reality, our experience typically follows a chronological process: (1) There is a challenge, criticism, or setback; (2) we interpret that challenge, setback, or criticism; and (3) a negative emotional or mental reaction follows in line with that interpretation. This chronological process is what Cognitive Behavioral Therapists call the "ABC Model," which stands for Adversity, Belief, Consequence. The ABC Model shows that your beliefs (B) about the situation precede the consequence (C), which is your mental or emotional response.[10] Thus, your belief or interpretation about the situation—which is always within your control—governs your resulting response. In other words, the real order is A, then B, then C. B is the key to your response or reaction to the event or action. You have the ability to change your emotional response by changing your thought, belief, interpretation, or perception about the event. This is the essence of mental control.

Often what causes our negative reaction or suffering is not the event itself but our own opinions and stories about those events. Our thoughts and beliefs about the challenge is what truly causes the negative emotion. It's the belief about the adversity and not the adversity itself that causes the stress or anxiety. Marcus Aurelius said, "If you are distressed by anything external, the pain is not due to the thing itself but to your own estimate of it; and this you have the power to revoke at any moment."[11] Shakespeare concurs: "There is nothing either good or bad but thinking makes it so." If we want to eliminate or significantly reduce the negative reactions in our lives, let's take control of our thoughts and perceptions.

This power of perception cannot be overstated. Think about a significant change in your life. How did you perceive the change? Could you have perceived it in a different manner? For example, imagine if you changed your job. If your thoughts about your new job are one of fear, the job change will likely create anxiety. If your thoughts are hopeful and excited, the new job creates a positive and encouraging state of mind. Same job, different thoughts based on your perception.

The key benefit of mental control is that by taking control of your thoughts, you can in turn manage your negative emotions. Feelings are created by our thinking; we evaluate the circumstances in our lives as positive or negative. Greek philosopher, Epic-tetus said, "It's not what happens to you, but how you react to it that matters." This first discipline of mental control allows and empowers our next two disciplines.

Emotional Resilience

The second discipline of emotional resilience deals with challenges, setbacks, and disappointments *after* they have already happened. When things fall outside of our control, such as a natural disaster, an illness, a car accident, or losing at trial, we use emotional resilience. The past has already happened. We have a healthy acceptance to life's ills and challenges. You can't argue with reality. You will lose every time—but only always. Many people find that a peaceful surrender to what has already occurred provides great freedom.

This does not mean we are passive doormats. Yes, we get knocked down, make mistakes, or take something too personally. This is where we become emotionally resilient. The word *resilience* comes from the Latin word *resilio,* which means "to bounce back or rebound."[12] Its essence is springing back into shape after being stretched, bent, or compressed. Resilience is recovering our strength, spirit, and good humor.

The palm tree doesn't break in storms or strong winds because it is able to bend and then rise back up. In fact, the more it has to bend, the deeper its roots grow, making it more pliable and stronger. In contrast, the mighty oak tree, which can last hundreds of years, will often break when faced with strong winds or a bad storm because of its rigid-ity and shallow roots. When we practice emotional resilience, we not only bounce back, but we are also not the same person after overcoming and dealing with the challenge. We are actually transformed and strengthened.

One of the best examples of resilience comes from Louis Zamperini's life, which was captured in the book and movie *Unbroken.* He faced numerous traumatic incidents as a youth but used his resilience to become an Olympian and a military hero. When his fighter plane crashed in the South Pacific during World War II, he was stranded on a tiny raft for forty-seven days, enduring the starvation of another crewmate, machine gunfire from a Japanese bomber, and several shark attacks. After he was "rescued" from his life raft by an enemy ship, he was held captive for two years in a Japanese prisoner-of-war camp. There, he suffered unimaginable physical and psychological torture. He survived but fell into a deep depression upon his return home.

It's when the going gets tough, the emotional resilient stay in the fight. They get back up. This is what Zamperini did, as he was able to bounce back and create a new life for himself. He was later awarded a Purple Heart and achieved many accolades. He had a successful and rewarding career devoted to helping at-risk youth. Years later, he returned to Japan several times to visit the prison guards who had tortured him to offer forgiveness. On his eighty-first birthday, he again travelled to Japan to run a leg in the Olympic torch relay.[13] Zamperini is as an exemplar of a true, resilient hero.

Fortunately, emotional resilience can be developed. Some of the most common traits to cultivate resilience include perseverance, optimism, perspective, and a sense of humor. Some of Zamperini's greatest traits were his perseverance and optimism. Also, keeping things in perspective prevents over dramatizing or catastrophizing a challenge. I find it helpful to step back and try to rise above a situation from a higher and detached perspective.

And, when appropriate, a sense of humor goes a long way to disarming an emotionally tense situation. Try to look at many of life's challenges as a game and start to cultivate a playful attitude. A lawyer told me her primary tool for resilience is something called "BS" for "Breath and Smile." She said it was amazing how effective it was to BS every time she got criticized.

My favorite practice for resilience is called the Equanimity game, inspired by Marcus Aurelius. In this game, you see how quickly you can bounce back to being your optimal self after experiencing some type of challenge. The term equanimity comes from Latin meaning "steadiness," "calmness," and "composure."[14] The goal is a quick turnaround. If something does not go your way, how long does it take you to get back to your flourishing self? Will you mourn, shutdown, or get stuck in a victim identity? Or will you turn your frown upside down and get back to business?

In the 2020 Masters, Tiger Woods, arguably the greatest golfer ever, took ten shots on the twelfth hole. It was the worst hole of his career in one of his biggest tournaments. What did Tiger do after his worst career performance on the twelfth hole? He responded with the best score of his career on the five closing holes. He had never played those five holes in five under par. "You just have to turn around and figure out the next shot," said Tiger. We too want to master quick turnarounds.

Have fun playing the Equanimity game. As you get better, you will become an emotionally stronger person and be able to handle bigger challenges. The great Nelson

Mandela said, "The greatest glory in living lies not in never falling, but in rising every time we fall."[15] The sooner we get back up and dust ourselves off, the sooner we can get back to flourishing.

Positive Attitude

When my kids were young, I had a tradition of taking them on Saturdays to Jamba Juice for delicious fruit smoothies. One Saturday, I was particularly busy as usual doing legal work at home. My son asked me several times when we were going to go. "Is it time yet?" Each time I responded, "No, not yet." My work project was challenging and taking me longer than expected. "Daddy, are we ever going to go?" he asked. "Soon," I replied. Then he changed the question on me: "Daddy, what flavor smoothie are you going to get? I'm getting the Mango-a-go-go!" I picked up my keys and took my kids to get their smoothies.

Much of the two previously discussed practices of mental control and emotional resilience are often used to play defense. You have a mental or emotional challenge and use these practices to get back to a well-functioning state of mind.

The legal profession seems to be a breeding ground for criticism and negativity. You cannot exercise critical thinking skills without being a "critic." You cannot effectively advocate without arguing. In fact, positive psychology pioneer Dr. Seligman found that success in law school was correlated to being pessimistic.[16]

However, like my son who took a positive approach to getting his Jamba Juice, flourishing individuals play offense with our mental and emotional well-being. Studies show a positive attitude and positive emotions are highly correlated with health and well-being. They are life enhancing. In fact, Dr. Seligman concluded that positive emotion is one of the necessary elements of well-being.[17]

Can you be an effective critic and advocate while also maintaining a positive attitude? Are lawyers doomed to a "Sophie's choice?" Must you choose between being a successful lawyer or a happy person? Is a "happy lawyer" an oxymoron? Fortunately, the answer is no.

In being a legal professional, there is nothing inconsistent with being confident, enthusiastic, and optimistic while also being an effective advocate. In fact, based on my years as a lawyer and judge, I have concluded those who display a positive mindset are *both* the happiest and most effective in their professions. Of course, you want to question authority and think about your client's potential pitfalls. But you can do so with a hopeful outcome and a positive attitude. Both objective and optimistic; critical and confident.

I'm not talking about a "rainbows and lollipops" positive attitude. That everything is wonderful all the time, no matter what. As lawyers and judges, our work stems from people's problems and tragedies. Rather, I'm talking about an authentic and grounded positivity.

In the literature on positive attitude, three key traits have been identified: Confidence, Enthusiasm, and Optimism. I call these the "CEO" of your own attitude. This is the third mental discipline, and it is always within our control.

Confidence is the first trait and comes from the Latin word *con-fidere*, meaning "with trust." We are talking about self-confidence. It's a sincere belief in yourself. Confidence results from trusting your own abilities and qualities. Firmly grounded in reality, confidence is the launching pad for achievement. Your belief in yourself is either the key or the lock to your flourishing.

Real confidence is earned. Former Navy SEAL David Goggins talks about his "cookie jar" method for confidence. Goggins was once obese, weighing 300 pounds and having asthma. He was repeatedly beaten by his father and almost flunked out of high school. He decided to turn his life around and ultimately became a member of Navy SEAL Team Five, then graduated from Army Ranger School as Top Honor Man, held the Guinness World Record for most pull-ups in twenty-four hours, and ran sixty ultra-endurance races.

Goggins credited his "cookie jar method" for his confidence to achieve his many successes.[18] Every time have you have achieved something or overcome an obstacle you place a symbolic cookie in your jar. "The cookie jar is a place in my mind where I put all things bad and good that shaped me. Some people try to forget the bad in their life. I use my bad for strength when needed, great lessons learned. In that cookie jar, I pull out whatever I need for the task at hand."

The second trait is enthusiasm, which comes from the Greek word *en theos* meaning "God within." We are connected to the divine within, our daimon. We are fully and radiantly alive. Enthusiasm brings genuine interest and enjoyment to life. Enthusiasm is in an outward demonstration coming from an inward thought or feeling. I am not talking about being loud or overly excited but rather a genuine zest for life, a cheerful disposition, and warm emotions.

Enthusiasm is your displayed life force. It is your positive energy. Have you ever been to a party where a person lights up a room? The co-worker with vitality and an infectious smile? They have a sincere effervescence about them. If you have ever seen a Beyoncé, Bruce Springsteen, or Garth Brooks concert, you know the kind of enthusiasm I'm talking about. Theirs is palpable from the stage.

The final trait is optimism, which reflects a belief in a favorable or positive outcome. An optimist sees and looks for the best in life. The optimist sees the half glass of water as full. In the David and Goliath story, nobody wanted to fight the giant Goliath because he was too big. But David was an optimist and figured Goliath was too big to miss. As Hellen Keller said, "Optimism is the faith that leads to achievement."

Fortunately, our attitude is malleable, and we can improve our confidence, enthusiasm, and optimism. The father of American psychology, Williams James, found the ability to change our lives by changing our attitude was the most important discovery of his lifetime.[19] So, if you really want to change your life, you can start by changing your attitude. Improving your positive attitude is much like a computer or a garden. What you put in; you'll also get out. Try being the Confident, Enthusiastic, Optimistic CEO of your life and watch your life flourish.

Euthymia—An Ancient Idea for a Modern World

We live in a hectic world. Constantly on the go. Always too much to do at work and home. Trying to keep up with the ceaseless information. Never-ending texts, emails, and social media. Staying connected with friends, co-workers, and family. A bombardment of stimulus and obligations coming at us from all directions. Never enough time to do it all. We feel overwhelmed.

But it doesn't have to be that way. We can play offense through one of my favorite concepts, *euthymia* (pronounced, you-thim-ee-ah). It's an ancient practice but more applicable than ever. I believe it's an ideal state of mind and one that can serve as your baseline or default attitude most of the time.

The word *euthymia* is Greek, and its translation comes from *eu*, meaning "good" or "well," and *thymos*, meaning "emotion" and "life energy." There are two aspects to euthymia: tranquil and energetic. At first blush, they seem opposite. But, in fact, they are a beautiful yin and yang providing harmony and flow to your life.

First, euthymia is a mental and emotional state that is calm and composed. It comes from nothing external, yet the feeling is infinite, a total contentment. *Tranquility* is the word most synonymous with *euthymia*. It is knowing that inner peace comes from within. It's a state of mind that is serene and free from strife. A true heart of peace.

Second, at the same time, euthymia also provides an energy and lifeforce. It's not passive; it's active, interested, and engaged. You are fully functioning and pursuing good health as well as meaningful work and meaningful relationships. It gives you the stability and confidence to follow your own path.

In short, euthymia is a mindset of both peace and strength; energized and tranquil.

As a judge, I love the concept of euthymia and believe it provides the ideal temperament for the bench. A sense of energized tranquility. Calm yet fully engaged. When emotions run high among counsel or the parties, my euthymic mindset allows me to remain courteous, balanced, and even-tempered. I believe this same mental state applies equally to lawyers.

When we talk about an ideal state of mind, it's not that we don't have negative emotions. Of course, life involves suffering, sadness, disappointment, despair, death, and more. You can't go through life without experiencing the full spectrum of emotions. You aren't supposed to smile at the loss of a loved one. These emotions are all a part of life and have as much, if not more, to teach us than the positive emotions.

However, as euthymia is practiced more regularly, you will have less stress and be better at dealing with emotions more effectively. You will trust yourself more and then recover so you can flourish again. Euthymia serves as a lighthouse or beacon to bring us back to genuine tranquility.

Euthymia also involves trusting you are on the right path. You believe you are heading in the right direction. Seneca said: Euthymia is "believing in yourself and trusting you are on the right path, and not being in doubt by following the myriad footpaths of those wandering in every direction."[20] Euthymia allows you to say "no" with confidence to things that waste your time or don't matter, so you can say "yes" to those things that you know are truly important. It also says "no" to the comparisons.

The best way to foster euthymia is to live with the three mental disciplines previously discussed in this chapter. Interestingly, those three disciplines comprise the same three aspects of the Serenity Prayer. The Serenity Prayer was first popularized by Alcoholic Anonymous and other twelve-step programs and continues to be used as part of its regular meetings. It states: "God, grant me the serenity to accept the things I cannot change; the courage to change the things I can; and the wisdom to know the difference."

Personally, I say this prayer in my own meditation, but I reverse the order and modify the language slightly, as follows: "God grant me the wisdom to know what I can and can't control; the serenity to radically accept those things that I cannot change, and the courage to act virtuously on all things within my control."

Either way, this prayer beautifully encapsulates the three different traits we have been discussing as part of mental and emotional well-being. First, for things we cannot change or control, we accept them and have emotional resilience. (Fact: There are many more items that fall in this category.) Second, for those things that we can control and can change, we exercise our courage to do the right thing, such as act with kindness, goodness, and a positive attitude. Third, we have the wisdom to distinguish between what is and what is not within our control and to see things as they are through mental control. (I put this first in my own meditation because we initially need to know whether something is in our control.)

When opposing counsel doesn't grant you that extension of time you so desperately need, how do you react? You can react emotionally (not good), or you can take it to a higher level by employing mental control (better), or you can have a euthymic mindset that you are at peace with those things you cannot control (best).

Consider applying this classical wisdom of calm confidence and energized tranquility to the ubiquitous noise and stress of daily living. A healthy mind and peaceful emotions will lead to a sense of well-being and a flourishing life.

The most effective practice I know to cultivate euthymia is meditation. If you aren't aware of the tremendous benefits of mediation, let me just say there are many books written about its advantages. In short, it is strength training for the mind. Meditation is a concentration practice. It will improve your focus, concentration, will power, peace of mind, tranquility, and physical health. Like drinking water, meditation is a no-brainer.

There are great books, articles, and apps on how to meditate. If you are new to meditation, just start with meditating for one minute or even one breath. Over time, your meditation practice will bring you greater peace and presence in your life.

CULTIVATE SPIRITUALITY

Many people have a spiritual dimension that is one of the most rewarding aspects of their lives. Spirituality is significant, irrespective of whether you are a religious person, which is why it is included in this book. You can be spiritual without being religious, and some people are religious but not very spiritual.

The term *spirituality* is broad but essentially describes a person living out his or her deepest meaning and values as a process of inner transformation or connection to a higher purpose. It is your true inner life as opposed to what is purely physical or material. *Spirit* comes from Latin word *spiritus*, "meaning breath of life."

Spirituality is important because it allows you to develop a deeper connection to the world in which we all live. You not only learn more about yourself and others but also what is genuinely important to you. Spirituality permits you to transcend your ego.

Let me say, however, that spirituality is a very personal and individual choice, and only you can choose which path to follow. If you are truly spiritual, you will love all your brothers and sisters in this world regardless of their chosen path. Spirituality should be unifying, not dividing.

Connecting to a Higher Purpose

I believe spirituality provides a higher purpose that is bigger than yourself. It gives life meaning. It's about making society and the planet better. This higher purpose offers a common ground for us all, whether you are religious or not. We ultimately want to become the best version of ourselves, so we can more profoundly love and serve others. This, in turn, helps make our world a better place. That's the essence of spirituality. Spirituality is looking vertically for purpose rather than just horizontally

For those who believe in God—such as Christians, Jews, Hindus, and Muslims—there is one supreme being, God. It is God who created the universe and all living things. The goal of the believers is to live a life connected with and living for God.

The great Mahatma Gandhi was a devout Hindu, and he led his fellow citizens in India to independence from British rule. Yes, Gandhi had a higher purpose, but all of this emanated from his spiritual roots. He said: "God is that indefinable something which we all feel but which we do not know. To me God is Truth and Love. God is ethics and morality. God is fearlessness. God is the course of light and life and yet He is above and beyond all of these."[21]

Secular humanists can have a "spiritual" dimension, even without a belief in God or a deity. They can believe the world was created for the sake of each other, which provides an opportunity to help one another. If spirituality provides a higher purpose, secular humanists can find meaning in the natural human characteristics, such as loving others and connecting to Mother Earth. They can have a sense of wonder through observations and insights into nature and the universe.

Cultivating Your Spiritual Connection

How do we practice connecting to our higher purpose? There are a variety of great practices for developing your spirituality. Some of these practices are focused on your inner life and others on your outer behavior.

The key inward practices to growing spiritually include prayer, gratitude, mindfulness, meditation, fasting, stillness, and study. For instance, Mother Teresa used the power of prayer as one of her primary spiritual disciplines. She is commonly quoted as saying, "I do not pray for success. I ask for faithfulness."[22] And for those of the Muslim faith, the main practices include professing a belief in God, praying five times a day, fasting, praying during the month of Ramadan, and making a pilgrimage.

While spiritual disciplines typically start with the inner life, they eventually transition to a life beyond the self. As we become more aware of our spirituality, we will find ourselves living an abundant and virtuous life dedicated to others. Dr. Martin Luther King, Jr. dedicated his life to equal rights for all. He based his trumpet call on biblical love. He famously said, "Darkness cannot drive out darkness; only light can do that. Hate cannot drive out hate; only love can do that."

When you develop your entire being, your whole person—your physical, mental, emotional, and spiritual dimensions—you will experience great flourishing and reach your full potential. Combine a strong body and strong mind with a deep spirituality and watch your life thrive.

With the foundation laid for our personal well-being, we are now ready to move to the next step in our flourishing life—our work. Remember the more we grow as individuals, the more we can give away to others in our work and service.

Chapter Summary:

- Personal well-being enables us to thrive and achieve our vision for the future.
- The dimensions of our physical, mental, emotional, and spiritual lives are interdependent; we need to thrive in each to live optimally.
- We thrive physically by eating, moving, and sleeping in a healthy manner.
- We thrive in the other dimension of well-being by maintaining mental control, practicing emotional resilience, having a positive attitude, and growing spirituality.

SIDEBAR _____

Think like a judge. Ask yourself: What does the judge need to know at today's hearing? If it's a status conference, the judge will want to know the most current procedural posture, what the parties are doing to resolve the matter, and when the parties will be ready for trial. If it's a hearing, the judge will need to know the governing law and the relevant facts to rule in your favor.

CHAPTER 9

WORK

• • •

*"Life's most persistent and urgent question is,
'What are you doing for others?'"*
—DR. MARTIN LUTHER KING, JR.

I t is ironic that, as a judge, the chapter on work was the one with which I most struggled to write. My struggle was not for the reason you might think. It was not due to the content but because every other chapter in this book is universal. It applies to everybody, regardless of your occupation. Every person has a unique calling in life, and that is a wonderful thing. Although this chapter is written with the legal professional in mind, I still recommend everyone read this chapter because many of the principles will apply to your own occupation. My experience is not just in the law but also in life, so these work principles are intended to be mostly universal. I am confident you will benefit from this discussion.

Being a great lawyer or great in your occupation obviously matters. It matters not only to your own career success but also to how well you serve others. In the law, there is the thrill of victory and the agony of defeat. I see it daily in my court. In an otherwise excellent legal system, one of the flaws is the disparate caliber of lawyering. The great inequality is the unequal quality of the lawyers. Good lawyers beat bad lawyers most of the time.

If you want to fulfill your vision for succeeding and thriving in your legal (or any) career, I have found there are five essential principles to follow. Although only five, each is critical: (1) make your work meaningful, (2) have a prosperous mindset; (3) build your career; (4) manage your business; and (5) build your book of business. Plus, we'll explore why it is important to properly managing the money you earn from work.

MAKE WORK MEANINGFUL

When I entered law school, my dream was to be a sports agent and sit in Dodger Stadium watching my clients perform on the field. However, in my first year of law school, I had a professor in constitutional law whose incredible class sparked my interest. He made me think deeply about my values and what was truly important to me. This began my shift toward civil rights and constitutional law and ultimately led to a meaningful career in those areas of the law.

We all understand the importance of work. Yes, work is a necessary means to money, survival, and life in the modern world. But it is also a great source of passion, purpose, and contribution. Work can make life sweet and fruitful. "Work is love made visible," says Kahlil Gibran.[1]

Since we are going to spend most of our waking hours working, we want to learn to thrive in our work. The first step in doing so is to find meaning in our work. Many studies show that people are happiest when their work is personally meaningful to them. Some work is easy to see as meaningful, but other work requires us to look deeper to find meaning. Every single job provides a service of some kind, so at a minimum, see how your service to others provides meaning. I encourage you to take a few minutes to get clarity on how your work benefits society or others in some way.

The important point is you can choose to see your work as meaningful. Each job provides an opportunity to serve profoundly. As Dr. Martin Luther King, Jr. said: "If a man is called to be a street sweeper, he should sweep the streets even as Michelangelo painted, or Beethoven composed music or Shakespeare wrote poetry. He should sweep streets so well that all the hosts of heaven and earth will pause to say, 'Here lived a great street sweeper who did his job well.'"[2]

Serving as a lawyer can provide incredible meaning. Knowing that you serve your clients by being the best lawyer you can, should be very rewarding. While some of my own cases as a lawyer were more interesting than others, I found that my daily work provided a great deal of meaning. We have the benefit of providing a lasting impact on our clients' cases and lives.

Do you have a job, a career, or a calling? The distinction matters. A "job" is some activity you do to earn a paycheck. It is perfectly good to have a job because of its ability to put food on the table, pay the rent, etc. A "career" also provides a paycheck but adds additional opportunities for advancement or promotion. However, a "calling" involves the same characteristics as a career, plus you feel a strong urge or impulse toward some deeper purpose. If you don't find your work meaningful or "if you can't work with love, but only with distaste," says Gibran, then consider how you can find your calling.[3] People with a calling are typically more enthusiastic and more willing to do the work necessary to achieve greatness.

So how can you find or at least move closer to your calling? The author Jim Collins offers an excellent tool called the Hedgehog Concept. He says that in order find your calling, look at the intersection of the following three factors:

1. What do you love to do? Write out the top pursuits you would love to do for work.
2. What are your best skills and abilities? Write out the top activities at which you excel.
3. Is there a demand for your service or product such that people are willing to pay for it? You need to be completely honest here. Yes, it's great to have a purpose and gift for your work, but you must ground it in economic reality.[4]
4. I recommend you think about the three factors in your own work. Do you have an overlap between some or all three factors into one great calling? If all three factors overlap, then you are on your way. If they don't align or you are unsure, don't worry; keep looking and learning. It's a process

I spoke with one family law lawyer, who realized all three factors converged. She had a strong awareness that nothing gave her greater satisfaction than helping a parent gain custody of her or his child after an extremely bitter divorce. She was good at her work. Because of her passion and skill, she made good money. It is not surprising she feels like her family law practice is a "calling."

It's equally important and sometimes easier to learn what you don't want to do. One of my very first cases as a lawyer involved defending an insurance company that denied cancer treatment to a mother. We ultimately got the case dismissed based on clear language in the contract. However, I subsequently heard she passed away. The legal decision was correct, but I decided this was not the type of case that personally resonated with me. Although I firmly believe all matters should have excellent legal representation, each of you must personally decide how you can give your gifts in greatest service to the world. Let me just state loudly and clearly that it is perfectly okay if you haven't found your calling yet. Don't force it but be open and ready when it does come.

As you pursue your work, it is important to have self-awareness, to know yourself and your values. If you want to flourish, seek to align your work with your values. What the world needs most is more people doing what they are best at and makes them come alive.

HAVE A PROSPEROUS MINDSET

The second step to excelling at work is to have a prosperous mindset. Most people think of being prosperous as having financial success or good fortune. And, while that's part of it, I'm talking more about a state of mind and approach to your work.

The etymology of *prosper* comes from the Latin word *prospere*, which literally means "to move forward with hope." The essence of hope is a belief that the future will be better than the past. In reality, hope is making progress toward a positive vision of the future. The opposite of prosper is despair. Hopelessness occurs when you believe you are stuck, not progressing, not learning, not growing, or feel like your future will be no better than the past.

So how can you bring a prosperous mindset to your daily work? There are three main qualities to having a prosperous mindset.

A Clear Future Vision

A prosperous mindset means having a strong future vision. It's having a goal other than just money. Yes, of course, you need to make money—what I refer to as the red blood cells of any business. Just like you can't live without healthy red blood cells, a business can't survive without profit. But, like red blood cells, that is not why you live. We want to have a clear vision of our ideal work in addition to wealth. This is the "yes and" concept. Yes, we want profit and to pursue our optimal vision as a lawyer.

Try to get specific with your vision. Prepare a one-year and five-year projection for yourself. What would your ideal work look like in one year from now if you're prospering? Then telescope out five years. What does that look like? Waive your magic wand. When somebody asks you what you do for a living, can you answer in one compelling sentence?

A purpose-driven lawyer is more likely to be a prosperous lawyer. Dr. Martin Luther King, Jr. said that lawyers have helped "the arc of the moral universe ... bend ... toward justice."[5] Think about the noble purpose of your work. As we progress as a society, I have grown to believe we should continue to move toward more conscious capitalism—one that is helping both others and society as a whole. How can your practice be a force for good?

Being a Professional

A prosperous mindset includes becoming a professional at what you do. A professional means you are at the top of your game; you are a true master. It's about how you approach your work. The opposite of a professional is an amateur. That's someone who does something purely for pleasure or pastime. But the pros move forward with intentionality in their knowledge and skill.

The essence of law school is to train students to enter the legal profession. To become a professional lawyer. This requires you to become an expert at what you are doing. How are you treating your own job? Are you a pro or an amateur? Turn "pro" and become a top-notch professional lawyer.

The key to becoming a professional is deliberate growth and preparation. You invest the time to master what you do. It will not be easy and will take years. You must do the right things with clear specific objectives in mind. Through hard work, you will start to gain a sense of competence at what you do. As your competence grows, you start to move forward toward becoming a professional. The person who becomes highly skilled or capable at what he or she does will feel a greater sense of satisfaction and accomplishment.

Serving Profoundly

Think of a time when you hired somebody or used a business establishment where they exceeded your expectations. Not just pleased you but truly astonished you with their service. What was it that was truly exceptional? When you have that sense in your mind, think about your own work, and what would serving profoundly look like. How could you truly astonish your clients or boss?

It's natural that you will want to exceed expectations, but please be careful as this is a two-fold endeavor. One is managing those expectations. And the second is attempting to exceed the managed expectations. For instance, I would notify my corporate clients in litigation that I would provide them with a status report about every two months. But I would calendar to send a report at least every six weeks plus any time something significant occurred. That allowed me to both manage and exceed expectations.

Starting today, let's possess a prosperous mindset with a clear picture of our future vision, while becoming a professional and serving profoundly.

BUILD CAREER CAPITAL

In 2007, the actor and comedian Steve Martin appeared on the Charlie Rose show to discuss his memoir, *Born Standing Up*. During the interview, Martin talked about his process of becoming a success in comedy, and Rose asked him if he had any advice for aspiring comedians. Martin responded, "Nobody ever takes note [of my advice], because it's not the answer they wanted to hear. What they want to hear is 'Here's how you get an agent, here's how you write a script',... but I always say, 'Be so good they can't ignore you.'"[6]

Martin is describing the process of intentionally building up expertise in a given vocation over time. Indeed, it took Martin ten years of purposeful improvement before he became a smash success. This idea of developing your skills and knowledge through an extended period of hard work is known as career capital.

As I reflect on my own career, both as a lawyer and a judge, I believe that this intentional process of building expertise was the single most important characteristic for my own success. Although I didn't have a name for it at the time, I was building and have continued to build career capital my entire career.

Author Cal Newport wrote a book on this very subject, aptly titled *So Good They Can't Ignore You*. Newport asserts career capital is built by committing to a craftsman mindset. Your focus is on getting very good at what you do. Becoming a true master. When you see an expert surgeon, skilled musician, or brilliant lawyer, you know what I mean. If you want to excel in your work, get very, very good at it.

Here's the amazing benefit: *As you gain more career capital, you will get more autonomy, more interesting work, and often more money.* You become more valuable. You will spend less time doing the monotonous work and more time doing more interesting work.[7] Indeed, studies show that as lawyers gain more competence, they become happier and more satisfied.

CHAPTER 9: WORK

Let's begin your official training and education program. Your number one job is to become the best version of what you are capable of as a lawyer. Next to being ethical, I believe the most important thing you can do as a lawyer is to formulate and implement a very purposeful education and training plan. There are internet articles, books, and seminars replete with information for almost every type of legal career. Take the time to identify the key skills and knowledge you need to become a master. Put this book down and ask yourself what are the top five skills in my particular specialty?

In developing a training plan, I'm going to use civil litigation as an example. But having coached and consulted with many individuals from all different occupations, I have found that these same principles apply to virtually all businesses. Based on my experience from practicing law and serving as a judge for over fifteen years, these are the top ten skills a civil litigator should acquire:

1—Legal Reasoning Skills

The chief function a lawyer performs is to think like one. Your ultimate objective is to help your clients. How do you translate legal reasoning skills into helping your clients?

Start with a deep awareness that litigators serve in two distinct roles—advocates and counselors. Lawyers wear two hats. The first hat is that of the zealous advocate. Know the law and the facts cold, and within the bounds of ethics, "persuasively" assert your client's position to the court, jury, or other side during negotiations.

The second hat is that of a counselor at law. A counselor analyzes the law and the facts "objectively" and provides clients with a neutral and accurate assessment of their legal rights. This is where most lawyers fall short. They think all they need to do is argue their clients' position, but they haven't taken the time to impartially analyze the particular case's strengths and weaknesses. After an objective assessment of the law and facts, a lawyer should be able to advise the client on whether to settle the case or take it to trial. With each case going forward, you should always wear both hats. (Again, for other occupations, you can substitute "client" for customer, boss, patient, etc.)

2—Civil Procedure

You need to start with the rules of the game, and those are found in the Rules of Civil Procedure. The lawyers who master these rules will walk securely, and those who don't will be constantly practicing law at their peril. I can tell you from a judge's perspective that many times lawyers have blown their case by their lack of familiarity with civil procedure.

I recommend finding a well-organized secondary source such as the *Federal Practice and Procedure Guide* and go through all the key concepts. You should become extremely familiar with the key chronological steps of the litigation process and have them firmly embedded in your memory.

Understand that most judges want to proactively manage their cases. Our goal is not only to do justice but try to get cases resolved efficiently. It is very important lawyers come prepared for hearings and be able to discuss the procedural status of the case. Judges will keep moving you forward through the process until ultimate resolution. I repeat myself purposely—learn the key chronological steps of the litigation process until they are deeply ingrained in your mind. (For other occupations, you should know the systems that run your specific business.)

3—Substantive Law

This is fundamental. You must know the substantive law of the case cold. This takes time and focused study. As you progress in your career, I encourage you to focus your expertise on a few areas of the law, such business litigation, real estate, employment, personal injury, or insurance. Become the very best in your field.

I found a few really good resources and created my own personal outline of the law in my practice areas. I put the outline in my own words and supplemented it often. By doing this on a regular basis, I started accumulating real knowledge in the key areas of the law I practiced. Could you give a detailed, organized presentation of the law right now in your specialty?

The law is dynamic and changing. Are you staying current with the most recent developments? Does it vary according to jurisdiction, federal or state, different appellate courts? I find the more I dig and research, the more my knowledge expands. That is your job.

4—Rules of Ethics and Civility

In the movie *Liar*, Jim Carrey plays Fletcher Reede, a hot-shot lawyer who is put under a spell that ensures he can't lie. When he realizes he can only tell the truth, he asks the Court for a continuance. The Court asks for good cause for his request. Exasperated, Reede responds, "I can't lie!" The Court humorously says, "Commendable, but I'm still waiting to hear good cause. Do you have one or not?" Reede quickly retorts, "Not." So the case proceeds with Reede having to tell the truth.

This shouldn't be so funny, but it is. The fact is that lawyers are often paid to "stretch the truth," and, even worse, they are called "liars." But there are bright lines that shouldn't be crossed. You must always act ethically. It's not only the law; it's the right thing to do. Trust me, it's better for you and your business. As the adage goes, one's ethical reputation is like a bubble, it can only be burst once.

I didn't list this item first because none of you would have read any further if I told you to start with the model code of ethics. But I absolutely recommend you read your state and/or the federal model rules of professional responsibility. And, then write down in your own words the ten most important principles for you to follow. Create your own Ten Commandments for your practice. When in doubt, which will be often, always take the ethical high road.

5—Evidence

A good lawyer understands the difference between fact and evidence. A fact is an assertion that something is true. The evidence is the source establishing the fact. An airplane flew across the sky is a fact. Jane's testimony she saw the airplane fly across the sky is evidence.

All lawyers need to know the rules of evidence and how facts are admitted into evidence. I recommend coming up with your own analytical framework for analyzing evidentiary issues, such as: "relevance, foundation, hearsay, privileges, privacy, and FRE 403." Evidentiary objections sometimes call for super quick reflexes at trial or depositions. As such, creating your own system will assist you in developing expertise in this area.

6—Writing Skills

In civil litigation, written communication is paramount. Judges decide much of your case on paperwork. If you don't write well, you may not even get to trial. Writing is a skill that can be improved, and you would be wise to hone this craft. Start with a good basic book on writing such as *The Elements of Style* and consider taking a good legal writing course.

Let me make a couple of fundamental points about writing for the court.

First, be well organized in your writing. Tell the court in a short, concise introduction exactly what you are requesting. Then, in the memorandum of points and authorities, support each point clearly, and finish with a short, pithy conclusion.

Second, for each point, make sure you have *both* the law and the facts supporting your position. Don't just state the law and not tell the judge the facts. Also, don't throw a bunch of facts at the judge without citing the law. Yes, the IRAC format—Issue, Rule, Analysis, and Conclusion—is still alive and well.

Third, proof your brief several times. Writing is a process. After you write your brief the first time, read it again with the aim that it is clear, logical, and flows. Then, review it a third time just to proof it for grammar, spelling, needless words, etc. By your third version, it should be a polished product worthy of submission to the court.

7—Trial Skills

One of the turning points in my career was when I finally got some trial experience. This is the final act for a case, and until you have conducted a trial you don't really appreciate how everything fits together. There is simply no substitute. Think of a trial as a wrestling match. You only get better by sparring with an opponent.

You need to get some trial experience. If you can't get it at your firm, then do yourself a huge favor and find one of the high-quality trial programs out there, such as the National Institute for Trial Attorneys (NITA) in which individuals participate in a mock trial over the course of a week. Or volunteer to handle cases on behalf of indigent clients. In fact, my very first trial was exactly that. That gave me the confidence and credibility to handle bigger trials.

I have presided over hundreds of trials in my career, so let me offer you three keys to being an effective trial lawyer. First, always remember what you are trying to accomplish in each phase of the trial. For instance, I had one of the best civil rights lawyers in Los Angeles representing the plaintiff. When conducting his direct examination, he was physically close to the witness. He didn't want the jurors to take their eyes off the witness. On cross-examination, it was just the opposite. He was typically as far away from the witness as possible as he wanted the jury to focus on him. During one cross-examination, he was so far away, I was afraid he was going to stumble into the clerk's desk. He knew exactly what he wanted to accomplish when examining witnesses.

Second, most trials are primarily determined by the credibility of the witnesses. Yet, it is shocking how few lawyers prepare their witnesses to give believable testimony. Think hard about what makes a witness believable. Even simple things like wearing appropriate attire, making eye contact with the jurors or the court, and being prepared for difficult questions goes a long way in enhancing credibility.

Third, with today's modern technology, I'm surprised how few lawyers use appropriate visual aids. They have a witness talk for hours to a jury when a single picture can be worth a thousand words. I strongly suggest using powerful and simple visual aids at all stages of the trial to make it as easy as possible for the court or jury to understand your case.

8—Investigation/Discovery Skills

I've found that many lawyers investigate their case or conduct discovery as if they're on autopilot. Without thinking, they follow a form interview outline or hire an investigator to gather the facts. They just check the boxes to serve basic discovery on the parties.

You will greatly benefit from crafting an investigation and discovery plan specifically tailored for your case. In creating such a plan, always start with the law. What needs to be proven by the plaintiff? If the defendant can punch one hole in an essential element of the plaintiff's claim, liability will be lost. Then, obtain that information methodically and tenaciously. Don't give up until you get what you need. If Plan A doesn't work, get those facts using Plan B or C.

9—Verbal Communication Skills

Lawyers who can effectively communicate face-to-face will have a huge advantage. You may know the law and the facts, but if you can't communicate them clearly, your client will suffer. If you've seen an articulate lawyer in front of the court, a jury, or with a client, you know what I'm talking about.

Like all other skills, good communication is learned and developed. The single biggest step is getting comfortable speaking in front of others. Jerry Seinfeld joked most people would rather receive a eulogy than give one. I highly recommend you invest in a good speaking course or join an organization like Toastmasters. There's no substitute for experience. When you are speaking in public, including to a court or jury, switch your mindset from "I'm afraid" to "I'm excited."

When addressing the court, be brief, respectful, and to the point. Let the judge know you want to make a certain number of points (three is a good number), but always look at the judge's questions as an opportunity to help them rule in your favor. "Thank you, Your Honor, for asking that question," is an excellent approach.

10—Negotiation

Most cases are overwhelmingly settled rather than tried. That is a fact. Yet, we spend so much of our time becoming trial experts and so little time at mastering the skills of negotiation. In my experience, there are two main aspects of settlement skills that are lacking.

First, most lawyers don't serve as adequate counselors of law in "objectively" advising their clients of the likelihood of prevailing. Studies show lawyers often overestimate their chances of prevailing. Maybe that's due to bravado, but in the end, it typically hurts their clients. For those cases that go to trial, both sides generally believe they have a good chance of prevailing. The fact is, however, it's logically impossible for both parties to win. One of the parties is going to lose. It is typically much more painful for the party who loses than it is good for the party who wins.

Second, learn and apply the basic skills of negotiation to get a matter resolved. Being creative and being open to negotiations goes a long way in getting a case settled. There are numerous excellent books, blogs, and courses on negotiation and settlement, and I highly recommend trying one.

11—Bonus: Find a Mentor

One of the surest ways to substantially improve your career capital is to find a mentor. When looking for a mentor, the person should have at least three attributes: (1) a high degree of ethics, (2) knowledge and experience they can impart to you, and (3) a willingness to invest in your life and/or career.

In my own career, I was blessed to find an early mentor in Dick Terzian. He was one of the best lawyers I ever met and an even better man. When I started at my first law firm, I wanted to practice in the civil rights area, so I hoped to work with him. As a new lawyer, it was my responsibility to take the initiative to let partners know I wanted to work with them.

Because of how busy he was, Dick was not easy to approach. When you first met him, he was a man of few words. He used silence better than any person I know. If you didn't have something worthwhile to say, he would just courteously smile at you.

I eventually mustered the courage, knocked on his closed door, and said, "Hi, Mr. Terzian. As you know, I'm a new associate here and have a great interest in civil rights law, so if you're looking for somebody to do some work, I would very much appreciate your considering me. Thank you." I waited for about ten seconds, but he just smiled and didn't say a word. I couldn't believe how uncomfortable it was just standing there waiting for a response. Finally, I just said, "thank you again," and left.

I heard nothing from him initially. But about two weeks later, I got a call: "Steve, this is Dick Terzian; please come to my office." I immediately went to his office. There were no pleasantries exchanged. Dick said, "I have a new case from the City of Pasadena regarding an officer-involved shooting. I want you to research whether the qualified immunity defense applies in this case and get back to me in one week." I replied thank you and left immediately.

I was excited for my opportunity. Of course, I did the best job I possibly could. I stayed late and researched the issue thoroughly. In a week's time, I had become a mini expert on qualified immunity. I wrote and re-wrote the memo many times. I even had one of my fellow associates review it.

The day before the deadline, I knocked on Dick's door and said, "Here's the paper you requested, and please let me know if you have any questions." He said, "Thank you," and gave me his trademark polite smile. Nothing else was said. The next few days I wondered if I still had a job. But, a week later, I got a call from Dick asking me if I was available for another assignment. I guess I did well enough.

Thus began my relationship with my mentor of thirty years. Our relationship blossomed over time, and I eventually earned his trust. I appreciated that it needed to be earned. He made me a much better lawyer and person. I owe so much to him. It can't be overstated how important it is to find a great mentor.

It is also invaluable, if possible, to find a contemporary, co-worker, or friend with whom you can bounce ideas; and you and this person can hold one another accountable. The Navy SEALs call them "swim buddies." When I was a mid-level associate, Richard, a new junior lawyer joined our firm. I was initially assigned to show him the ropes. He was truly my equal, if not superior, in so many ways, and this new lawyer fast became one of my close friends and a great "swim buddy" at my firm.

MANAGE YOUR BUSINESS

Is the practice of law a business or a profession? The answer is it's both. Most lawyers understand the practice of law is a profession, but those same lawyers struggle mightily to recognize the business aspect.

I have stressed the importance of thinking like a lawyer as necessary to excelling as a lawyer. However, it's also imperative to think like a businessperson. You are both a lawyer *and* a businessperson. You can ignore that fact and stick your head in the sand. But that won't change reality.

If you want to thrive as a lawyer, you would be well served to develop certain business skills. Those skills will vary depending on the type of practice you have—a solo litigation lawyer will have different responsibilities than a transactional lawyer working for a large governmental agency. In helping lawyers, I have found it's not the lack of legal acumen, but rather the neglect or ignorance of business skills that most torpedoes their career or practice.

To start, there are three specific plans from which all lawyers will benefit.

First, you need to have an individual business plan. "You, Inc." Carve out time to plan you and your business. The most successful individuals find time by themselves to sit and plan out their own careers and business. Who are you as a firm/business? What type of practice do you run? What is your specific vision for your legal business?

You don't just work "in" your business, you work "on" your business. You are in the business of providing legal services. You and your firm are a business. Hopefully a profitable one. You need to have a profit in the business if you want to get paid. What is your minimum viable profit for your business? Do you have a specific goal of how much you or your firm desires to make financially per year? Regardless of what it is, having a specific goal is what matters.

I was a business major in college, and it is Finance 101 that all profitable businesses pay attention to both revenues and expenses. From a revenue perspective, you must have a strong system in place to track your time, get out invoices, collect payment, etc. From an expense perspective, you must monitor all your costs, and be especially mindful of not only your fixed/predictable costs but the enormous variable costs of each case, such as experts, depositions, data collection and storage. Make sure you are confident with your financial system to ensure on-going viability.

Second, you must have a management plan for your practice. This is commonly referred to as a "practice management plan." While your business plan essentially sets your vision as a lawyer or firm, your practice management plan implements how you operate your practice. As author and management consultant Michael Gerber states, a practice management plan answers, "What do I need to do to fulfill the expectations of the client on time, every time, exactly as promised?"

It's hard to imagine thriving in your practice without an excellent practice management plan. Such a plan should include, at a minimum, a calendaring system, deadlines, case management software, file organization, and a trial preparation system. It makes sure you keep your commitments and don't miss deadlines. It's your daily calendar and daily reminders. By setting up key tools, habits, and structures, it frees you up to practice law. It is why Gerber says: "Practice management" is "practice liberation."[8]

As a mid-level associate, I learned an indelible lesson of just how critical blown deadlines can be. I was the lead lawyer for a company facing serious allegations of gender discrimination and harassment. An employee claimed an unknown person had painted a swastika on her door, made offensive remarks, and the company had done nothing about it.

These were inflammatory allegations, and I knew it was going to be a tough case. I decided to file a motion for summary judgment to hopefully defeat some of the legal claims and flesh out plaintiff's evidence. I believed the motion was strong and anticipated what the opposition would say. When the opposition due date came and passed, I verified online that no opposition had been filed. I immediately filed a "notice of non-opposition." About five days later, and just one day before the hearing, the plaintiff filed a request to file a late opposition. The court denied the request and granted the summary judgement motion. When I informed the client, he almost fell out of his chair. Plaintiff had missed a critical deadline, resulting in a dismissal of the entire case.

Another crucial aspect of an excellent practice management plan is to ensure that your technology is current and fully functional. Technology is indispensable to the modern practice of law. Much of our practice management is now run by sophisticated software. With courts going to electronic filing systems and remote appearances, you need to make sure you are properly invested in an excellent program.

The third and final aspect of a successful practice is an "employee-relations plan." You will be more successful if you have excellent and satisfied co-workers, whether a legal assistant, paralegal, associates, or fellow lawyers. You are all going to work with others.

In addition to the obvious people skills, such as respect, consideration, and open lines of communication, there are other key aspects of an employee-relations plan. Think through a positive staff accountability and team building system. Training, retaining, and growing positive, productive employees takes effort but is well worth it.

Most lawyers switch jobs within five years.[9] Therefore, the lawyer or firm who can retain highly skilled, dependable, people-friendly associates or co-workers has struck gold. Not only is such an associate profitable for the firm, but it is also very costly to continue replacing associates, especially when you factor in the time and expense. When retaining employees, compensation and extrinsic rewards are important, but so is their happiness. Quality of life, location, work-life balance, flexibility, autonomy, and mission are factors in work happiness.

In short, by focusing on these three aspects—a business plan, a practice management plan, and an employee-relations plan—you will maximize your potential for a flourishing practice, one that provides high income to its lawyers, high-standards of service to its clients, and high job satisfaction to its employees. You will become the "In-N-Out Burger" or "Chick-fil-A" of lawyers or law firms, doing it the same excellent way every day.

BUILD YOUR BUSINESS

You can have a prosperous mindset, excellent career capital, and effective business plan, but without having and retaining clients, your practice won't succeed. The last essential component for a flourishing practice is building your clientele. You must have clients to serve. This is an economic reality.

Early in my career, I saw how plainly evident this was. The "rainmakers" in the firm had the corner offices and power. Those that didn't have their own clients were beholden to those who did. If you want real job security and a successful practice in the private sector, I encourage you to have your own clients.

Some lawyers find the notion of marketing distasteful or beneath them. "I am a lawyer, not a salesperson," he or she might say. Well, what do you think you do when you present your case to a judge or jury? You're selling your position and hoping to make the "sale." Like it or not, lawyers are in the business of sales.

There is no specific formula for building your business. There are as many creative and varied ways as there are lawyers. Each approach will be unique to what fits you.

Start by putting yourself in the shoes of a client. Why would they want to retain *you*? Why would somebody hire you over someone else? Is it because you are the best lawyer? Because you have built a relationship? You are trusted? You're a good communicator? Your rates? Your flashy website? Something else or all the above? Before moving on, are you able to answer those questions?

Let me first start with the assumption you're already a great lawyer. This is by far the most important aspect in building your business. No marketing effort will overcome being an incompetent or mediocre lawyer.

When I was a mid-level associate, my mentor told me he was leaving the firm. I asked if there was a position at his new firm, and he said yes. I informed the clients on my cases that I was leaving the firm and that they would be in excellent hands with the newly assigned lawyers at the old firm. Surprisingly, a number of those clients sought me out at my new firm, essentially saying they loved my work and wanted to stay with me. One client in particular was a Fortune 500 company, and it became my single biggest client overnight. I never would have asked the client to leave, but the in-house counsel approached me based on my past service.

With that said, there are at least four common characteristics to most successful marketing plans.

First and foremost, build trusted relationships. Business will come from another person. Relationships are the bread and butter of getting business. Ultimately, your cases will come from other people. Always understand that. If you don't have relationships, those cases will go somewhere else.

Creation of relationships starts with connection. Connection should come before retention or solutions. Once you have a connection, consider some type of invitation. Lunch, an email, an article. Reach out and take the next step that fits you. Some type of movement from connection to invitation.

Join clubs, organizations, and groups that are closely connected with your interests. At a minimum, get meaningfully involved in an organization in your practice area. Networking is a long-term, relationship-based strategy. It does not happen overnight. You can't attend one or two bar events or educational seminars and expect to develop business. Relationships take time and trust. Once a person has gotten to know you or your reputation well, the business will start to come.

Second, communicate early, often, and effectively. Every communication with a client or prospect is an opportunity. I encourage you to be thoroughly prepared when you first talk about the case, so the client is confident you can successfully handle the matter.

I was once invited to make a proposal to a school district being sued by a prominent plaintiff's lawyer. Three other firms were also asked to bid. When it came time for my interview with the school superintendent, I had spent several hours analyzing the case, researching the claims, and doing some background investigation on the plaintiff and the plaintiff's lawyer. I believe it was my familiarity with and research on plaintiff's lawyer as well my ability to communicate my strategy that won the day. I left the interview with a new client.

Once you have a client, ensure he or she knows what is happening during the case. It's the single biggest source of complaints to the Bar—clients don't hear from their lawyers. Have a system or protocol in place for communicating on a regular basis with your clients. Your clients will love you for it. For example, "Hi Sandra, today the court scheduled a trial setting conference for June. Hopefully, we will get an early trial date at that time. I'll keep you posted." If your practice thrives on repeat business or word of mouth, you should place great emphasis on this. It's much more cost-effective to keep existing clients than to find new clients. Keep your lines of communication open to ensure they are happy and there are no problems.

Third, be cost-sensitive. There is incredible competition. All things being equal, clients often decide based on cost. If there are two good lawyers, and one is charging substantially less, they will likely go with that lawyer. While we often get what we pay for, we need to be cost-sensitive in our overall marketing plan. Be extremely strategic in setting your rates. It's partly a function of supply and demand.

Early in my career, a partner asked me to take the lead on a personal injury case involving a roller coaster. It was a soft-tissue injury, and even if the plaintiff prevailed, she could have recovered a maximum of $50,000. The ride manufacturer wanted us to aggressively defend the case but not spend any money doing so! As the case neared trial, our lawyer's fees were only about $15,000. Although we opined there was a strong likelihood of prevailing, the client decided to settle the case for $5,000 because it didn't want to spend any more money. It's important you have an agreed upon cost plan that makes sense for both the client and the lawyer.

Think about how you can use fees and costs as a marketing tool. By way of example, consider not charging clients for phone calls. You know how many clients abhor those charges or don't call their lawyers because they don't want to get charged for it. I, for one, loved when my clients called because it gave me an opportunity to interact with them and show that I was on top of their case. Now this may not work for all types of practices but is worth considering. When a clients have a positive experience with you, they are more likely to tell others and to give you repeat business.

Fourth, garner attention. Like it or not, we live in an attention economy. We need potential clients to know what we can offer and why they should retain us. There are so many ways to attain good attention, but here are some proven methods:

Create a good online presence. The various approaches lawyers use to find clients, and vice versa, have undergone a revolutionary change, and it's driven by technology. A good website is not expensive but indispensable. Everybody looks to see what your website says about you. Do you have a compelling or inspiring vision of your practice? Social media, LinkedIn, Facebook, Twitter, etc. are other business tools to demonstrate your legal acumen.

Hire a marketing consultant. Depending on your type of practice, professionals can assist you in getting consistent referrals.

Build your resume. When I began my career, I approached partners with an idea to write an article that might be of interest to their practice and asked if they wanted to co-author it. I offered to do the initial writing. Then, I started writing articles myself. As I got more experience, I looked for opportunities to speak at conferences.

I encourage you to do some type of active marketing on a daily or weekly basis. Whether it is making a phone call, attending a meeting, writing a blog, or sending a thank you email, you want to keep your marketing momentum going. One of the best things I learned from my mentor is he never stopped marketing, whether it be attending meetings, going to lunches, or taking them to a sporting event. Although extremely successful, he kept up with his relationships, continued to speak at events, and showed his smiling face. He was never pushy or high pressured. He was pleasant, respectful, kind, and an exceptional lawyer. And his business overflowed.

MASTER YOUR FINANCES

Yes, work should be meaningful, but it is also the lifeblood of your financial security. It pays for your home, car, food, and clothes. It allows you to go out to dinner, on vacation, and pay for the kids' school. Money matters.

We have discussed how to make money, but what do you do with your money once you get it? How do you flourish in your finances?

The first step is to determine your financial goals or objectives. Everybody is different. At a minimum, you will want to be able to cover your regular expenses and save for your retirement. Most of us want some type of financial security.

The word *security* derives from the Latin word *securus*, meaning "without care." Having a life in which we don't have to constantly worry about money is a vision we can get excited about. Almost two-thirds of Americans worry about money. Money is also one of the top three sources of conflict in relationships. It will be challenging to flourish if you are constantly concerned about how you are going to get by financially.

Taking control of your finances will help you in the other aspects of your life. Certainly, your mental and emotional health will improve. You will improve your physical health by reducing your stress. Your relationships will get better when finances are not an issue of contention. And you'll have a greater sense of freedom as you can spend and give money without having to worry whether you can.

If I summarized financial planning into one sentence, it would be: Spend less money than you make. But, of course, there is more to it than that, so let's cover the fundamentals to get you started toward financial flourishing.

The first step is to always pay yourself first. This is non-negotiable. When you get a paycheck, the first person you pay is yourself by depositing a portion of it into a savings account or investing it in the stock market (more on that shortly). Even if it is just $50 a pay period, get in the habit of putting money away. At first, this money can provide for your emergency fund. The purpose of having an emergency fund is to see you through a serious illness, unemployment, or other unforeseen setback. Once you have put away three months of pay in your emergency fund, then money can be used for savings or investing. An excellent goal is to save or invest at least 10 percent of your net income.

The second step is to invest your money wisely. You want to use sound investing principles. This includes investing consistently, so you can make compound interest work for you. Become an educated investor. The penalty of a foolish risk is the loss of your money. Blue chip stocks and index funds have been solid choices for the long run. Once you have invested your money. Let it grow.

Where do you start investing? In his book the *Capitalist Code,* Ben Stein looks at the investing philosophy of the one of richest men in America, Warren Buffet, and concludes: "All you have to do is buy and hold an 'index' of the largest stocks in the United States of America and hold onto them and add to them regularly."[10] He specifically recommends buying shares in the Standard & Poor 500 Industrial Stock Index fund.

The third step is to be frugal with your money. Notice I didn't say be "cheap" or live a monastic lifestyle. The term "frugal" means getting value for your money or being fruitful with what you have. It means spending money on what gives you worthwhile fulfillment. It means harmonizing your money with your values. As discussed beautifully in the classic, *Your Money or Your Life*, it's about transforming your relationship with money, so that your spending reflects your life's values.[11] If you absolutely love high quality clothes and can afford them, go for it. It's also important to learn to be content with "enough." Just because you would like a scoop of ice cream doesn't mean a triple scoop is better. Frugality is good for you and good for the planet.

The fourth step is to stay out of debt. There may be exceptions, for example, your home mortgage, but these should be rare. In general, if you don't have money to pay for it, then don't buy it. Americans are so used to buying things on credit and paying interest on that money. If you want real security, just say no to debt.

The fifth step is to make a written budget and stick to it. I know budgets are no fun. But there is no better way to track your money. It's simple—your income needs to exceed your expenses. The budget is the best way to see if this is happening. It gives you a snapshot of where you are spending money.

Dave Ramsey tells the story of a man who didn't have enough money at the end of the month to save for retirement. Each month, his income exactly matched his expenses, with nothing left over. He met with Ramsey, who had him do a budget. It became clear the man spent an enormous amount of his money eating out. When he saw this, the man commented he had been literally "eating his own retirement." By seeing it on his budget, he was able to make an adjustment that included both going out to dinner *and* saving for retirement.

These five steps provide a very solid foundation for you to flourish financially. Of course, there are plenty of other wise steps to take, such as owning your own home, investing in a retirement account, having adequate insurance, and minimizing your taxes.

Lastly, let's remember that money is a means to an end. It's never an end in itself. It allows you to buy things and to help others. Money is like a brick. You can use a brick wastefully or even harmfully by throwing it through a window, or you can construct a beautiful home or building with it. The same with money. It can be a great source of security, freedom, and joy. Or it can be wasted and a source of anxiety and dissatisfaction. Let's learn to use our hard-earned money well and watch all other aspects of our lives improve.

....

Chapter Summary:

- **Make work meaningful; have a vision for a purposeful, thriving work life.**
- **Have a prosperous mindset so that you might rise to flourishing heights in work.**
- **Build career capital, manage your business, build your business, and master your personal finances.**

SIDEBAR _____

Make sure your technology works well. Before your court appearance, double-check connections, lighting, and microphone. Remember a virtual appearance is still a court appearance.

CHAPTER 10

RELATIONSHIPS WITH OTHERS

• • •

"I shall pass this way but once; any good that I can do or any kindness I can show to any human being, let me do it now. Let me not defer nor neglect it, for I shall not pass this way again."

—RALPH WALDO EMERSON

At my wedding, as my wife-to-be walked down the aisle, my best man leaned over and whispered to me, "Remember this moment." And I have never forgotten that beautiful day and how my beautiful bride looked. While a wedding is one day, a marriage lasts a lifetime and is perhaps the most important relationship of your life.

In the delivery room awaiting the birth of my first child, just as my daughter was about to be born, the nurse asked, "Do you want to cut the umbilical cord?" I did, and then as the nurse handed my daughter to me, I was struck by the lightning bolt realization that my life would never be the same, as I would be a parent the rest of my days.

Back when I was in kindergarten, my best friend and I had a bad-tempered substitute teacher. As we walked to school, we "pinky swore" if that substitute was there again, we would ditch school. Upon arrival, we peeked in the window, and sure enough, she was back. We left school and went to my friend's backyard where we played until we were caught by his dad. But I had a friend for life, and we still laugh about that moment fifty years later.

There is no question that when you look back at your life, the most central part of it will be marked by your significant relationships. Whether it be with your spouse, significant other, children, parents, friends, co-workers, or even strangers, meaningful relationships matter. A lot.

When you are on your deathbed, you won't be wishing you spent more time at the office. Hopefully, you will be surrounded by loving family and friends. It's what we most desire. They are what make life so incredible and precious.

You will measure your life in large part by the quality of your relationships. If you want to flourish, you must develop and nurture real, meaningful relationships. The failure to do so will undoubtedly lead to loneliness, sadness, and despair. In fact, when I speak with lawyers, the two most common complaints are they have no time to live a balanced, happy life or to devote to meaningful relationships. A life where you had no meaningful relationships—no family, no friends, no colleagues. The world would be a dark and lonely place indeed.

Humans need each other. We need a human connection to thrive. "Connection is why we are here. It is what gives purpose and meaning to our lives," says author Brené Brown.[1] There is no vision of flourishing that doesn't include thriving relationships.

Given its critical importance, it's not surprising science shows that loving relationships make us more positive, emotionally resilient, satisfied, and healthier. Love is biologically good for our health and happiness.[2] As professor and scholar Barbara Fredrickson writes: "Love is our supreme emotion ... When you experience love—true heart/mind/soul-expanding love—you not only become better able to see the larger tapestry of life and better able to breathe life into the connections that matter to you, but you also set yourself on a pathway that leads to more health, happiness, and wisdom."[3]

In fact, numerous studies have firmly established that meaningful relationships are more important to your health, happiness, and flourishing than any other factor. In a famous seventy-five-year study out of Harvard Medical School, the director of that study found: "You could have all the money you've ever wanted, a successful career, and be in good physical health, but without loving relationships, you won't be happy ... The good life is built with good relationships."[4] In short, meaningful relationships are essential to flourishing.

The good—no, great—news is that there are many things we can do to improve a meaningful relationship. Let's commit or recommit to pursuing meaningful relationships in our lives. The first step is a recognition of their fundamental importance. Then, we move from that recognition to putting our knowledge into action. How do we do that?

We will examine the five primary types of relationships in which we can flourish. Note that love and meaningful relationships are expansive in nature. The more comprehensively and broadly we include love in our lives, the more flourishing we will experience.

LOVE 1.0—LOVING YOURSELF

As a teenager, Phyllis thought she was ugly. Every time she looked in the mirror, she became depressed. This carried into her adult life. At the age of thirty-seven, she was a discouraged and directionless housewife on welfare. However, her life began to turn around after she read *The Magic of Believing* by Claude Bristol. For the first time, she accepted herself and even noticed some of her own gifts. One of her best talents was making people laugh. She started doing stand-up comedy routines, mostly poking fun at herself.

Eventually, Phyllis Diller went on to become one of the most successful comedians of all time as well as an actress, author, and musician. She recognized her poor self-esteem was the root of her problems, and her life completely changed once she genuinely accepted who she was.

Yes, a flourishing life involves meaningful relationships with others. But those relationships first require a healthy relationship with yourself. Leo Buscaglia in his book, *Love,* said it best: "To love others you must love yourself ... You can only give away what you have yourself." The opposite is also true: You can't give what you don't have.

Brené Brown states, "We can only love others as much as we love ourselves."[5] Because healthy love for ourselves is so foundational, I call it Love 1.0. You must begin by loving you.

When you are on an airplane, you are told that before assisting others, you should put on your own oxygen mask first. Once your own oxygen mask is on, you can then safely help others. It's the same way with relationships. You must take care of yourself before you can take care of others. A healthy self-love is a condition precedent to loving others.

The primary terms we use to describe a healthy love and acceptance for the self are "self-esteem" and "self-worth." While they mean different things, they are very much interrelated and, for our purposes, convey the concept of acceptance, appreciation, and belief in yourself.

The leading expert on self-esteem, Nathaniel Branden, in his book, *The Six Pillars of Self-Esteem*, says: "Apart from disturbance whose roots are biological, I cannot think of a single psychological problem—from anxiety and depression, to underachievement at school or at work, to fear of intimacy, happiness, or success, to alcohol or drug abuse, to spouse battering or child molestation, to co-dependency and sexual disorders, to passivity and chronic aimlessness, to suicide and crimes of violence—that's not traceable, at least in part, to the problem of deficient self-esteem. Of all the judgment we pass in life, none is as important as the one we pass on ourselves."[6]

Hopefully, you are sold on the connection between a healthy self-love and a love of others. Please take some time exploring your own acceptance and worth. Perhaps it is time for a tune-up, an upgrade, or even a massive rebuild. Like all the principles in this book, self-esteem and self-worth are not just vague ideas, they are a specific practice. They can be cultivated. You can move from knowledge to daily practice.

To start, we can have a healthy self-acceptance of who we are that is not based on what we have achieved in our lives. Rather, we must develop a sense of knowing that we are enough. Renowned author, Brené Brown, has done extensive research in this area and describes developing this kind of self-acceptance as "cultivating the courage, compassion, and connection to wake up in the morning and think, 'No matter what gets done and how much is left undone, I am enough.' It's going to bed at night thinking, 'Yes, I am imperfect and vulnerable and sometimes afraid but that doesn't change the truth that I am also brave and worthy of love and belonging.'"[7]

Take those healthy thoughts of your own value and put them into action. Two of the best daily practices include setting your intentions and doing your number one self-care habit.

First, each morning, take a few minutes to set your intentions for the day by connecting with your higher purpose and yourself. It could be prayer, meditation, journaling, breathing, positive self-talk, or something else. Whatever is most effective for you.

While there is no single magic bullet, I encourage you to establish a ritual involving some type of recognition of your good traits and/or accomplishments. For instance, I start my morning by journaling about the positive virtues I want to embody. It's a healthy way to re-affirm your best attributes. Your thoughts about yourself are a self-fulfilling prophecy. You will become what you believe about yourself.

Second, identify your single most important self-care habit. Ask yourself, what's the number one thing I can do for myself? By being creative and experimenting, you will figure it out, and it will likely change over time. It could be a good night's sleep, prayer, meditation, inspirational reading, going for walk, healthy eating, exercising, or breathing. The key is to know what is most important for you and then to do it daily.

Be patient with yourself (and others) as you grow in a healthy self-acceptance. No self-shaming. Like a baby learning to walk, loving yourself too takes time to grow. Imagine what we could achieve if we had that type of patience and discipline with ourselves. As Dan Millman counsels: "So be gentle with yourself; show yourself the same kindness and patience you might show a young child—the child you once were. If you won't be your own friend, who will be?"[8] Just like the baby who continually gets up and falls, we, too, keep trying. Quitting is not an option. We take the next step—one at a time—and eventually attain a genuine love and acceptance for ourselves. No other person can make you feel inferior without your permission. When you begin to accept yourself, you will have laid the foundation not only for loving others but for a flourishing life.

LOVE 2.0—LOVING YOUR FAMILY

Loving Your Spouse or Significant Other

A longtime friend of mine recently told me he was separating after twenty-five years of marriage. I remember when his first child was born; it was one of the happiest days of his life. He eventually had more children. We talked regularly, but I noticed he always talked about his work and kids but never about his wife or marriage. He had a good job and great kids. When his youngest child graduated from college, he and his wife were alone as a couple for the first time in twenty years. He looked at her and realized he hardly knew her anymore. Their marriage had been almost exclusively dedicated to raising kids and taking care of the house. They had essentially forgotten about each other.

It's obvious that a bad marriage or relationship can significantly impact one's happiness. I won't detail how often marriages or committed relationships fail. I won't cite the latest depressing statistics about high divorce rates. On the other hand, a committed, intimate relationship between two people is one of the best aspects of life. A good marriage or partnership can provide the deepest and most meaningful form of companionship a person can encounter. Because of a family's critical importance to our lives and society, I call this Love 2.0.

Let me ask you: How's your marriage or significant relationship? Do you feel like your relationship is flourishing and fulfilling? For purposes of this chapter, I will deal with marriages and committed relationships (hereinafter "partners" or "partnerships") in the same manner.

One of the biggest challenges facing a partnership is that it involves two individuals who each control their own lives but don't have control over the other. You can't control what the other person says or does, how they feel or how they feel about you. We have different interests, personalities, temperaments, habits, and upbringings. We have our own expectations. So it's not surprising partnerships can be both exhilarating and excruciating.

The good news is partnerships can survive and thrive. You can learn how to make yourself a better partner, to improve the relationship, and to help your partnership grow. It takes both knowledge and work.

I have read many books on partnerships, attended conferences, and done extensive research on what makes a partnership thrive. Dr. John Gottman is widely regarded as one of the foremost relationship experts in the world and able to predict divorce with a 90 percent accuracy rate. In his book, *The Seven Principles for Making Marriage Work*, Dr. Gottman first articulates no marriage is perfect. And yours won't be the first. Even successful partnerships have numerous conflicts and challenges. Partners need to navigate many of the common issues that confront most partnerships, such as money, sex, in-laws, work, kids, and chores.

Dr. Gottman emphasized there is no one way for a happy marriage. Every marriage has its own uniqueness. However, based on over forty years of research, Gottman found that successful couples share several principles in common.

The chief principle—which is corroborated by many other experts—is to demonstrate genuine fondness and admiration for your spouse. This emanates from the virtues of love and kindness. Gottman rather bluntly states "if fondness and admiration are completely missing, reviving the relationship is impossible."[9]

If you stop watering a plant, it will die from neglect. A plant needs to be watered and nurtured. So does a relationship. Our closest relationships are nurtured through our loving actions toward our partner. I agree with Gottman, who advises those in relationships to look at each other through rose-colored glasses and to be good finders. It starts with thinking about what is special about your partner. What do you admire about him or her? Why did you fall in love with him or her? That's admiration. Then, tell them often. Love is an action verb.

In his uber best-selling book, *The Five Love Languages*, Dr. Gary Chapman shows how couples can express love for each other better by recognizing the unique way their partner feels love. He identifies five different ways that couples show love: words of affirmation, quality time, gift giving, acts of service, and physical touch.

If your partner's love language is "words of affirmation," then you can give him or her genuine compliments or praise often. If your spouse craves "quality time," you can set up date nights, trips, or walks together. If its "gift giving," both big and small presents can demonstrate how much you love them. Another love language is providing "acts of service" by helping them out—working in the yard, doing dishes, helping with kids' homework. Remember, a helpful partner has a happy partner. The final love language is "physical touch," including holding hands, kissing, cuddling, and making love.

I am close with a couple, Bob and Peg, who have a wonderful marriage. Bob's love language is "physical touch," and Peg's is "quality time." You can see it in their marriage. They are regularly affectionate and affirming. As a result, they light up in each other's presence. Bob loves how affectionate Peg is, and she appreciates Bob spending time with her.

Bob tells a story about how he ran into a friend who hadn't seen him in a year. "How are you doing, Bob?" asked the friend. "Peggy and I are separated," he replied. "What? You two were so in love and always together. I'm shocked." "Don't worry," Bob said, "Peg's just at the grocery store. We'll only be apart an hour."

Yes, there will be times where life is ordinary, routine. There will be long roads of flat highways. Yet it is during those times we can continue to kindle the relationship through fondness and admiration of the little things. Like Bill Murray in the movie *Groundhog Day*, we, too, can approach our daily partnership by adding sprinkles of positive connection and words of appreciation.

There is a win-win-win in showing affection and admiration in that it benefits both the giver and receiver as well as the relationship. We want to help our partner become the best version of him or herself. In short, this is all about demonstrating the virtue of love. There are so many different, beautiful ways we can show our partners we love them. If you want to flourish in your relationship, connect with your spouse in loving, admiring ways.

Being a Parent

A good friend's son recently left for college on a baseball scholarship. After the semester, the son flew home and was met by his parents. The son had shaved his head and died it yellow, a stark contrast from his long, brown hair. Both parents were surprised but happy to see him. "All of my teammates did the same, and it was a team-bonding experience," said the son. They supported their son and laughed with (not at) him.

If you're a parent, you understand there is little else in life that can bring you the happiness and satisfaction of your family. From my own experience, I remember feeling love like never before when my children were born. The most powerful type of love may be a parent's love for a child. The privilege of loving and raising, as well as being loved and taught by, my children has been one of my greatest sources of happiness.

Unlike other relationships, the parent relationship is truly unique. Nobody else can be their parents. Only your children will call you dad or mom. Your children can't trade you in for different parents, and you can't exchange your children for different ones. It is hard to overstate the importance of parenting.

Given its critical importance, it's remarkable how little parents invest in educating themselves about being a good parent. They spend countless hours mastering their work or even a hobby but little time learning to be an excellent parent. Isn't it ironic that you need a license to drive a car or own a dog, but anybody can be a parent?

I believe the most important principle of being a great parent is to be an exemplary role-model. As with all your roles in life, it's not just your words but also your actions that matter. That is particularly amplified with children. Recognize the awesome power your words can have on your children, but more importantly your children watch you like hawks. So, your words and deeds should be consistent. Model the behavior you desire in your children.

Your role will change over time along with your children. As they grow and mature, so too will your parenting style. Child psychologists often list five different stages of child development and the parent's primary role at each stage:

- Infant—meet their needs,
- Toddler—protect and educate them,
- Elementary—provide for them,
- Teen—nurture a relationship and provide boundaries,
- Young adult—encourage flourishing through responsibility, love, and goodness.

One of the best ways to bond with your young children is by providing physical attachment and closeness. Connect with your child early and often. Respond to your baby's cues. Pick them up when they cry. Hold your baby. One of the foremost childcare experts, Dr. William Sears, states: "The single most important function in a healthy baby is physical attachment with a loving parent."[10]

As your child goes through the elementary school years, you start to get parenting down. Soon you will enter the dangerous water of adolescence. As your child transitions into a teenager, you too must transition as a parent. Things will change, as they should. What worked for you when your children were young will likely backfire with your teens. Don't get stuck being that overprotective, overindulgent, or overproviding parent with your teenager.

I really admire the wise and commonsense approach of Mark Gregston in his book, *Tough Guys and Drama Queens*. He states that a parent's first priority is to preserve the relationship with his or her teen. He says, "A parent's success has little to do with either the validity of their words or their intent as messengers, it's more about how they approach their child and engage with them."[11] By building stronger relationships with your teen, they won't try to find it elsewhere. When things inevitably go wrong, or your kid faces a real challenge, you will be so glad you have that relationship.

The twin pillars of love and responsibility are the best principles to follow. Experts agree you need to have some set limits for your children. These serve as guardrails the children cannot cross. Yes, you give them age-appropriate freedom and at the same time, safety, structure, and security as they're growing. Renowned psychologist Angela Duckworth notes children flourish in an environment of authentic love and reasonable discipline.

Be careful not to be overly critical. Constant criticism and correction will destroy your relationship with your kids. "If every time you saw a person," says Mark Gregston, "that person always corrected you, never quit telling you what you are doing wrong, and always had a better way of doing things, how would you feel about that person?" Pick your battles carefully, and let the other items go for the sake of the relationship.

The other side of the discipline coin is to be an active, encouraging, loving parent. "Love" to children is spelled "T-I-M-E." When my kids were toddlers, I loved playing and reading with them daily. During elementary school, I was involved in their activities and sports. During their teen years, we had date nights and took regular trips together. At each phase, I showed them how much I loved them by spending time.

The focus is on them, their needs and wants, and just plain loving them. My daughter and I love baseball, so we played catch and still follow our local team, the Dodgers, as well as go to games together. This has created an amazing, fun bond between the two of us. Mark Gregston writes: "The fact that you are spending time out of your schedule lets your child know that you value him. Value is determined by the importance you place on this time together." [12]

Our goal is to create a wonderfully warm relationship with our kids. To make memories and produce lasting positive emotions in your child's life that will serve as one of their foundations for flourishing. Your relationship will not only serve as a secure launching pad for their lives but also as a safe harbor when the storms hit. Aptly summarized by Fred Rogers in his book *Many Ways to Say I Love You*, "My wish for my children and parents alike is that they learn to find love and joy even amidst the world's and their own imperfections." [13]

By loving our spouse, significant other, and children, we grow closer in our most meaningful relationships, which directly leads to an increase in flourishing in our lives.

LOVE 3.0—LOVING YOUR FRIENDS

The beautiful book *Tuesdays with Morrie* by Mitch Albom shares a true story of an amazing friendship. Morrie was Mitch's favorite professor in college, and Mitch took every class he taught. At graduation, Mitch gave Morrie a monogrammed briefcase as a thank you and promised to stay in touch. Life got busy, however, and Mitch lost contact with Morrie. In fact, several decades passed until one day Mitch just happened to see Morrie on a TV episode of *Nightline*, where Morrie talked about his ALS disease, known as Lou Gehrig's disease, and how he is coping with his impending death.

Mitch immediately reached out to Morrie, who agreed to meet with him. Their first meeting lasted several hours, and Morrie invited Mitch to come back again for another visit. The relationship was rekindled. Mitch returned every Tuesday for months and took notes from their conversations, in which Morrie talked about life and death. Morrie encouraged Mitch to write a book about their conversations, which he did.

On their fourteenth Tuesday together, they had to say goodbye. Morrie was weak and could barely give Mitch a hug. It was an emotional farewell. A few days after that meeting, Morrie passed away. At the end of the book, Mitch offered his biggest lesson learned: He wished that he had reached out to his friend Morrie earlier.

I probably don't have to tell you that close friendships are critical to flourishing. The philosopher Epicurus said that of all the different paths to happiness, the most important by far is the acquisition of friends. I'm talking about real friends. Meaningful friendships. The type where you wish the best for your friends regardless of what they can offer you in return. Aristotle calls this a "complete ... friendship between people who are good and alike in virtue."[14]

A friend who is there for you in good times and bad. When one of my children was diagnosed with a life-threatening illness, I was not surprised the first call I received was from my friend, Dan, who was in tears. He immediately started helping our family by arranging a "meal train" where families came by and dropped off dinner. He called or stopped by daily to see how we and our child were doing. He was a rock and support every single twist and turn of the way. It's not surprising my kids refer to him as "Uncle Dan." A priceless friend indeed.

Because you will likely have only a few close friends at any one time, it is important you choose them wisely—both with your head and heart. Jim Rohn says you are the average of the five people you spend the most time with. Having good and close friends will undoubtedly shape you and your life.

While we all know close friendships are vital, fewer individuals are experiencing such relationships. Loneliness is reaching epidemic proportions. The causes are certainly numerous and varied, such as our hectic lifestyles and lack of real connection. Nearly 25 percent of Americans say they do not have a close friend they can confide in.[15] Do you have a close friend or two with whom you can share life?

This is why it is so important we learn how to maintain good friendships. While there are several qualities necessary to maintain close friendships, I believe the key principle here is to make proactive efforts toward staying connected. It takes effort. Ideally, you can see the person face to face. At a minimum, you need to talk regularly.

I am grateful to have had close friends throughout my life. As a young boy, I had a best friend, Rick, who lived across the street until we graduated from middle school, when he moved. (He's the one with whom I ditched kindergarten.) Growing up, we did everything together. We have remained the closest of friends. It is not often you get to know one of your closest friends for fifty years! But it took effort and work. When we were both busy with young kids and growing careers, we had to carve out time to see each other.

When Rick moved away, I met some great new friends on my high school soccer team. Soon, we had an amazing, close group of friends we nicknamed "Da Boyz." It was a magical group that laughed, made memories of a lifetime, and grew together. We enjoyed each other's company and spent regular time together. One of the best things we did was establish a regular fall trip together. Every year, we all know we are going to plan a trip and go away together. To this day, it's still one of my favorite trips of the year.

Today, that same group—some thirty-five years later—continues to thrive. We have all been in each other's weddings, watched our kids grow up, and continue to see each other. Recently, when we turned fifty, we took all our families and kids to Hawaii together—about thirty strong—for a "Hawaii 5-0" extended family reunion.

In their book, *Big Friendship*, the authors, Aminatou Sow and Anne Friedman, make the case for the critical importance of friendships. The authors tell their own story of the need to nurture friendships. The two of them worked together and co-hosted a popular podcast called *Call Your Girlfriend*. However, they barely spoke outside of work and were not close. They rekindled their friendship through intentional effort.

Big Friendship is also noteworthy for its excellent handling of race. Sow is Black; Friedman is White. They stress the importance of not only devoting energy to our relationships but also being sensitive to misunderstandings that can arise with race.

To have a friend, you must be a friend. Some of the best advice in this regard is offered by Dale Carnegie in one of the best-selling books of all time, *How to Win Friends and Influence People*. The essence of Carnegie's message is to try making people feel appreciated and understood. Carnegie says, "the single most important desire is for people to feel important."[16] Be genuinely interested in *their* lives. Be a good listener, so you learn what is important to them. The common thread in all these ideas is making a prioritized effort toward genuine friendships. Those that have friends make them a priority and expend effort toward those friendships. Those that don't make friends a priority or make a genuine effort, typically don't have close friends.

Then, when life's challenges and struggles happen, which we know they will, you will not go at it alone. You will hopefully be surrounded by close family and friends to love, comfort, and support you. As this anonymous quote says, "When you have been through hard times and come out the other side, look around you. The people still there are your true friends."

So, yes, friends do matter. A lot. It is hard to imagine living a long, flourishing life without meaningful friends. Invest the time and the effort in those friendships. This should be part of your vision. It will pay dividends beyond what you can imagine.

LOVE 4.0—LOVING OTHERS

Dr. Leo Buscaglia taught a class at the University of Southern California called "Love." His class became so popular he eventually wrote a book about love. Buscaglia brain-stormed numerous creative titles for the book but was surprised to learn the title *Love* had never been claimed. That became the title of his book, and Buscaglia humorously claimed he owns the copyright on *Love*.

In his book, Buscaglia tells one of his favorite stories about how we can love others, even strangers. During his class, Buscaglia required each student to do something to help others without receiving anything in return. One of his students came to Buscaglia because he couldn't think of anything to do. "What is there to do?" asked Buscaglia incredulously. "Just look around. There is so much to do, so much love and help we can show to others."

Buscaglia suggested a nursing home not far from U.S.C. So Buscaglia and the student, Joel, visited the home together, where they found many elderly individuals lying in their gowns staring at the ceiling. Joel asked what he should do, so Buscaglia told him to go over and say hello to a woman sitting by herself. Joel walked over and said, "Uh, hello." She looked at him with suspicion and bluntly asked, "Are you a relative?" "No," replied Joel. "Good! Sit down, young man." They sparked up a wonderful conversation, talking about life, love, pain, and suffering.

Joel visited the home every week, and it became known as "Joel's Day." Everybody loved that day. One of the elderly women even dressed in a nice gown and had her hair done. One of the highlights of Buscaglia's teaching career was when he was on campus on a Saturday and saw Joel leading a group of the elderly from the home, like the pied piper, to a U.S.C. football game.[17]

When it comes to loving a person who is not our friend or acquaintance, most of us just look the other way. We walk by strangers daily without even acknowledging them. We pass by co-workers and don't say hi, let alone know their names.

The directive to "love others" is not limited to our family and friends. Love is such a big word that it is intended to include loving everybody. Love needs to be expanded in its interpretation. This is precisely why psychologist, Barbara Fredrickson, defined love as "that micro-moment of positive connection that you share with another."[18] This simple definition can become life-changing once you understand it.

This upgraded version of love not only provides great benefits to the recipient of the positive connection but also to the giver. Studies show the individual who initiates the contact benefits physically and emotionally. For the science nerds, these micro-moments of positive connection increase your oxytocin (the hormones responsible for your capacity to love) and strengthen your vagus nerve (which connects your brain to your heart). You are literally making yourself healthier every single time you make a positive connection with another.

One of the easiest ways to make a positive connection with others is to simply start with a smile and eye contact. Nothing more is required. Up your game by adding a hello or how are you doing? Perhaps this can lead to asking, "How was your weekend?" or commenting on the nice day outside. The possibilities are endless.

Once you realize how beneficial and easy it is, you will be constantly seeking out tiny moments of positive connection. Fredrickson urges us to get out of "our cocoon of self-absorption" and look for those brief encounters where you can positively connect with others. "Spread love everywhere you go. Let no one ever come to you without leaving happier," said Mother Teresa.

I'm amazed at the number of lawyers who don't use this opportunity with the clerks and others when they appear in court. Lawyers should always be very professional and act with the highest level of courteousness and respect when dealing with Court staff. Be polite, address them by their titles (e.g., Madam Clerk), say hello, please, and thank you. Use this as another occasion to practice Love 4.0.

Most interactions with others can be placed in one of two categories. First, as we just discussed, many of your interactions with others will involve positive connections. However, everybody also faces challenges, setbacks, and suffering of some kind. What's interesting is that almost everybody has both positive and negative experiences occurring simultaneously in their lives. For instance, a person might be doing great at work but facing a serious health challenge.

When people face those negative events, we can offer a genuinely compassionate connection. Specifically, we show micro-moments of compassion to others. Compassion essentially means a sympathetic concern for other's distress and a desire to alleviate it. Not surprisingly, research has confirmed you get similar benefits by providing a compassionate connection as you do with a positive connection.

Our compassionate connection can be in the form of expressing loving concern, offering a helping hand, or giving encouragement in overcoming an obstacle. It could be as simple as a warm touch, gesture, or, if appropriate, a hug. A few sincere words of hope and positive thought. "I'm thinking of you and hope things get better."

Remind yourself daily that you are likely to see people who have faced either good news or bad news, either fortune or misfortune. No matter which one, you have the choice to offer love ... either celebratory or compassionate love in the form of connection. At each moment, seek a positive or compassionate connection with others.

Love is in the heart, but love is not in the heart to stay, for love is only love if you give it away. Although it starts in the heart, love calls for action. Hanging on my office wall is a single quote from Ralph Waldo Emerson, which states: "I shall pass this way but once; any good, therefore, that I can do or any kindness that I can show to any human being, let me do it now. Let me not defer nor neglect it, for I shall not pass this way again." Love 4.0 is one of the most powerful ways to flourish and demonstrate our love to others.

LOVE ∞—LOVING HUMANITY

Throughout history, people have relied on communities, tribes, and groups to survive and thrive. Now, in our modern world, we are more independent than ever before. All we need is a phone or computer, and we can literally do our work, order everything we need, and keep in touch with others. That technology is amazing, but at the same time, we have lost a sense of community and togetherness ... our connection to humanity.

If we truly want to love, we need to love our community and all people. It is a fact that we are all a part of the same human species. As our world is getting both simultaneously smaller and more dangerous, there is a greater need than ever for us to love all humankind. In fact, the time is now for such a clarion call to love.

The Greeks had a word for this love of humanity called *sympatheia*, which means "an affinity for all parts of the whole" and "an understanding of our mutual interdependence." It recognizes that life is both dependent and interdependent. We are all interconnected. I call this love "infinity," because our love has no limits. (The symbol for "infinity" is "∞.")

For many people, sympatheia or infinity is the love that exits in the universe. Some would equate that love with God. Whether you believe in God or an infinite love, I believe nearly all of us can agree that we should love our planet. I'm not getting political, but it's hard to dispute that a clean, green, healthy planet is good for humans and that a warming, polluted, and toxic planet is bad. We all share the same planet, one world. We all depend on the earth's awesome resources to live, such as clean water, healthy soil, and clear air. So, let's all love and care for our planet. Sympatheia.

Have you ever seen the famous picture of the earth called the Blue Marble, taken from the Apollo space craft? This iconic photograph was the first ever taken showing the whole round earth, a beautiful blue in color. It also dramatically demonstrates how we all share this same, small place. Sympatheia.

How about our interconnectedness to others? The book you're reading, the chair on which you're sitting, the light in your room, the clothes you're wearing, and the food you've eaten today, all came from others. We all rely heavily on others to live our lives. We are truly dependent. Sympatheia.

At the time of my writing this book, the entire world was enduring a pandemic known as the Coronavirus. It ranks among the deadliest pandemics in history. Yet can you imagine how much worse it could have been if not for the incredible actions of so many individuals in health care working together? It was only through mutual cooperation and effort that the virus was able to be subdued. Sympatheia.

The world is littered with countless problems to solve: the homeless, crime, drugs, the environment, veterans, children, the sick, the impoverished, racism, religious freedom, world peace, and so, so much more. Opportunities for serving our community, for giving, and for helping humanity are as wide and varied as our own work. It's only together that we can truly solve these problems. Sympatheia.

I love that the U.S. celebrates Independence Day. It symbolizes America's birth, freedom, and self-governance. At the same time, with the world becoming smaller and needing each other more than ever, we should also celebrate an "Interdependence Day."

A day where we recognize all humanity is inter-dependent. Imagine if the world signed a Declaration of Interdependence. Here's a poem I penned regarding this idea:

Yes, we are all part of a common humanity.
We all want so many of the same things in life.
So, we need to have a community.

Yes, it's important to think about ourselves and our immediate concerns.
But we also need to move from "Me" to "We."
What's good for the hive is good for the bee.

"We" is a message of hope and togetherness.
Let's evolve to a higher form of a love: a love of all of humanity.
This requires us to act selflessly, not selfishly.

We are necessary to solve the world's biggest problems.
We are necessary for a better future.
Only together can "We" make the world a better place.

The planet and the world are calling for us to act in love.
We can make choices that are good for us and good for the planet.
Only together can we make the environment healthy.

Only We can solve homelessness.
Only We can cure cancer.
Only We can achieve world peace

The two opposites of love are apathy and hate.
Apathy and hate are overcome through the combination of love and humanity.
Imagine a world consisting of one beloved community.

We are all part of the same circle of life.
Life and Death.
Sunrise and Sunset.

A flourishing individual helps society flourish.

A flourishing society helps individuals flourish.

Thus, there is an interconnectedness between both society and individuals flourishing.

We Need.

To Love.

Humanity.

THE MOST ESSENTIAL INGREDIENT TO MEANINGFUL RELATIONSHIPS

An unknown disease caused Helen Keller to lose her sight and hearing at just nineteen months old. Unable to see or hear, she described her life as living "at sea in a dense fog." Nevertheless, she became the first blind-deaf person to earn a bachelor's degree in college and was a prolific writer, including her famous autobiography, *The Story of My Life.*

When asked how she learned to read, write, and break through her isolation, Keller gave the credit to the loving support and work of Anne Sullivan. As you can imagine, the two of them worked closely together but also had many conflicts. Unable to communicate or understand what was happening, Keller exhibited consistent behavioral issues and tantrums. It was only through Sullivan's patience and persistence that she was able to get through to Keller. Sullivan eventually earned Keller's trust and became a pseudo-parent.

Anne Sullivan became famous for her brilliant work with Keller. Yet, Sullivan's story is equally compelling. At age five, Sullivan contracted a painful eye disease, causing severe vision loss. When Sullivan was eight, her mother died. Her father abused and abandoned her. Left destitute, she was sent to a "poor house" where she was locked up in a mental institution and considered hopelessly insane.

However, one nurse saw "Little Annie" Sullivan for what she was—a young child. The nurse would take her lunch and just sit outside of Sullivan's dungeon. Although Little Annie often acted like a caged animal, the nurse focused her love on Annie and consistently visited her, bringing her brownies, and speaking words of caring. The nurse's continual support never wavered, and years later Sullivan recovered and was released.

Fast forward a few years, when Helen Keller's parents were looking for someone to help their daughter, and Anne Sullivan got the job. The rest is history. The two of them changed the way the world saw disabled individuals.

What do the two stories have in common? Both the nurse and Sullivan faced enormous challenges in their relationships. To the nurse, Sullivan acted like a caged animal. Helen Keller was wild and stubborn toward Sullivan. Yet, both the nurse and Sullivan unilaterally displayed consistent love toward the young girls.

Yes, meaningful relationships often provide us with our greatest sense of happiness and enjoyment. At the same time, however, relationships can also cause our biggest challenges, frustrations, and suffering. It seems meaningful relationships are more difficult than ever.

When I was speaking to one of my lawyer friends, he confessed he had decided to stay single because relationships were too much trouble and too complicated. "Every time I get close to somebody, it seems like we get into a conflict, or they let me down." He said his work was much easier to manage, and "it didn't talk back" to him. In his last relationship, his partner always wanted to go out, and he preferred to stay home.

The primary challenge of relationships stems from the lack of control over others. In relationships, you must interact with and rely on others. My lawyer friend is correct that when pursuing a career over relationships, you have more autonomy and control over your life. As much as you would like, you simply can't control what other people say, think, feel, or do.

As we conclude this chapter on love, let me offer you what I believe is the most important principle for developing meaningful relationships. This principle applies to all forms of loving others from *Love 0.0 to Love* ∞. It will be the key to unlock your ability to bettering and deepening your relationships. It is the most essential ingredient to meaningful relationships. Yes, there are many other ingredients to positive relationships, but if you follow this one, all the others will be much easier to apply. What is this key?

Approach every relationship not for what others can do for you, but on how you can best love and serve others. In other words, focus on your own loving actions, not their actions.

This was the exact approach taken by the nurse loving Anne Sullivan and then Sullivan later caring for Hellen Keller. They acted unilaterally notwithstanding how difficult and stubborn the other person was. They acted with kindness and patience, even when the other didn't deserve it.

This principle applies to all your relationships. At work, concentrate on your actions toward your co-workers and colleagues. Ask yourself: How can I best serve my co-workers or clients today? For your kids and friends, live by the motto: How can I best be a blessing to them today? For your spouse or significant other, how can I best love and support him or her?

When you are unhappy with another person or not getting your needs met, say, for instance, the other person isn't helping around the house, is spending too much money, or is not having enough sex, your typical response may be to criticize or to focus on the other person's behavior. You then go into a victim mentality.

While these issues may be addressed appropriately and lovingly, let me ask you – how's your own attitude and behavior? Are you displaying anger? Withdrawing love? Being cold and distant? Instead of focusing your energy on how the other person could improve, consider spending most of your time looking within to change yourself. Honestly ask yourself: "Does my partner feel like he or she is married to or living with a flourishing spouse?" Does my child or friend see me as being an optimal, loving parent or friend?

Yes, it takes character and maturity. Yes, you ought to learn to deal with your own ego and expectations. However, the primary cause of suffering stems from our consistent expectations of, and cravings for, other things or people. Learning to manage your expectations of others will reduce your own frustrations and anxieties.

I am willing to bet that one of the biggest challenges in your relationship is that the other person (spouse, significant other, parent, child, friend) is not living up to your expectations or desires. Seriously, pause for just a moment and answer this question—in one of your meaningful relationships that you wish were better, what is the main obstacle or challenge? Is it that the other person isn't helping, working, or loving enough? Or is it that they are too serious, too lax, too distracted, too impatient, too loud, too quiet, too critical? If not, congratulations.

Erich Fromm poignantly stated, "Most people see the problem of love as that of being loved, rather than that of loving, of one's capacity to love [others]. Hence the problem to them is how to be loved ..." This places the responsibility to love squarely on somebody else, not on yourself.

We all have our mistakes, failures, and foibles. This means other people will also make mistakes and maybe even do things that hurt you. What are your options? Blame, shame, forgive, and/or learn. Blaming and shaming are virtually never good choices. The number one problem in relationships is blame, says famed psychiatrist, David Burns, because it worsens conflict.

Do the right thing and forgive people who make mistakes. Forgiveness means to wash away the transgression. It means not holding grudges or withholding love in the relationship. If you want to be forgiven yourself, then you need to forgive. Forgiven people forgive people. When asked for his secret to peace and happiness, Pope Francis said, "Move forward and let others do the same."[19]

All of this can be appropriately summed up in one great rule, the "Golden Rule." Treat others like you would want to be treated. Dale Carnegie noted the well-established historical roots for the Golden Rule:

"Philosophers have been speculating on the rules of human relationships for thousands of years, and out of all that speculation, there has evolved only one important precept. It is not new. It is as old as history. Zoroaster taught it to his followers in Persia twenty-five hundred years ago. Confucius preached it in China twenty-four hundred years ago. Lao-tse, the founder of Taoism, taught it to his disciples in the Valley of the Han. Buddha preached it on the bank of the Holy Ganges five hundred years before Christ. The sacred books of Hinduism taught it a thousand years before that. Jesus taught it among the stony hills of Judea nineteen hundred ago. Jesus summed it in one thought: 'Do unto others as you would have others do unto you.'"[20]

When in doubt, let's follow the Golden Rule. This will serve as a single reliable guide for your relationships with others. Don't like when others gossip about, criticize, or attack you? Don't do it to others. You like when people are kind, encouraging, complimentary to you? How about if you do the same to others? The Golden Rule focuses on you and your behavior. Do this and watch your meaningful relationships thrive.

Chapter Summary:

- **Meaningful relationships are critical to your own personal flourishing.**
- **A healthy love for yourself is foundational for healthy relationships with others.**
- **Your immediate family will thrive more when there is abundant affirmation and encouragement.**
- **Close friendships require consistent effort and being present for them.**
- **Expand your concept of love to look for micro-moments of positive and compassionate connections with others.**
- **Loving humanity is ultimately the highest form of love, as we are all part of the same interconnected world.**
- **The key factor in having meaningful relationships is for you to focus on your own loving behavior.**

SIDEBAR _____

When you are in court, know how to address individuals appropriately. Always refer to the judge as "Your Honor," not "Sir" or "Judge." Refer to the clerk, as "Madam or Mister Clerk." Refer to the court reporter as "Madam or Mister Reporter." When examining witnesses, don't use first names; rather refer to them by their last name, Sir, or Ma'am. If referring to opposing counsel, either use their last name or simply, "Opposing Counsel." These references are not only out of respect for the institution and the individuals but also for the solemnity of the proceedings.

CHAPTER 11

RECREATE

• • •

"Just when the caterpillar thought the world was over, it became a butterfly."

— PROVERB

I was presiding over my third consecutive jury trial; this one involving allegations of serious racial discrimination, and there was great animosity between opposing counsel. Everything was a fight. One day during that trial, my son was in the hospital, and my daughter had been involved in a car accident. It was a very challenging day.

I tried hard to stay 100 percent focused on the trial at hand. The plaintiff was cross-examining one of the defendant's witnesses, when there was an objection to a question. The objection was not well-taken, but instead of saying "overruled," I blurted out "overwhelmed!" I immediately caught my mistake, and with a smile, said, "Sorry about that counsel; strike that, overruled." In truth, I was overwhelmed, and it was a classic Freudian slip.

We all get tired, burned out, restless, even exhausted at times. If we want to flourish in our lives, we must consciously take time for restoration. A reset of our body, mind, and soul. We do this primarily through the four main practices of restoration: rest, balance, recreation, and play.

REST AND RENEWAL

Stephen Covey tells the well-known story of the lumberjack strenuously cutting down trees in the forest. Over time, the lumberjack's productivity diminished. Right about then, a traveler walks by and asks the lumberjack how it's going. "Exhausted," replies the lumberjack. The person then asks the lumberjack why he doesn't take a break and sharpen the saw he is using. The lumberjack replies he doesn't have time to sharpen the saw because he is too busy sawing.[1]

This is how many of us live our lives. Overworked and too busy to stop and sharpen our saws. Hard work is good. However, if we don't also take the time to stop and rest in order to sharpen our saw, we will be more inclined to burn out, suffer health maladies, be less productive, and ultimately be less happy. For lawyers, burnout in particular is worn like a badge of honor.

The failure to adequately rest is particularly bad for your health. Those who are constantly on the go are setting themselves up for all types of health ailments, especially the number one killer, heart disease. Studies show that individuals working eleven to twelve hours a day have a higher risk of coronary heart disease and heart attacks.[2] Another study demonstrates that overworked and overstressed individuals have a 45 percent greater chance of developing diabetes.[3] For more than fifty years, stomach ulcers have been attributed to overwork and stress. There is a well-publicized case of a thirty-one-year-old woman who died from overwork. People, wake up!

In addition to poor health, the lack of restoration not surprisingly leads to decreased energy and performance. Of course, we are tired. Many of us try to power through like that incessantly sawing lumberjack, and we tell ourselves, "I don't have time to take a break. I'm too busy working. I have this project due. I have too many things to do."

Not only does our physical energy get depleted, but our mental energy does also. We must allow our mental and emotional self to have time for rest and recovery. "There is no way to get dark out of a room other than to let light in. The only way to get stress out of your being is to let in relaxation."[4]

Not surprisingly, most lawyers don't have a problem with turning it on—Go! Go! Go! —their problem is turning it off.

This is what the authors of *Peak Performance*, Brad Stulberg and Steve Magness, aptly call the "paradox of rest."[5] While we want to keep working and pushing, we are much better off if we take time to rest and restore. Both physical and cognitive recovery are crucial to be at our best in all aspects of our lives.

The truth is that you cannot—I repeat, cannot—be your optimal best without rest. We need to continually renew ourselves and recuperate if we want to reach our full potential. I can do a certain number of push-ups but eventually get to failure. It's amazing how after just a one-minute rest, I can perform another set of push-ups. Plain and simple, you cannot be at your best without proper rest.

To "restore" means to bring back again and to "renew" means to make like new again. It's during rest where the caterpillar turns into the butterfly. There is a crucial connection between your work and your rest. The more you renew and restore, the more you can prosper in your profession. There's a direct link between the two. You can't proceed on your journey unless you re-fill your gas tank.

There are several very specific practices you can use to maximize your rest and recovery. The number one thing is taking short breaks throughout the day. While we are awake, our bodies follow a daily cycle called ultradian rhythms. Ultradian rhythms or cycles are shorter than a day but longer than an hour. For most individuals, this incremental period lasts between ninety to 120 minutes, with the average being ninety minutes nonstop. This means that most of us can perform at a high level for up to ninety minutes to two hours before our cycles of energy start decreasing.

THE ULTRADIAN PERFORMANCE RHYTHM

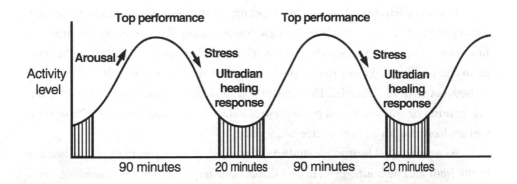

After about ninety minutes, our willpower is diminished, and we start to feel tired, hungry, unfocused, irritable, or restless. When that happens to me, I often feel like picking up my phone to check the latest scores from ESPN. Others might start feeling hungry, needing caffeine, or craving sugar. Your body is sending you a clear signal that you need a break. When you take a fifteen to twenty-minute break, your body clears the oxidative waste products and free radicals that have built up from your mental work. Your mind is replenished, and your mental energy restored.

In his book *The 20 Minute Break*, Dr. Ernest Rossi recommends about ninety minutes of activity and twenty minutes for a break. Thus, sustainable peak performance is best achieved when we combine periods of <u>both</u> intense focus and deliberate rest. Below is an excellent diagram showing the ultradian rhythms of work and rest.

Practically, what we do on our break is not as important as that we down shift and rest from what we are doing. If you take a real respite, your body and mind will reset itself naturally. There are so many ways to take a short break: Take a walk; call your spouse, kids, or a friend; look out the window or at nature; pet your dog; meditate, move, stretch, or drink water. Even something as simple as taking a walk in the hallway or going outside or out to lunch can give you the break you need, and you will find that you will come back able to do more deep work and be more productive.

Start incorporating regular, short rest breaks into your day and monitor how your body and mind feel. Over time, you will feel healthier, happier, and revitalized.

BALANCE

Lawyers often aim to bill eight hours per day (forty hours per week; 160 per month, 1,900 per year). This is considered a magic minimum number for many law firms. At first glance, this seems very doable. I mean, it's only eight hours! The typical worker puts in an eight-hour day. What's the big deal? However, the difference here is "billable." Not all hours at work are "billable." Those hours don't include all the administrative, marketing, continuing education, and *pro bono* work. Thus, to get eight hours of billable time, you are likely working ten to twelve hours a day.

As a professor, I hear many students concerned about becoming a lawyer because of the high billable hours. Even if the billable hour requirements are reasonable, there is always more to do, more to bill. U.S. Supreme Court Justice Joseph Story famously observed: "The law is a jealous mistress and requires a long and constant courtship."

In fact, when I spoke with numerous lawyers to write this book, their *number one complaint* was finding a good work-life balance. This is backed up by numerous studies showing that a lack of balance is the primary source of dissatisfaction. There; now you know. It is worth repeating for emphasis: Finding an appropriate balance between your professional and personal life will likely be your most difficult challenge.

If you are regularly at work more than nine hours, you are also likely not attending to other important facets of life. Do you find yourself speeding to get to your kid's game? Not able to get your workouts in or eat healthy, or do you get to bed too late? Do you regularly find yourself with too much work and not enough time for the rest of your life?

Everything in our lives is interconnected and synergistic. Thus, it's good to have a vision of the big picture. The key point is to take some time to reflect on whether all the essential aspects of your life—your health, work, relationships, and rest—are all getting proper attention.

We work to provide a service to society, but at what cost? Why would we sacrifice our personal lives for work? The reality is we have a mortgage to pay, kids to put through school, food to put on the table, and we really enjoy that vacation to an exotic destination. Those all take work and money. It is important in thinking about both balance and satisfaction to make sure you get really clear on what you want *and* the cost of obtaining it.

One of the best ways to help you find your balance is to understand the concept of "enough." John Bogle, who founded the extremely successful Vanguard Mutual Funds, experienced the addictive and destructive cost of the never-ending pursuit of financial success. Bogle essentially put work far above anything else in his life, because he had not learned the true meaning of "enough."

Bogle turned his life around by understanding this simple idea of "enough." He writes in his book *Enough* that the never-ending pursuit of wealth prevents us from living the life that is truly worthwhile. This concept of "enough" is graphically represented in the Peak Fulfillment Curve below.

At some point, once you find your level of peak fulfilment or satisfaction, the continued pursuit of more leads to overconsumption, dissatisfaction, anxiety, and being out of balance.

The Fulfillment Curve

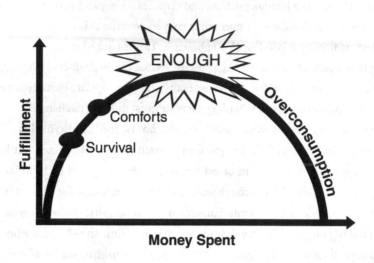

Source: *Your Money or Your Life*, Penguin Books, 2008.

Most people would say the definition of courage is to act in the face of fear. I think it is just as important to define courage as how you act when you face temptation or greed. We all want more, more, more. It's easy to expand your definition of what is "enough" and remain in perpetual pursuit of more. Everyone seems to do it. But do you have courage not to?

It's well worth your time to think through the most important aspects of your life and understand your own unique "enough." Know that constantly striving and setting your aims higher costs you time and energy. Every time you say yes to something, you are, by default, saying no to something else.

Once we have a sense of our own level of satisfaction, then we need to come up with a specific plan for getting our life in the right balance. Let's begin by looking at the idea of "free time." Most of us think our time falls in three separate boxes. There's the work box, the relationship box, and the free-time box. For most of us, the work box is our biggest box, and we spend the most time in it. Whatever time remains, we will put some into our family and social lives. But after those two boxes, any other "free time" is again usually devoted to just keeping up with life, such as errands, chores, and appointments.

As the diagram shows, most people flow in the direction from work to relationships to free time.

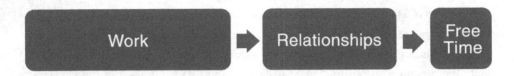

Although a perfect balance among these three boxes is often unrealistic or not feasible, most people often have too much of an imbalance. Too much work, not enough love, health, and free time. As the old proverb goes, "All work and no play make Jack a dull boy."

There comes a time when we need to make a decision—no, a commitment—to close our briefcase, shut off our computer, put our phone away, and start making time for the other vital aspects in our life. We need to be very intentional about "all" aspects of our life, not just work. This, of course, is going to be unique to each person because one person's meat is another person's poison. Let's call it "life/work" planning because life is why we are here—to have a thriving, happy, abundant, rich, and full life.

The big question is how to find more time. Your frustrations might be voiced as something like, "I'm already running a busy firm or a busy household. I can barely squeeze in a 5,000-step walk while returning calls or listening to a podcast at the same time." Well, I'm sorry to be the one to say this, but you do have control over much of your time. You are not prioritizing what really matters in your life if you don't say "no" to the less important things. Most of us can find the time for those things that are very important. Honestly, if your child had an emergency, you would find the time to take her or him to the doctor, right?

One helpful model is looking at how ancient civilizations balanced their day. They didn't have a day planner or iPhone calendar app. Their day naturally included all three aspects of work, love, and play. They woke up just before the sun rose to get their work done to maximize the daylight. When it was nearing dark, they returned to their village where their families and friends would gather for a meal, story time, and play. They didn't need to go to the gym because they got plenty of movement during their work. They went to bed when it was dark and got plenty of sleep. The beauty of this life is its harmony with the rhythms of nature.

In an upcoming chapter, I will show you how to get very specific in planning your day to provide for a healthy and optimal balance. For now, let's carve out time for all the vital aspects of your life, recognizing it is not only good for your health and well-being but also part of a flourishing life. Many workers, and lawyers in particular, often feel like they must choose between family and work. You are not what you do for your occupation. Don't measure your life solely by your career or money. You are much more than that. The persons who can find true satisfaction and balance in each of the key areas of their life will significantly increase their happiness and flourishing. One of the most important measures of whether you are flourishing in life is how you allocate your time.

RECREATION

I happen to love sports. Growing up, I played a wide variety of sports and dreamed of being a major league baseball player. However, when pitchers started throwing curveballs by me, it was time to hang up my cleats—or was it?

Since high school, I have played in a variety of softball leagues from college intramurals to lawyers' leagues. When my friends decided to attend the Los Angeles Dodgers Fantasy Camp, I was all in! I was in my early forties and had not played baseball for a while. So, we started training, and I was having more fun than when I was a kid.

When the day finally arrived, my five friends and I flew to Vero Beach, Florida, which was then home to the famous L.A. Dodgers Spring training facility. I had watched countless games on TV from Vero Beach, so when we drove into the facility, it felt almost surreal. We put our bags in our dorm rooms and headed over to the locker rooms. There, hanging in my locker, was my full LA Dodger uniform with my name on the back, just like the pros. Right next to my locker was the locker of Steve Yeager, the former Dodger great. He was one of the coaches at the camp.

We began by doing drills the "Dodger Way." One of the drills involved catching pop-ups. The coaches used an electronic pitching machine to shoot baseballs high in the air. At the end of the drill, the coaches held a friendly competition. If a player dropped the pop-up, he or she was eliminated. The coach would increase the height of the pop-up in each successive round. With just a few players left, one of my friends, Brian, took his turn. The machine hurled the ball so high I couldn't see it in the bright blue sky. Unfortunately, neither could Brian. As the ball came down, it hit Brian smack on the top of his head and bounced straight up. Fortunately, Brian was not hurt, but the entire group was on the ground laughing. Even writing this, I can still picture the moment, and it makes me laugh.

The camp lasted one week, but the fun and incredible memories will last me a lifetime. I mean, seriously, how many times does a forty-year-old guy get to put on a Los Angeles Dodgers uniform and play real baseball in a real stadium for an entire week with his best friends? I felt like I had died and gone to heaven.

Life is to be enjoyed, celebrated, and lived to its fullest. Yes, we need to take time to rest and restore, but we also can add so much more meaning and happiness to our life through recreation, adventure, and leisure.

By recreation, I mean spending time in pleasurable activities during your free time (*i.e.*, not during your work or the daily requirements of life). I love the etymology of the word recreation, as it comes from two Latin terms, the first being *re*, which means "again," and the second being *creare*, which denotes "creating or bringing forth." So, the spirit of recreation is to literally re-create yourself or to create a new self.

Recreation, leisure, and fun are vital parts of flourishing and should be enjoyed at every stage of life. Many individuals think leisure and recreation are mostly for kids and the retired. But for those who have "real jobs," we hopefully can muster a one-week vacation where we can just sit, veg, and enjoy a piña colada. In reality, making time for recreating and enjoyment is especially important during our working years.

When it comes to recreation, it's not about what you do as much as how you do it. Do you bring a sense of pleasure and well-being to your recreation? I have several friends with whom I occasionally play golf. One friend is super relaxed, and we laugh and have fun on the beautiful golf course. We get to whack a stationary object and drive golf carts around—It can't get much better than that. I have another friend, a truly great guy, who is as competitive as Tiger Woods on the golf course. It's not fun and games; it's serious business. After he hits the ball, it is almost always followed by an expletive, angry grunt, or self-criticism. He is driven for perfection on the golf course.

Golf, like anything, can be a recreational sport, but it can be approached with different mindsets. It is the attitude you bring to the activity, and not the activity itself, that makes it recreational. The first friend had a much more leisurely attitude while the second brought a work like mentality to his recreational golf game.

This doesn't mean you can't try to excel at an activity and approach it with an appropriate level of seriousness. In fact, as you improve in something, you often find it more satisfying. I strongly encourage you to pursue depth and proficiency in those activities you love and enjoy.

When exploring various recreational activities, consider the following two factors: It would be something you freely choose to do (you want to do it) and something you would enjoy doing. Nobody tells you what to do; you choose to do it because you would enjoy it. What truly makes you come alive? Is it health and fitness? Is it a hobby? Travel? Reading? When it comes to recreation and leisure, there's no right or wrong, other than it should be pleasurable and not harmful.

During my junior year of college, I attended school abroad in England for a semester. After dinner, many of the students would head to the pubs to enjoy lively conversation. They rarely talked about their future careers or business. They seemed much more interested in world issues, politics, economics, travel, books, culture, and philosophy. I appreciated how well rounded they were and how their lives reflected much more than what they would do for a living. Travelling to other countries is not only eye opening but truly expands your perspectives and broadens your horizons.

No matter what you do, the key is to understand the importance of recreation and to devote some time to it. Create some space to let it happen. Pursue recreation in your life and watch how much more your enjoyment and happiness increase.

PLAY

Play is a separate but related concept to recreation. Play is defined as an activity engaged in for enjoyment. It's more of the way you approach your activities with a joyful, fun-loving attitude. The primary difference between recreation and play, as I define the terms, is that recreation is typically an end in itself, whereas play can be both an end and a means to approaching other aspects of your life. My hope is you can incorporate more play into your daily activities.

In fact, it is especially play that will lead you to greater flourishing. When we talk about play, it's not all about being giggly and silly. It's about being joyful, free, openminded, creative, and in the moment.

When you think about kids sitting and playing, what does that look like? Yes, they might be lighthearted, but they are also fully engrossed, creative, curious, adaptable, and active, getting lost in time. Aren't those great skills you might want to bring to your own life? Imagine approaching your work with such concentration, joy, creativity, adaptability, etc.

The benefits of play should be obvious. There's no question that play energizes our lives and is fun. Play makes us feel free, connected, and creative. Abraham Maslow said: "Almost all creativity involves purposeful play." Another has noted: "Necessity may be the mother of invention, but play is certainly the father."[6] Yes, play and creativity are close relatives. Play helps us realize our full potential.

Stuart Brown is a medical doctor who has devoted most of his life to studying play. His book *Play* is considered the foremost guide on play for adults. He boldly asserts that "understanding what play is all about and making it a part of our daily lives are probably the most important factors in being a fulfilled human being." In contrast, he notes that a "lack of play should be treated like malnutrition—it's a health risk to your body and mind."[7] Yes, life is serious at times, but we must also find times to be lighthearted. Our health depends on it.

Many of us simply take too many aspects of our lives too seriously. Paradoxically, when we take things too seriously, such as our careers, marriages, or self, it often has the opposite effect. Everything improves with a sense of play. For instance, when I coached high school softball, I noticed my players would approach the batter's box all tight and nervous. Not surprisingly, they struggled at the plate. When we took a different approach of "relaxed focus," going up to the plate while having fun, staying calm but alert, and ready to hit the ball, they became better hitters.

We did not just take the approach of relaxed focus when the players were hitting, the other coaches and I also brought that same mindset to our practices and games. We had fun working hard. We blasted music before the games. For one practice, I rented an ice cream truck. Near the end of practice, I sneaked away and got into the ice cream truck that was parked out of the players' view. With the fun music blaring, the ice cream truck drove up, and I got to serve everybody their favorite ice cream.

Research indicates that younger adults are spending considerably fewer hours playing and more time taking life seriously. For kids in school, it's even worse—grades at school, tutors, athletic trainers, test preparation, volunteer activities—it's all about resume building. But that lack of play has serious consequences on our kids, including higher levels of depression, obesity, addiction, narcissism, and suicide.[8]

Play also provides additional motivation and keeps us in the game longer. When my training partner and I were running hills for an upcoming Spartan Race, it was grueling. It was fun at times but also hard and challenging. Yet, we stuck to the process, enjoyed the overall experience, laughed many times, especially when I couldn't hang onto the monkey bars. We trained during the hot summer for that race. So, of course, on the day of the race, it was cold and rainy. We playfully switched into rain gear and added an extra layer of clothing. Ultimately, we had a blast during the race and got into the best shape of our lives training for it.

The same goes for our work. We understand that work is often difficult, a grind, and competitive. Yet, it is remarkable how a playful approach can completely transform your work for the better. Abraham Maslow found that the self-actualizing individual no longer lives with the dichotomy between work and play; rather, the two dissolve into one; your work gives you enjoyment and pleasure.

I spoke to a lawyer just three years out of law school who was looking to change careers. Her work was a constant grind. She couldn't see how she could keep her sanity and be a lawyer. We worked on redefining play and joy for her in her job. I asked her to focus just for one day on being fully engaged, alive, and even having a sense of fun. We touched base at the end of the week, and she noticed a difference.

We continued communicating about how to expand her sense of play at work from one day to one week. After seeing the results—and although work was still challenging at times—she had a dramatic change in mindset. She made a commitment to bringing fun and play into her work environment. When I visit with her on occasion, she still has that playful mindset and is now happy practicing law.

As a judge, I am extremely careful about using humor in the courtroom. But smiling and having an appropriate, light-hearted touch often go a long way to de-stressing and relaxing the environment for the parties and jurors. I can see their faces and posture relax.

In one case, a defendant entered a plea of no contest to a minor infraction. He was a nice man, and we exchanged pleasantries in open court. After imposing a minimal fee, I asked if he had any questions. He responded, "No, Your Honor, but has anybody ever told you that you look like Judge Brad Pitt?" I laughed (and so did my staff, almost too much!) and said, "Thank you, Sir. You made my week."

Play also positively impacts relationships. I don't know about you, but when my wife and I are in a playful mood, or things are fun and light between us, our relationship often seems the happiest and healthiest. Even your sex life can be improved by a sense of play.

When your kids are young, get down on the ground at their level and play with them. One of my daughter's all-time favorite memories is when the two of us played with her Barbies in the mud. When one of the Barbies got stuck in the mud, I tried to lift it out by its head, which popped off. I was horrified. But my young daughter burst out laughing, "Look Dad, it's a headless Barbie!" As your kids get a little older, one of the best ways to stay close to them is through having fun as a family, laughing, joking, playing games, watching movies, getting outdoors, and a myriad of other things that cement your relationship.

I highly encourage you to incorporate a sense of play in all facets of your life. As George Bernard Shaw said, we grow old because we stop playing, not the opposite. You have a choice of whether to approach your life, work, relationships, and health with a sense of play and youthful vigor.

We don't want to take ourselves or others so seriously all the time. Let's infuse our lives with a sense of playfulness. In short, play positively impacts our big three missions—health, work, and love. Enjoy it!

Chapter Summary:

- If you want to be at your best, you must take time to "sharpen your saw" by resting and recovering.
- Carve out time to find a satisfying balance in your life.
- Recreational activities provide one of the best ways to enjoy life.
- Bring a playful vision to your health, work, relationships.

SIDEBAR _____

Respect others' time. Plan ahead to arrive at least ten minutes early to court, and always check in with the staff to let them know you are present. If you are going to be late, notify the court and opposing counsel in advance. This means you should have the phone number for each.

The Second Pillar of Flourishing

ACTION: Have a Process

CHAPTER 12

PRIORITIZE

• • •

"Greatness is not in where we stand but
in what direction we are moving."
—JUSTICE OLIVER WENDELL HOLMES, JR.

rials follow a logical process. First, a jury is selected. Next, the lawyers give their opening statements. Then, each side presents their evidence. After each side has rested, they make their closing arguments. Finally, the jury deliberates until it returns a verdict. Each step builds on the previous. For instance, you wouldn't start with jury deliberations. The order of the process makes logical sense.

In the law, the concept of "due process" typically means that certain steps or procedures must be followed before depriving an individual of life, liberty, or property. These procedures ensure that an accused defendant is provided certain legal safeguards to ensure a fair trial.

Most worthwhile accomplishments require a process. By way of a few examples: The construction of a building follows a precise plan, the manufacture of a car uses a system of production, and the flying of a plane requires certain steps before taking off. You wouldn't just willy-nilly engage in these endeavors without a clear system in place.

Likewise, if we want to flourish in our life, we need to have a process. Here, however, we are going to "do" process as opposed to "due" process. The term "process" is commonly understood as a series of actions or steps taken to advance toward a particular end. It's a strategy to obtain a particular goal. It's the method to accomplish a specific result.

CHAPTER 12: PRIORITIZE

In the first Pillar (Vision), we began identifying the targets and goals for our lives. Now, we move to the second Pillar (Action), which provides the process and tools to achieve those targets and goals. It's the important link that connects our goals with our actions. The process is what allows us to turn our dreams into reality.

You will not reach your goals if you lack a process. Imagine a football team without a game plan. The coach just tells every player to run around and do what they want. Without a process in your life, chaos would likely reign.

Since a process involves a series of steps toward a specific goal, we should identify and make clear what those steps are. Our goals will change over time, but the process will remain consistent. Our life can be defined by "events" or "activities." At any given moment, we are engaged in some type of event or activity—whether it is sleeping, eating, working, talking, playing, reading this book, and so on.

We manage our lives through our process. Management is the act of controlling things or events. So, our process aims to bring some degree of control over our time and events. This life management process consists of three simple steps. While they are simple to understand, they are not always easy to apply.

First—prioritize—decide what is your most important priority or priorities today. Second—plan—determine when you will work on those priorities.

Third—act—focus and take action on those plans.

We will discuss the principles of prioritizing in this chapter, planning in the chapter 12, and action in Chapter 13.

Once you turn these steps into a routine or habit, you will see how incredibly efficient, effective, and beneficial they are. Indeed, a "successful life," writes Ari Kiev, "does not result from chance nor is it determined by fate or good fortune but from a succession of successful days."[1] We should aim for crafting a successful day using this proven three-step process.

Let's begin with prioritizing. The first step in our process is to get clarity on our main priority or priorities each day. To really know what matters most. We begin this process by creating or setting specific goals. Then, once we have created some goals, it is vital we prioritize our goals to determine which is the most important and their relative importance to one another.

Why is it important to prioritize? Because we can only live one day at a time. The reality is almost all of us find we cannot squeeze everything we want to do on a given day. We finish the day saying, "Where did all the time go? I wish I had a few more hours in the day." We have many competing roles, desires, and obligations. Do I relax and watch TV or exercise? Spend more time working or with my family? When I get to work, should I check my emails first or work on that legal brief?

Remember, our time each day is finite. Whenever you say "yes," to something, you are in essence saying "no" to something else. As a result, we must intentionally decide on our true priorities.

WE MUST HAVE TARGETS

Apollo was the Greek god of archery. He was a master of the bow and arrow. Unrivalled in his accuracy, he was known as the "far shooter" for his prowess to rain down arrows with precise accuracy. Apollo used his bow and arrow to kill the famous one-eyed giant, Cyclopes. He has been immortalized in statues, the world's museums, and classic books such as Homer's *Iliad*.

As good an archer as Apollo was, I am confident you could beat him in an archery contest. We would set up the traditional bullseye about twenty yards away. Each of you would be given a bow and some arrows. I would then put a blindfold on Apollo and spin him around multiple times, so he had no idea in what direction he was facing or where the bullseye was located.

Given those facts, you would more consistently come closer to the bullseye than Apollo. Now, you might say, "Wait, he's blindfolded, so it would be impossible to hit a target he couldn't see." That's true. So, let me ask you a related question. "How can you hit a target you can't see?" The exact point of this make-believe story is that it's critical we have targets in our life. We do this through goals. Goals are defined as a specific object, target, or destination. A desired result.

A famous study out of Harvard University found that the three percent of their graduates who wrote down their goals earned more than the other 97 percent combined who didn't write their goals just ten years after graduation.[2] They found that having written goals was the difference. Not only are you more successful with goals, but you are happier as well. Whether it's mastering your career, acing an exam, or showing up more powerfully for your family, we need goals that inspire us.

Take Ruth Kundsin; she always had goals. She retired at the age of eighty-one as a microbiologist, having published five books and 150 papers. Still going at the age of

103, Ruth reflected on her life and concluded the secret to living a happy and long life is having goals. "You've got to have something to look forward to. That is the secret." As a spry centenarian, Ruth has her daily goals of working out and enjoying the people at the gym.[3]

You cannot fully flourish in life or reach your full potential without goals. We need to have targeted thinking. Aristotle made it clear that humans are teleological (goal-oriented) by nature. Goals provide the targets you need to reach your optimal best. You've got to have goals.

When we talk about goals, I highly recommend that we start by making goals in our big three areas of life—our health and well-being, our work, and our relationships. Sure, goals are obvious for our career, but they are just as important for the other two areas.

Your goals should emanate from the missions and identities you have previously created. For each of these missions and identities, you begin by creating long-range goals. Your long-range goals are further broken down into intermediate and daily goals. Thus, you can see from the diagram below this beautiful congruity between your missions and identities all the way up to your specific daily actions. When this amazing consistency occurs between your missions and your daily actions, you will possess and feel the highest level of flourishing.

ACHIEVING GOAL CONTINUITY

ACHIEVING GOAL CONTINUITY

Daily-Action Goals

Intermediate Goals

Long-Range Goals

Mission & Identity

As you move though the diagram, you can ultimately boil everything down to daily action goals. You move with the same goal from the general to the very specific. From mission and identity to long term goal to intermediate goal to daily action goals.

You've probably heard the saying, "How do you eat an elephant? Answer: One bite at a time." Let me encourage you toward the idea of bite-sized, daily actions. Everything you do must be made small enough so it can be accomplished within the time allotted for that day.

Yes, you want big goals, but you also want to break them into daily, bite-sized actions. For example, if my long-range goal is to take a European vacation for next summer, it's very hard to know what needs to be done. But if I divided that goal into smaller, actionable items, such as decide where to visit, book flights, research hotels in London, etc., those are doable.

I did the same as a lawyer with my work. For instance, if I wanted to file a summary judgment motion, I broke that motion down into specific steps. My first step might be to perform legal research on the plaintiff's first claim for breach of contract. Divide each action item so that it is something you can specifically do that day.

In his famous autobiography, Benjamin Franklin stated that by breaking his projects into smaller, specific parts, he increased the chances his project would be accomplished. Franklin himself found he achieved far more by breaking tasks into small, action steps than by trying to take on a large task.

HOW TO WRITE GOALS

Now that we understand the necessity of harmonizing long-range goals with daily actions, let's turn to how to create goals. Although there are many different tools for goal creation, the best framework that has personally worked for me is using the acronym "SMART."

"S" *is for significant.* Select a bold goal that stretches you past your comfort zone and truly excites you. Jim Collins calls these "BHAGs," for Big Hairy Audacious Goals.[4] What do you most want to accomplish in your life? Find time to get away and really let your mind think, wander, and dream.

It is very important to be completely honest with yourself here. Set goals that are big enough for your mind and noble enough for your spirit. Get out of your comfort zone! Most people gravitate toward what makes them comfortable, or they're afraid of failing, so they stay where they are. But if you never leave your comfort zone, it is impossible to grow. By definition, getting out of your comfort zone is uncomfortable. "Aim for the stars, and you might still hit the moon." (Note for those who don't have a bold goal right now, that is more than OK, as it will come in due time. For now, until you can spend time alone with your inner thoughts, go through all the steps for SMART goals using a smaller goal to understand the process.)

"*M*" *is for measurable.* Goals must be specific to know if you hit your target. You don't want to be a wandering generality. Ideally, a measurable goal should be quantifiable. For example, don't have a health goal such as "get more sleep;" that's too vague. Rather, say "I will get eight hours of sleep per night." Or if you have a certain number of hours you need to bill at work, put a specific number on it. Some goals are not as easy to measure such as character goals, like being honest or having a certain emotional disposition, like not getting angry. For those goals, I prefer to use words like "consistently" or "habitually," and measure my success by how many times I succeed or not in a given day.

"*A*" *is for achievable.* Yes, you want to stretch yourself with a significant goal, but you also want to make sure it is realistically attainable. The goal should be both ambitious yet not ridiculous. I like to use the term, "grounded in reality."

"*R*" *is for rewarding.* You want to be clear on the specific benefit for your goal. Your goal is spending an hour with your kids each night. Great! What is the positive result of that? You have an improved relationship with your kids. Your kids are happier. You are enjoying and grateful for the family time. Just make sure the present, tangible outcome of achieving your goal is clear.

"*T*" *is for time-based.* Your goal needs to have a specific date or time that it will be reached. For example, I will earn straight A's in my classes this semester, or I will bill 2,000 hours by December 31st. Frame your goal as I will go from X to Y by a date certain. Be reasonable in setting a deadline, as an unrealistic time frame can lead to frustration.

Once you have created your goals, it is imperative that you put them in writing. Famed coaches John Wooden and Pete Carroll stress the fundamental importance of written goals. John Wooden's success only began after he developed his written philosophy. Coach Pete Carroll credits his profound change in coaching to putting his goals in writing. Writing gives a sense of permanence and significance to your goals. It allows you to review them and remind yourself of them.

There is no one particular format for writing goals. Some people write them out in a paragraph, others in one sentence or add a drawing or picture to make it more personal. Make sure whatever format you decide on you can review and edit daily each morning. We will discuss this in more detail in the very next chapter.

Remember, too, goals are part of your ongoing pursuit of happiness, and you should consistently review and modify them moving forward. Have a regular plan to measure and check your progress. This ensures you stay on track, maintain momentum, and hold yourself accountable.

PRIORITIZE YOUR DAILY GOALS

In the movie *City Slickers*, actor Billy Crystal played the lead role of a man going through a mid-life crisis. He was depressed by his lack of clarity on what was important to him. For his fortieth birthday, his friends took him on a cattle drive to help cheer him up. In a poignant scene, while searching for a lost calf, the lead wrangler, a tough but wise cowboy named Curly, asks Crystal, "Do you know the secret to life?" and Curly holds up one finger. Crystal responds sarcastically, "Your finger?" "No," responds Curly, "It's one thing." Crystal sincerely inquires, "What is that one thing?" Curly answers. "That's up to you to find out."

Every single day, you will want to ask yourself what's the most important thing I can do today? I recommend you do that for each of the big three areas we have discussed—your health, your work, and your relationships. If you could only accomplish one thing in each area, what would it be on any given day?

I also suggest you distinguish between activities that are truly important versus trivial. An important activity is connected to a vital priority or goal. It is something aligned with your highest goals. In contrast, a trivial activity has little or no value. And, of course, there is the middle ground, as some projects may have a certain amount of value.

Often the biggest obstacle to doing what is important is being distracted by things that are urgent. In other words, rather than deciding what is important, we instead look at what is urgent. Often, the things that are important but not urgent—such as drafting that motion, spending time talking with your friend, exercising, sleeping—do not get done. Instead, the things that are urgent—that are screaming for our time—get most of our attention.

We live in a continually connected world where emails, texts, smartphones, social media, and interruptions are never-ending. Thus, determining urgent versus important is a critical distinction in your life management strategy. Most people are so busy doing trivial and urgent matters that they don't take the time to do what is really important. We want to turn that type of behavior on its head and focus almost exclusively on those activities that are truly important.

The Italian economist, Vilfredo Pareto, came up with the 80/20 rule. This came to be known as the law of the vital few. In essence, the rule states that 80 percent of your benefits come from 20 percent of your behavior or actions.[5]

A lot of people are experts at what shouldn't have been done in the first place. If you spend your day reacting to emails and texts and pushing projects from one pile to the next or ingesting lots of social media but never really accomplishing anything of real importance, then you are not following the Pareto principle. As author and lifehacker, Tim Ferris, said: "Doing something unimportant well does not make it important."[6]

To put this principle in action, Stephen Covey popularized the big rocks concept. The "big rocks" is a metaphor for the vital few things that are the most important in our life. In essence, if you put the big rocks in a jar first, then you can also add smaller rocks, pebbles, some sand, and eventually even some water. If you didn't put the big rocks in first, you wouldn't be able to fit them in the jar. All the smaller rocks, pebbles, sand, and water would have taken the space for the big rocks.

So, let me ask you, do you know what your vital few big rocks are today?

For some, one of the rocks might be spiritual in nature, such as spending time in prayer, study, or meditation. For others, one of the rocks might be your family and spending time with them. Still others will identify their work as one of their big rocks.

Although everybody's rocks are unique, I suggest having at least three of your big rocks as health/well-being, meaningful work/service, and meaningful relationships. Start by identifying and putting those three big rocks in your jar daily.

Once you start to get familiar with the big three rocks, consider adding a fourth rock of "renewal or recreation" to give some priority to this important aspect. Something that makes *you* happy or brings you joy. Reading a book, working on a hobby, planning a vacation, or simply relaxing. This last big rock allows you to sharpen your saw and make sure you stay in the game for the long run.

Here's my own big rocks list for one of my days:

Big 4 Rocks	#1 Actions
Health	Get eight hours of sleep
Work	Finish writing decision in Jones trial
Love	Dinner date with my wife
Play	Book flight for family summer vacation

If you got nothing else done on a given day but your four big rocks, I suspect you might feel pretty good about your day.

On your deathbed, you will never say, "I wish I'd spent more time checking my emails, looking at social media, watching more TV." Many wise mentors add you will also not say you wish you spent more time at the office. Rather, you will likely say you wish you loved more, played more, had more adventure in your life. No amount of money, material goods, or success can replace your family, loved ones, and meaningful relationships.

"Sounds good," you may say, but it never works that way. Trust me, from a person who used to try pleasing everyone, so I rarely said "no" to anyone. When I learned to say "no" more often, it ironically improved my life and my relationships with others. Time is our most precious commodity in life. You can never get it back. We must make decisions among competing priorities. You can't do it all. By saying yes, to one activity, you are saying no to other things. When you really say no to things, then you know you are truly committed to your big yes. I aim to do less but better. It's hard, but really learn how to say no.

A Russian proverb says: "Chase two rabbits, catch none." The more you diffuse your priorities, the less likely you are to succeed. That's why it's so important we get clear on vital priorities.

I suggest you take some time of solitude to identify your highest priorities. I begin each morning re-affirming mine. I recommend you do this first thing in the morning, so you have a clear vision of what you hope to get done in your day. Once you start to get a clear picture of your most important priorities, then you can start to plan your day, which is our next topic.

Chapter Summary:

- In order to achieve our meaningful goals, we need to follow a process of action.
- The first step in the process is to set "smart" goals.
- Those goals should be broken down into specific daily goals.
- Then prioritize those goals to get very clear on what is most vital for you to flourish today.

SIDEBAR _____

Speaking of priorities, don't get caught up in irrelevant minutiae. Whether in oral argument or in your legal briefs, lawyers should focus on their strongest arguments rather than argue the picayune. There's an old saying in card games like bridge: Lead through strength.

CHAPTER 13

PLAN

• • •

"A goal without a plan is just a wish."
—ANTOINE DE SAINT-EXUPERY

S cott Adams is the cartoonist for Dilbert, one of the most popular comic strips of all time. Dilbert portrays the everyday office worker and his often incompetent, co-workers. As he did in the comic strip above, Adams was one of the first cartoonists to focus on the workplace. Adams wanted to be a cartoonist from an early age but had no idea where to start. So, he placed most of his emphasis on his work process. Adams stressed it is the process that moves people toward their goals.

Adams creates cartoons every day. He does this by making a clear daily plan. In 2013, Adams published a book called *How to Fail at Almost Everything and Still Win Big* in which he wrote he knew exactly what he would be doing four years in the future on any given Saturday. He writes: "If you ask me today where I will be at 6:20 a.m. on a Saturday morning in the year 2017, I'll tell you I will be at my desk finishing the artwork on some comics I drew earlier in the week. That's what I was doing last Saturday at that time and what I plan on doing this Saturday as well. I can't recall the last time I woke up and looked at my options for what to do first. It's always the same, at least for the first few hours of my day."[1]

Adams is a man with a plan. He first gets clarity on his priorities and then makes a plan to achieve them. A plan is essentially a detailed proposal for achieving something. It's deciding and arranging activities aimed at accomplishing a goal. Some experts in the field of time management also refer to it as a system or strategy.

We all have the same amount of time every day—twenty-four hours, which is 1,440 minutes per day. How you intend to use those hours or minutes is your plan. It's the ability to manage your time. Author Brian Tracey declared: "Time management is really life management, personal management, management of yourself. People who value themselves highly allocate their time carefully. They give their time usage a lot of thought. When you love your life, you love every minute of it. You are very careful about misusing or wasting any of the precious minutes and hours of each day." By managing our time, we are managing our life. Manage your time well, and you'll manage your life well.

Let's now take the priorities we discussed in the previous chapter and create a plan to accomplish them. I will offer you very specific and doable planning tools to flourish. Let's begin with the first tool, weekly planning.

START WITH WEEKLY PLANNING

Now that we have divided our priorities into bite-sized, daily action items, we are ready to start scheduling those items. I encourage you to consider reviewing your entire week before doing your daily scheduling.

At the beginning of the week, you look at the items or appointments you don't nec-essarily do every single day but want to make sure they get handled at some point during the week. Examples of things that might happen during the week include a weekly date with your spouse, a school event with a child, workouts that occur several times a week but not every single day, scheduled work meetings, a doctor's visit, or hair appointment.

You would then put those in your daily planner under the appropriate day and time. Then, when you get to each individual day, you already know that part of your day has certain appointments or scheduled commitments.

Although there are many variations, here is an example of a calendar where you can quickly peruse your week:

WEEKLY PLANNER

MONDAY	TUESDAY	WEDNESDAY	THURSDAY

FRIDAY	SATURDAY	SUNDAY	*Notes*

By viewing the entire week, you can see what you have scheduled and where you have free time to do your discretionary work. Besides scheduling events that don't occur every day, another benefit of weekly planning is to make sure you are not too over-loaded on any given day. It allows you to look at your week from a higher level and get perspective on all aspects of your life, including the big three of your well-being, work, and relationships.

I don't recommend using two different calendars—one for your week and one for your day. Simply enter your weekly appointments or scheduled events into your daily calendar for that particular day.

To get really specific, I suggest sitting down every Sunday and planning your big three or four priorities for the week. For example, while you may not exercise every single day, you are able to exercise three times for the week. Then put in your work schedule. Next would be your relationship time, and finally your rest and/or recreation. All four of your priorities, your four big rocks, have been given a place in your schedule.

Be mindful of not letting your highest priorities, your biggest rocks, get pushed out for other seemingly important meetings or activities. I hope I have made it clear that your highest priorities should not get superseded unless they are truly more important.

DAILY PLANNING—CREATE YOUR MASTERPEACE DAY

Carpe diem is the Latin phrase for "seize the day." First popularized by the Roman poet, Horace, carpe diem has been used as a great reminder to make the most of the present moment. In the movie, *Dead Poet Society*, the late actor Robin Williams played an English high school teacher who famously tells his students: "Carpe diem. Seize the day, boys. Make your lives extraordinary." I love this quote because it connects the day to your life ... by living each day to the fullest, you can make your lives extraordinary.

You can only live one day at a time. One moment at a time. A series of moments make up the day. Coach John Wooden recognized this and encouraged people to strive to make each day a masterpiece. When you architect a truly great day, it is not only a masterpiece, but it also gives you great peace of mind, knowing you have identified and implemented a plan to accomplish what is most important in your day. To get the most out of our day, create a masterpeace day. (Yes, I know I misspelled "masterpiece," but I love this play on words.)

Creating a Masterpeace Day Plan is our second planning tool. Let's get very practical. How do we architect a masterpiece day? We do it through three simple and systematic steps, which are set forth below:

AM AND PM BOOKENDS

It is critical that we control the controllable. In general, people have the most control over the beginning and the end of the day. It is more likely that interruptions and urgent matters will arise in the middle of the day.

Darren Hardy in his book, *Compound Effect,* refers to these endpoints in our day as AM and PM bookends[2] Implementing AM and PM bookends is our first step in creating a masterpeace day. Some people refer to them as their morning and evening rituals, but I like a slightly more expansive definition because it is much more than just having coffee in the morning or brushing your teeth before going to bed.

Instead, we want to use our bookends to really begin creating a masterpeace day for ourselves. My mentor, Brian Johnson, often repeats that a great day starts the night before—by getting a great night of sleep. I mentioned earlier the incredible impact this one change has had on my life. It's why I start with the PM bookend before the AM bookend. This action alone will move you closer to flourishing.

PM Bookend

It bears repeating: If you want to have a great next day, then have a great night of sleep the night before. That's right; the number one thing you can do to have full energy the next day is to get a good night of sleep the night before. It's that important.

Please see the strong connection between your previous night and your next day. Are you waking up tired, groggy, and already thinking of when you can go to bed? Or do you wake up feeling refreshed, energized, and ready to go?

The very end of our night, the PM bookend, is designed to help us get a great night of sleep, so we can start off our next day full of energy. While your PM bookend will be unique and personal to you, there are three key practices that everyone can use.

The first practice is called "shutdown complete." This comes from author, Cal Newport, and it's what he and I do at the end of each workday.[3] The shutdown complete is both physical and mental. It's physical in that you take a moment to make sure your workday is done. You review your to-do list to capture any loose items, check that there are no urgent emails, and move any unfinished tasks to the following day. The goal here is you have closed any open loops for the day and have a sense of completion as well as peace of mind knowing you have captured what needs to be done for the next day. Your work is now done for this day.

The shutdown complete routine also has a psychological component. After you have physically shut down, it's also important to flip your mental switch as well. Make the mental switch from work, so you can attain a peaceful mind like water at the end of the day. Having a mind like water is a mental and emotional state where your mind is clear and still. When Cal Newport is done, he verbally says, "Shutdown complete." When I start my commute home, I let that drive serve as the transition from work mode. When I arrive home to my family, I'm in family mode, not lawyer or judge mode.

The second practice occurs a little later in the evening, and it's an important part of your PM routine. It's powering off and putting away your electronics. Brian Johnson calls it a "digital sunset," and I like to think of it as an "electronics shutdown." You want to start your electronics shutdown at least an hour before bed.

Scientific research is strong that our cellphones and computers keep us up at night. Using these devices causes us to take longer to fall asleep, and we don't sleep as well. Our electronic devices are both biologically and psychologically stimulating. According to the National Sleep Foundation, a whopping 95 percent of people look at their digital device within an hour before going to sleep.[4] The problem is the blue light emitted from these devices transmits a signal to our brain that it's still daytime and blocks the melatonin which makes us sleepy and regulates our sleep cycles.

Based on the substantial evidence and research, I'm about to tell you something you know is the right thing to do, but it's still one of the hardest to accomplish. When you do your digital sunset, put your cellphone somewhere out of reach. Ideally, you don't look at your texts and emails again until after your AM bookend. My own personal exception is I set my phone to ring for my family, but everyone else is on silent. If you say you are shutting down and turning off your phone, but then you regularly check your text and emails throughout the evening, are you really shutting down? Or are you now back in reactive work mode? Even a little peak can open the pandora's box and get your mind going again.

The third practice is to do all the routine things at night that you used to do in the morning. This may include laying out your clothes, checking for keys, making your lunch, showering, or anything else you routinely do in the morning. Sounds easy, and it is, but the ultimate goal is to not waste any brain power in the morning on these items. Studies have shown the morning is when individuals have their most creativity, willpower, and energy.

Ultimately, the PM bookend is one of the most powerful tools for creating a masterpeace day. When I'm at work, I'm fully focused and energized. When I'm home, I'm fully present and engaged. The PM bookend allows me to shut down my work and electronics as well as focus on other vital aspects of my life. At the end of the day, ask yourself – "Do I want to be entertained tonight or optimized in my life?" If the answer is you want to optimize your life, then you will power off your electronic devices and follow the PM bookend to get a good night of sleep.

AM Bookend

The AM bookend allows you to be creative before being reactive and to put your number one project first and make sure it gets done. The AM bookend enables you to resist the magnetic attraction to check the stimulating emails, texts, and social media. Instead, by not even looking at your phone until you have done your morning routine, you will have a much greater sense of calm energy. This can be life changing.

What would your ideal morning look like? If you had thirty minutes or an hour before you started working, how could you make your morning a masterpeace? Here are a few suggestions to consider:

- In his excellent book, *Make Your Bed*, Admiral William McRaven encourages us to begin our day with a sense of accomplishment by making the bed. I think it's a great practice and suggest that if you live alone, or if your partner is already up, then "make your bed."
- Drink a glass of water—most of us don't drink enough water.
- Do a little movement (such as yoga)—to get the blood flowing and gently ramp up mentally.
- Pray, meditate, and/or read—tapping into your spiritual, mental, and emotional energy to set your intentions for the day.
- Daily planning—this is what I call the Carpe Diem Journal. Take some solitary time and proactively plan out how you will architect your masterpeace day ahead.

It is crucial in achieving your goals to take time each morning or evening in solitude, without inputs, to get clarity on your priorities and to plan your day around those priorities. Every single day for the past twenty years, I have done exactly that. First thing in the morning, I take about ten minutes by myself to plan my daily goals and my day. But it doesn't have to be ten minutes. One lawyer I know does it in two minutes; another person I know takes a full thirty minutes. Do it when your mind is clear, before all the inputs and interruptions hit you.

The beauty of daily planning is it allows you to see how your day works together and how you can fit the big rocks into your day. After the big rocks are in, then I see whether and how to fit the other items in my day.

My AM bookend is a dramatic change from the past. I used to wake up and immediately checked my phone, responded to all my texts, reviewed my emails, and then checked the weather, news, sports, etc. The first forty-five minutes of the morning were gone, and my mind was already overly stimulated. I would say to myself, "Where has the morning gone already?" What a contrast to my current AM bookend, where I feel energized tranquility and a sense of accomplishment.

Start your day by focusing on what is important before you enter the digital world. Each morning, you get enthusiastic for at least one of your big rock goals that day. Something that gets you out of bed excited. Calm, confident, focused, and energized. The AM bookend is the beginning to a masterpeace day.

PUT FIRST THINGS FIRST

Now that we have installed AM and PM bookends, the second step is to plan when we will take action on our big rocks each day. The principle here is to do your first things—that is your highest priorities—first in the day. When the time management experts, Peter Drucker and Stephen Covey, say, "Put first things first," they take it literally.

Whatever you have identified as your number one goal, that is the first thing you do in your day or make sure it is clearly scheduled for when it will done. On a weekend, for example, after I did my AM routine and my hike, I sat down and did a ninety-minute writing session on this book. Boom, number one rock was in my jar. Now the rest of my day is dedicated to my second big rock, which is my family and friends, and then doing a few items around the home.

I did the same thing as a lawyer. When I got to work, I would do a quick check of emails for emergencies, and then dive right into my number-one priority at work. However, my biggest challenge as a lawyer—and it was a big challenge—was finding time for my relationships, as I often worked late.

I spoke with a lawyer who always focused on the urgent first. She wanted to handle her emails and discretionary urgent items first "to get them out of the way" and then focus on her work project, such as preparing for the deposition she was taking tomorrow. However, when the inevitable urgent matters arose later in the day, she liked to get those handled. Not surprisingly, she went to her deposition woefully unprepared. That is why you must discipline yourself to prioritize your projects and plan them in advance to make sure you have enough time to do them in a timely and effective manner.

How would you put your own "first things first?" You have a blank slate at the beginning of each morning, so let's start creating your own masterpeace day. If you feel so inspired, consider identifying your number one priority in health, work, and relationships for the day. Let me ask you right now:

1. Health—When and what are you going to do for your health today? What is your number one health priority? Again, for me, it's sleep. Knowing how important it is to get seven to eight hours of sleep, I prioritize my day to make this happen.

2. Work—What is your number one work priority and when are you going to do it?

3. Relationships—With whom and when are you going to nurture a meaningful relationship?

Navy SEAL Commander and instructor Mark Divine calls this simplifying your battlefield.[5] You reduce, not increase, the number of your goals. Get super clear on your number one goal—keep it simple. Line up that single domino, knock it over, and move to the next. Maybe your first priority in your morning routine is meditation, which moves you to do your workout—health domino done—then you get to work, and you do your number one priority in the morning at work. That's another domino, so now when you get home and spend time with your spouse, friends, kids ... each successive domino has been knocked over.

Hopefully, you can see that starting your day by knocking over those dominoes will have a huge impact on how you finish your day. And, interestingly, how you end your day—with time in meaningful relationships and a good night of sleep—will increase your chances of having your next day be a masterpeace.

SCHEDULE DEEP-WORK TIME BLOCKS

The owner of a German digital consulting firm, Lasse Rheingans, has been testing a novel idea – reducing the workday to only five hours per day. His employees all start work at 8:00 a.m. and end at 1:00 p.m. They focus those five hours exclusively on work and then leave. To get the same amount of work done as in eight hours, all cellphones are put completely away; social media is banned, emails are only checked two times per day, and meetings are limited to fifteen minutes. The remainder of the time is focused on uninterrupted time blocks of deep work. Rheingans found that his employees got just as much work done as if they had been working eight hours. The company has remained profitable, had higher measurements for customer service, and the employees are happier.[6]

Rheingans is on to something, as are other thinkers about how to schedule and use our time most effectively. This brings us to the "magic ingredient" of time management and the third step in building our masterpiece day— "time blocks."

Scheduling chunks of uninterrupted time is hardly new or a secret. Benjamin Franklin created time blocks every day to manage his time and avoid interruptions. In particular, Franklin scheduled two different blocks of four-hours each—from 8:00 a.m. to 12:00 p.m. and from 2:00 p.m. to 6:00 p.m. This may help explain how Franklin was not only a founding father of the United States but also a successful business owner, inventor, scientist, best-selling author, founder of the University of Pennsylvania and the Philadelphia Fire Department, violinist, composer, and diplomat. I am tired just thinking about all that.

More recently, Cal Newport wrote an excellent book about time blocks called *Deep Work*. He defines "deep work" as "Professional activities performed in a state of distraction-free concentration that push your cognitive capabilities to their limit. These efforts create new value, improve your skill and are hard to replicate." Time blocking is so powerful, author Gary Keller says, "It's productivity's greatest power tool."[7]

Newport suggests, and science corroborates, that the ideal time block is about sixty to ninety minutes in length. After that, our willpower and concentration tend to diminish. That's when we take a break and recover.

The key to deep work is the distraction-free focus of time. To facilitate deep work, we now add blocks of uninterrupted time to our daily schedule. How you install deep work into your daily routine may be personal to you but let me offer a few suggestions. I schedule daily deep work blocks like they are appointments. For example, if I schedule a doctor's appointment, I am going to keep it. Likewise, if I set a time to write an opinion on a case, write my book, or prepare for a lecture I'm teaching, then that becomes scheduled uninterrupted time. I shut my door and let others know I'm unavailable during that time unless it's a true emergency. I put my cellphone away and on silent mode. I don't look at my cellphone or emails during my deep work time blocks. Once you have established a habit of deep-work time blocks, watch your productivity skyrocket!

But what's the harm of checking your texts, emails, or social media quickly during your time blocks? Multi-tasking is a myth. What we are really doing is task-shifting. Research shows our focus and attention are diminished by task-shifting. When you shift from one task to another, your brain is still processing the prior task and has what is called "attention residue." When you have attention residue, your performance and focus will decrease, sometimes dramatically.

Let's run a little experiment to see how good you are at task-shifting. First, let's focus on just one task: count from 1 to 10 as fast as you can. Most people can do that task in 1.5 to 2 seconds. Now, let's focus on one more singular task: say the letters in alphabetical order from A to J as fast as you can. Again, most people can do in 1.5 to 2 seconds.

Now, let's do a third task, but doing it a task shift. Say 1, A, 2, B, 3, C, etc. as fast as you can. For most people, it typically takes 10 seconds to task shift. That's more than twice as long if had you done each task separately.

In the book, *The One Thing,* Gary Keller tells us the average worker loses 28 percent of their day to task-shifting.[8] Think about that. More than a quarter of your day. This amounts to thirteen weeks a year. What could you do with thirteen extra weeks?

Deep-work time blocks have been so profound for me, I have expanded the concept to other areas of my life. For example, I block out a focused, one hour for my workouts and have found that my workouts are much more effective. I get more done in less time and feel more energetic than ever.

When I'm home with my family, I often consider those sacred love blocks, where I'm fully engaged, present, and connected with my family. I want to make sure I am spending quality, focused time with my loved ones. Of course, you'll have spontaneous, light-hearted, joy-filled moments. Hopefully, lots of them. But you also do not want to leave your time with your family and close friends to chance or be constantly interrupted by your smartphone. In fact, you don't even want to be seduced by that shiny object. Put it far away.

Now that we have deep time blocks scheduled for our big rocks, we have the foundation for a masterpiece day in place. Just one more thing to plan—all the other smaller rocks and pebbles that eventually need to get accomplished. We have other work obligations, like responding to emails, returning calls, meeting with co-workers, answering questions, handling problems, working on other projects, and so much more. Then there's the personal side of life—grocery store, dinner, car maintenance, errands, home, kids, gifts, anniversaries, birthdays, hobbies, fun, oh my!

If we poured all these small and medium size rocks in our day, our jar would either explode or the rocks would cascade out of the jar and spill all over the floor. Our masterpeace day would be a master disaster. So, we need to be thoughtful about how we handle these other items in our day.

I call the time to handle your emails or other less important items as "monkey work." It's lower energy but still important to handle these items. Because this work typically takes less concentration and brain power, it is often best to do in the afternoon after you have used your highest energy for your most important tasks. Try to find a plan that is the least disruptive to your number one task. Same idea: just block out time for those tasks.

Also allow for time in your schedule to meet with people. I called this my "teamwork" time. When I was a partner, my staff, close associates, etc., knew when I was doing my deep work time so as not to interrupt me, but they also knew when I was available for my teamwork time, which was typically at the very beginning of the day, right before lunch, and later in the afternoon. I found it was beneficial for the people who needed my input, because like the deep work time blocks, I was able to give them my full and undivided time.

Of course, they also knew that if something was urgent or important, I had an open-door policy. But, once they knew I had a set time for them, it was amazing how the urgent things were no longer so urgent, and the important things could wait.

By allocating my deep work, my monkey work, and my teamwork times, I was able to handle more than 90 percent of what I wanted to accomplish every single day. In short, your masterpiece day ideally should consist of six parts

1. A.M. & P.M. Bookends,
2. Deep health block (eat and exercise),
3. Deep work time block(s),
4. Deep love/relationship time block,
5. Housekeeping work and teamwork time, and
6. Sleep.

These six components served as the building blocks for my days as a lawyer and currently serve me as a judge. Think through your fundamental building blocks and find what works best for your own masterpiece day.

HAVE A TRUSTED PLANNING SYSTEM

A vital aspect of creating a masterpeace day is to have a place where you can capture all this great planning. We need to have a system or tool that will store and help us access those components of our planning. A system is trusted if you can count on it to give you the information you need when you need it.

When you find a system that works, you will not only become more effective but also more at peace. You are not always wondering ... did I miss that deadline? When is my haircut appointment or my boss' birthday? A good system saves you time and often saves your bacon.

The specific system you use is up to you, but I highly recommend using some type of daily or weekly calendar. Of course, you can just use the old fashion pen and paper method by writing out your daily plan and to-do list. This is the first generation of time management tools, which works for many people and is elegantly simple. However, there are also so many great tools out there that let you be even more effective and productive. It doesn't matter if you use your computer, an electronic calendaring app, or a paper calendar.

The most important thing is to pick a tool, software, or an app that you will use consistently. You will want to use this tool for both work and personal life. One tool is most efficient and effective. Whatever tool you pick, it should have at least the following three functions: A place to see your number one priorities/projects for the day, a calendar and place for your appointments, and a place for to-do lists.

First, as we have thoroughly discussed, your planning tool should make it super easy for you to identify your most important priorities and big rocks.

Second, this tool will serve as your calendar for events, appointments, meetings, birthdays, concerts, etc. Anything that has a specific date and a corresponding commitment, you put it in your calendar. I also find it beneficial to include your spouse's or significant other's important dates or appointments, as well as your kids' games or special activities.

Third, your system should track all your key projects in your personal and professional life. This not only includes a "to-do" list of things that you need/want to get done today but also a discretionary "to-do list" that is not time sensitive but hopefully/ someday maybe in the future?

By capturing all your information in one or a few places, you are not constantly being bombarded by competing lists and thoughts of what you need to do swirling in your head. The goal is, as Bruce Lee said, to empty your mind, so it can be like water, where you are free to focus undistracted on your most important priorities. The beauty of having a trusted system is that it frees your mind. Again, a master "peace" day.

This idea of capturing your to-do lists and thoughts, organizing them, reviewing them regularly, and then getting them done is a time-tested system that will work for 99 percent of your tasks. It doesn't matter your occupation—lawyers, professionals, stay-at-home parents, students, and your home projects. Work and home. The key is to have a reliable process that works for you.

Now, taking the big three priorities we have discussed throughout this book—our health and well-being, our work, and our relationships—here is an example of a typical workday. Remember, the AM bookend includes reviewing and creating your plan every day.

WHEN	WHAT
8:00 p.m.	PM bookend (Remember a great day starts the night before.)
5:30 a.m.	AM bookend: Wake up, hopefully without an alarm. Brush teeth, drink a glass of water, and put on clothes laid out the night before.
	Meditate.
5:45 a.m.	Sit at table, eat breakfast, prepare calendar for masterpeace day, and journal. (Sometimes your journal is one word. Other times
6:00 a.m.	it's a lot longer, and that's OK.)
6:45 a.m.	Drive to gym.
7:00 a.m.	Exercise, shower, and change into work clothes.
8:15 a.m.	Leave gym and drive to work.
8:30 a.m.	Check my emails and texts for first time.
8:40 a.m.	Work block #1: Take the bench at 8:40 a.m.
10:00 a.m.	Take a 15-minute recess where I stand and walk.
10:30 a.m.	Work Block #2: Take the bench during trial or chambers work.
12:00–1:00 p.m.	Lunch.
1:00-1:30 p.m.	Respond to email, texts.
1:30 p.m.	Work block #3: Take the bench at 1:30 p.m. or chambers work.
3:00 p.m.	Teamwork Block and Housekeeping (Finish all emails, texts, and written decisions for day.)
5:00 p.m.	Shutdown complete.
5:30 p.m.	Drive home, greet family, change clothes.
6:30 p.m.	Dinner and quality time with family.
8:00 p.m.	PM bookend: Put out clothes, keys, etc.
8:30 p.m.	Digital Sunset: Read.
9:30 p.m.	Bed.

THREE PRINCIPLES TO THRIVE (AND MAINTAIN SANITY) IN THE PROCESS

No. 1—Keep It Simple

Whatever system you pick, try to keep it simple. If your system becomes too complicated or takes too much time, you won't use it. Not using your system is like not having a system at all.

For all his numerous accomplishments, Benjamin Franklin had an incredibly simple planning and time management system. He incorporated all the key components we discussed previously and did it in a simple and easy-to-use system. Take a look at his daily planner.

The morning question, What good shall I do this day?	5 6 7	Rise, wash and address *Powerful Goodness;* contrive day's business and take the resolution of the day; prosecute the present study; and breakfast.
	8	
	9 10 11	Work.
	12 1	Read, or overlook my accounts, and dine.
	2	
	3 4	Work.
	5	
	6 7 8 9	Put things in their places, supper, music, or diversion, or conversation; examination of the day.
Evening question, What good have I done today?	10 11	
	12 1	Sleep.
	2 3 4	

What should jump out most about Franklin's daily planner is the empty space and its simplicity. He only has six specific time blocks in his schedule.

First, he scheduled an extended AM bookend to plan out his days and set his intentions for accomplishing his priorities.

Second, he scheduled two deep work time blocks, each four hours in length. He was guided by one single question: "What good shall I do this day?"

Third, the middle portion of his day was carved out for reading, relaxing, overlooking his accounts, and lunch. This was essentially his monkey work and teamwork time.

Fourth, after his second, deep work, time block, which ended at 6:00 p.m., he had a "shutdown complete," which he called "put things in their places." After shutting down, he turned his attention to his deep love block, diversions, and conversations.

Fifth, Franklin carved out seven hours of time for his sleep.

Let's keep Franklin's principle of simplicity in mind in our daily schedule; it's detailed enough to block out time for our most important priorities but simple enough to be super user-friendly.

No. 2—Be Flexible

Many of us hard chargers want to accomplish everything on our "to-do list" and strictly follow our daily plan. However, it's equally important to counterbalance these goals with being flexible in life. The mighty oak tree has the potential to live a long life, but due to its rigidity, it's also susceptible to being blown over or toppled by strong storms or winds. Bruce Lee said: "Notice that the stiffest tree is most easily cracked, while the bamboo or willow survives by bending with the wind."

Yes, we need to have a daily plan and road map. Yet, at the same time, we can't remain so rigid that we break. We need to have structure, but at the same time, remain nimble and flexible. If an important or spontaneous situation arises—a child, spouse, or co-worker is sick; an urgent but unforeseen important project arises; or your spouse needs to talk to you—you should remain flexible and resilient, like the palm tree bending in the wind.

Neuroscientist Dr. Dan Siegel suggests we try to have a dynamic equilibrium—where we are simultaneously structured and flexible.[9] Like a flowing river—one bank of the river provides strength and structure, and the other bank provides for flexibility. Seigel says healthy humans find a happy medium between rigidity and chaos. As we proceed with our plan each day, let's find that balance between structure and spontaneity, the dance between discipline and flexibility.

No. 3—Enjoy the Process

"The road is always better than the inn," said writer Miguel de Cervantes. We are so immersed in achieving our daily plans and future goals, we fail to realize that most of our time is spent on the road getting there. The road is the process. It's our life journey.

Because nearly all our time is devoted to the journey and not the destination, it is important we try to enjoy the process. Of course, not every single minute is going to be enjoyable. When my child was hospitalized with a potentially life-threatening illness, it was the farthest thing from joy. There is death, illness, tragedy, suffering, and misfortune. We can't expect to face those with a big grin on our face. We are not always going to be making forward progress. But hopefully, you find a process that you mostly relish.

In my own career as a lawyer, this is where I most often fell short. I was so overly focused on my goals—winning the case, billing hours, getting clients—that I frequently failed to enjoy what I was doing. Tom Morris aptly notes in his book, *The Art of Achievement*: "We don't have to choose between accomplishment and enjoyment. We can have both. We can be both teleological, purposive workers, throwing ourselves into meaningful challenges, and at the same time lovers of the present moment. In fact, I've come to believe that we can't be workers at the highest levels of excellence, over the long run, unless we do find that joy in the process now, in a warm embrace of immediacy ..."[10]

Cervantes and Morris are referring to our power and potential to enjoy the process while striving toward our goals. Don't wait to celebrate only when you have reached the destination. Because for every goal you reach and mountain you climb, there will be yet another interesting goal or mountain ahead.

Chapter Summary:

- After we have clarified our vital priorities, the next step in our action process is to have a plan for achieving those priorities.
- Start your overall planning by looking at your entire week to make sure that all your key priorities, appointments, and events are captured.
- Then create a "masterpeace day" by planning AM/PM bookends, putting first things first, and scheduling deep time blocks.

SIDEBAR

Be overly prepared. Certainly, know the facts and the law of your case better than the judge. The law does not "cast a sympathetic eye on the unprepared."

CHAPTER 14

TAKE ACTION

• • •

*"Do you want to know who you are? Don't ask.
Act! Action will delineate and define you."*
—THOMAS JEFFERSON

Nick Saban is arguably the greatest college football coach of all time. As of this writing, he has won seven national championships, the most ever by any coach. While coaching at the University of Alabama, he has won close to 90 percent of his games and done so in the most competitive conference in football.[1]

Coaches are most often judged by their championships and winning percentage, which is why Nick Saban is so highly regarded. Ironically, however, Saban rarely, if ever, talks about them. Instead, Saban talks about "the Process." Rather than focusing on some distant goal, such as winning a national championship, he focuses on the action a person can take right now.

Yes, Saban follows the first two steps of the Process by identifying the priorities for his players and creating a plan, but it is his fierce commitment to the execution of those plans that is his distinguishing characteristic. His players relentlessly focus on what's in front of them. Whether it's watching a film, lifting weights, or practicing a particular play—all action words—the players give 100 percent to that present moment.

When it is game day, the players don't focus on winning the game. Rather, their entire focus is on just one play. Nothing else. In short, Saban's process is to focus all of one's energy on the present moment. I call this "present action."

In this chapter, we focus on the third and last step of the Process. We move from prioritizing to planning to performing. This third step is all about working single-mindedly toward accomplishing your priorities. This is the chapter where we go from dreamer to doer.

I also want to make an important distinction between planning and action. Yes, planning is a form of doing something, but they are not the same. The action is what ultimately produces the benefit. For instance, you might plan when and where to plant the seeds for your garden, but the actual digging of the soil and putting the seeds in the ground is the action. Planning to study at the library and actually studying at the library are big differences.

It's all about taking action now. That is why action, and the present are discussed together. You can only act in the present moment. Such present action is the most difficult of all the steps. Many people know what to do, but often they don't do it.

If we know just our priorities but never take action, we are dreamers. Similarly, if we act without knowing our priorities, we are wanderers. True flourishing starts once you focus on and act toward your highest priorities. The ability to align your priorities with your actions is the single most significant thing you can do to optimize your life.

Depending on what you are hoping to achieve, there are some significant principles for taking effective action. Running a marathon is different than writing a report or meditating. But the commonality in all of them is the "action." Whether running, writing, or meditating, they are all verbs. Indeed, life is a verb.

Let's now look at the essential principles and practices for taking effective action.

FOCUS FULLY ON THE TASK AT HAND

Olympic gold medalist Lanny Bassham once trained a professional golfer. Interestingly, Bassham is not a professional golfer. He didn't work with this golfer on improving his swing. Instead, Bassham works with athletes on the mental aspect of their performance. Bassham told his student and professional golfer Ben Crane to focus solely on a proper and relaxed swing on each hole, not on winning a tournament.

CHAPTER 14: PERFORM

At the prestigious San Diego's Torrey Pines Golf Tournament, Crane found himself only thirty inches from the cup on the 18th hole. "The crowd knew Ben needed to make the putt for the win, but Crane had no idea. When the ball rolled in, his playing partner offered his hand in congratulations. Thinking this was just the customary handshake after the round, Ben shook his hand and did not realize he had won until [Ben's wife] ran out to the green ... 'Did I win?' Crane asked. This is proof that a player can cause his mind to think about the process instead of outcome even with the possibility of winning pulling at him."[2]

How do we most effectively take action? We begin by being fully focused on the task at hand. Focus is central to every kind of success—work, health, and even our relationships, and is our first and most essential practice for taking effective action. Our ability to concentrate is linked to our ability to learn, memorize, achieve goals, and ignore what is irrelevant.

Focus on the wrong things, the unimportant things, and you won't thrive. Where you chose to put your focus will dictate the quality of your life. The Star Wars Jedi Master says: "Always remember: Your focus determines your reality."[3]

Focus is synonymous with attention and concentration. "If there is one 'secret' to effectiveness, it is concentration," says Peter Drucker. We place our focus, our attention, our concentration on what is most important at the present moment. Focus on accomplishing your identified priority to the exclusion of all else. Give your full attention to the one vital thing in front of you right now.

At work, imagine drafting a motion with complete focus and without distraction. How much faster and better would you be able to draft the motion? Or in your relationships, imagine being able to give your full and undivided attention to being with your kids, spouse, friends.

The opposite of focus is being distracted and inattentive. It's when someone is talking to you, but your mind is elsewhere. It's when you're at the gym but really thinking about work. It's when you are sort of, kind of, doing your work but constantly checking your phone for texts, sports scores, or social media. It's when you are only half-hearted about what you are doing.

Practically speaking, focus and concentration can be developed like a muscle. Practice doing focused deep work for some specific period of time, without any distractions, including not checking your emails, texts, or phone for any reason. For example, read, study, write, or work on a project for fifteen minutes, distraction free. If you can do that, try stretching it by another five minutes. Slowly and gradually, you will build up more mental stamina and greater concentration. In time, you will be focusing for periods of 30 minutes or longer.

This brings us back to Bassham's golf story. We want to be 100 percent focused on the Process, not on the outcome. We are all in on what we are doing, but at the same time, we want to remain unattached to results. Remember, we want to be rational in knowing what we can and can't control. Ben Crane could only control his swing; he couldn't ultimately control whether he won the tournament. One of the great secrets of living a happy life is we can strive for success and still maintain a sense of peace and calm by becoming detached from the outcome. Our ego often makes it difficult to let go of outcomes. But the ego also results in negative emotions and unhappiness, which hinders focus and performance.

Instead, focus fully on your current task and do not let anything else disturb or disrupt you. I would be willing to say that focus is so important that you can't flourish without it. Indeed, focus is at the very heart of all that we do.

BE PRESENT

Living in the "present" is closely related to our previous discussion on "focus." However, focus tells us to direct our attention to something. We can place our focus on the past, the present, or the future. We can focus on something that is important or unimportant. Focus tells us on what we are placing our attention.

Being present is more about time—telling us to specifically focus on now, this present moment. It is axiomatic you can only live in the present moment. This is what we truly have control over—our present thoughts and actions in this moment. Period. The present moment is all that exists. Being present at all times is our second essential practice for taking effective action.

When you think about the past, you are re-activating a memory trace but doing it in the now. For the future, it is only imagined in the now; it is a current mental projection of what lies ahead and is often portrayed as a worst-case scenario. When the future ultimately arrives, it is in the now. Therefore, the past and future have no reality of their own.

In his exceptional book, *The Power of Now*, Eckhart Tolle explains: "Realize deeply that the present moment is all you ever have."[4] "There is never a time when your life is not 'this moment.' Is this not a fact?"[5]

In one of my criminal trials, a defendant faced a misdemeanor charge of theft. In attempting to reach a resolution, the prosecutor offered to allow the defendant to perform community service instead of serving jail time. However, the defendant rejected the offer and insisted on going to trial. The defendant testified he did not commit the crime. The prosecution showed evidence to the contrary, and the jury disbelieved the defendant's testimony and unanimously found him guilty of the crime. I sentenced the defendant to one year in county jail. The defendant was immediately handcuffed, and while being escorted to the holding cell, he asked, "Can I still get my community service?" Well, the obvious answer was no. That ship had already sailed.

By living in the present, we free ourselves to create a new beginning each day. A fresh day. That's the way to live fully. One of my all-time favorite characters in literature is Zorba from the novel *Zorba the Greek* by Nikos Kazantzakis. The book tells the story of an uptight young man who travelled to the Greek island of Crete, where he met Zorba. They ended up working together. Immediately, the young man noticed Zorba lived fully in the present moment, passionately embracing whatever he was doing.

When the two were at work in a coal mine, the young man observed: "I hung the lamp up again on the nail and watched Zorba work. He was completely absorbed in his task; thought of nothing else; he was one with the earth, the pick, and the coal."[6] As they later talked about Zorba's approach to life, Zorba stated:

"I've stopped thinking all of the time of what happened yesterday. And stopped asking myself what's going to happen tomorrow. What's happening today, this minute, that's what I care about. I asked: 'What are you doing at this moment, Zorba?' 'I'm sleeping.' Well then sleep well. 'What are you doing at this moment, Zorba?' 'I'm working.' Well, work well. 'What are you doing at this moment Zorba?' 'I'm kissing a woman.' Well, kiss her well. And forget all the rest while you are doing it."[7]

If you are with your spouse, children, or friends, then fully focus and be present with them. Your presence is the best present you can give them. Presence is life infusing and nurturing to others. I can't think of anything more powerful than to give your presence to a person.

"Yesterday is history,

Tomorrow is a mystery,

Today is your gift,

It is why it is called the present."[8]

Because of the critical importance of presence, I wanted to go slightly deeper by examining two specific applications of being present – mindfulness and the flow state – and showing how they can further enrich our lives.

Be Mindful

Mindfulness is defined as "paying attention in a particular way, on purpose, in the present moment, non-judgmentally." Leading mindfulness expert Jon Kabat-Zinn says, "Mindfulness" is "the practice of maintaining a nonjudgmental state of heightened or complete awareness of one's thoughts, emotions, or experiences on a moment-to-moment basis; ..."

I find it helpful to think of mindfulness as having two basic aspects:

First, focus your attention on the present moment. Just be fully aware in the present. Second, have non-judgmental awareness of what is happening – knowing your own senses, thoughts, and emotions in that moment.

In short, it is seeing the truth of what is in the present moment – not judging it – just paying attention to it.

Mindfulness is similar to, but different from, presence. The difference is subtle but important. Presence is being "engaged" in the moment... whatever you are doing, you are fully engaged in that moment.... while mindfulness is being "aware" of the moment.

Being mindful involves active observation. You want to learn to witness your own thoughts and emotions. Think of having your own internal "observer" who is noticing your thoughts and emotions. For example, when you are walking, pay attention to your physical senses – your feet touching the ground, the gentle breeze against your face, the sounds you are hearing, and the sights you are seeing.

I began practicing mindfulness in earnest after attending the Navy SEALs camp. Mindfulness is one of the key concepts in which these elite special forces are trained. I immediately realized how applicable this training would be to lawyers and judges.

Although mindfulness has been around for centuries in Eastern religions, it has grown enormously in the West. Mindfulness training is now widely used throughout education, government, military, business, and the law. Law schools now offer mindfulness classes, and there are numerous mindfulness programs for lawyers. "Lawyers position themselves on the front lines of personal, moral, ethical, and cultural battles. Our work puts us directly in the midst of conflict and hostility. Yet, being an effective advocate requires both composure and clarity. How can we be passionate and aggressive, but cool, calm, and collected? And how can we do this, and still protect our own well-being and the well-being of our clients, our firms, and society? One word: mindfulness."[9]

Judges, too, are regularly offered mindfulness training. In fact, in his seminal work on judicial conduct, the Hon. David Rothman discusses mindfulness as one of the foundational pillars of being a judge: "Mindfulness and awareness in court involve consistency of focus on your mission as a judge in proceedings. This means being conscious of what you do and say and being attentive to what others do and say. Always notice your own reactions, feelings and thoughts in regard to what is taking place."

Mindfulness is especially important given that legal professionals are consistently dealing with conflict. When we intentionally pay attention in a nonjudgmental way to what is occurring, we can make better decisions, remain calm, and increase our focus.

Also, being mindful heightens our sense of being alive. We can exercise mindfully, eat mindfully, parent mindfully, work mindfully, love mindfully, and play mindfully. Just being aware of the present moment and enjoying what we are doing.

Get in the Flow

The second related application of being present is flow. As we start to regularly practice living in the present, we can move into a state of "flow." This term was first popularized by author and psychologist Mihaly Csikszentmihalyi (pronounced, "Cheeks-sent-me-high"). It's the peak optimal state that humans can experience.

Being in a state of flow is also referred to as "being in the zone." We often think of athletes being in the zone. Michael Jordan was famous for losing track of time when playing basketball. He was one with the game, fully engrossed in the moment. Flow is related to what Dr. Seligman calls "engagement," which is one of the essential characteristics of flourishing. It's "being one with the music, time stopping, and the loss of self-consciousness during an absorbing activity."[10]

Flow happens at work when you are thoroughly engrossed in a project, especially with no interruptions. While our work also involves aspects of non-flow projects, such as tracking billable hours, replying to emails, and taking calls, we can carve out deep work blocks to maximize our ability to get into the flow. Aim to spend more time in deep work in a flow state. At the end of your day, you will find the time spent in your flow state was the most productive and enjoyable part of your day.

Treat the present moment—whatever you are doing—like it's the most important thing in the world. Because it is. As we practice being present, we are fully engaged in life. This is the hallmark of flourishing—being at your energetic present best, moment to moment.

PURSUE MICRO-WINS

It's a fact that actions can only be taken one moment at a time. At this very second, I'm typing these words on this page. When I exercise, it's one repetition at time. Each moment provides a concrete opportunity to take action. To get a small win. Accumulating one win after another leads to bigger wins.

Yes, we want to seize the day, but in reality, a day can only be lived in brief intervals of time. As author Dan Millman says, "Most of us have heard the saying, 'carpe diem'— Seize the day. A valuable reminder to live fully, but not a realistic idea since you cannot seize the day. You can seize only the moment—this moment." Seizing the moment in Latin is *carpe punctum*.

Another essential step in taking effective action is to pursue "micro-wins." You can use the terms "small wins" or "micro-wins" interchangeably. Either way, aim to achieve a very specific win at each moment. Once you've identified your priority—your "what's important now"—then you take present action for the micro-win on that priority. As Martin Luther King, Jr. said, when you climb the mountain or ladder toward a larger goal, "You don't have to see the whole staircase. Just take the first step."

In her book *The Progress Principle*, Harvard Professor Theresa Amabile writes about the power of small wins. In her extensive research, she found the most effective tool in accomplishing your goals is to make small progress. It's the hour-by-hour wins, day after day, that produces the health, happiness, and success we seek.

Amabile states: "Of all the things that can boost emotions, motivation, and perceptions during a workday, the single most important is making progress in meaningful work." The beauty of small wins and tiny actions is they are simpler to accomplish. With small behaviors, there should be no excuse for procrastination or delay. We just need to take the first small step toward our goal.

When training for the Spartan Race, I read some great advice from the founder of that race, Joe DeSena, in his book *Spartan Up!* "The way to get through anything mentally painful is to take it a little at a time. The mind can't handle dealing with a massive iceberg of pain in front of it, but it can deal with short nuggets that will come to an end. So instead of thinking, ugh, I've got twenty-four miles to go, focus on making it to the next telephone pole in the distance. Whether you're running 20 or 120 miles at a time, the distance must be tackled mentally and physically one mile at a time. The ability to compartmentalize pain into these bite size increments is key."

If you have a big work project, such as opposing a summary judgment motion, that's freaking you out, just break it down into small actions. Go micro with your actions. What's the smallest, tiny domino you can knock over next? Go conquer that and then celebrate it.

This is true of any task, regardless of whether it's physical or mental, personal or professional. Navy SEAL Mark Divine, in his book, *Way of the SEAL*, stated:

"The tougher things get, the smaller your goals should become. These 'micro-goals' should be laser-focused on achievement of a target or a refined subset of your overall mission – this is benchmarking at work. While my trainees' arms are shaking, I don't encourage them to focus on holding their push-up position for forty-five minutes but for just one minute."

Because of its importance, I'm intentionally repeating myself that small wins will lead to big wins over time. Let's take massive action on your number one priority today. But we do that moment by moment with small actions. One repetition after another. One baby step, then another. We want to intentionally pursue small wins throughout our day as we make progress toward our vital few priorities. Micro-wins are the magic elixir to performance. You can only accomplish your bold goals through moment-to-moment actions.

HAVE RESOLVE

Resolve means to concentrate on and accomplish one thing at a time. It means to decide firmly on a course of action. It's finishing the race. It's easy to start writing a book but much harder to finish it. Finish what you start… that's resolve. It's not quitting or giving up.

Often when things get tough, tedious, boring, people give up. They quit. There is a Sanskrit term called "arambashura," which denotes a person who starts out full of passion and excitement, and then after things get tough or tedious, they throw in the towel. It can apply to our healthy New Year's resolutions, our relationships, and our work.

In our daily life, once you have decided to act on your priority, then you focus with great persistence until that task is completed. That's a commitment. In his book, *Focal Point*, Brian Tracy writes:

"Once you have thought through your work and decided on your most valuable task, you must discipline yourself to start it immediately and stay with it until it is complete. When you concentrate single-mindedly on a single task, without diversion or distraction, you get it done far faster than if you start and stop and then come back to the task and pick it up again. You can reduce the amount of time you spend on a major task by as much as 80 percent simply by refusing to do anything else until that task is complete."

George St. Pierre was a young man who faced numerous struggles growing up. He was bullied repeatedly and had his money and even his clothes stolen by other students. Tired of being bullied, St.-Pierre decided to learn karate. He made a commitment to become a master in martial arts. To support himself financially, he worked as a garbage man. In a real-life *Rocky* story, St. Pierre went from garbage man to the best Mixed Martial Arts (MMA) fighter in the world.

If you ask St-Pierre, it started with a commitment. Once he made that commitment, he had the resolve to stay with it. He made a conscious choice to do something with his life and the fierce resolve to finish what he started. As St-Pierre states in his book, *The Way of the Fight*: "And then, all my energy, everything I had inside of me, went toward achieving that goal [of becoming an MMA champion]. I wasn't making sacrifices anymore; I was making decisions. Train instead of party. Work instead of play. Perfect practice instead of casual repetition."

Every day, we too must bring new resolve to complete what is before us. It's not a one-time static commitment. Limit the little voice in your head that wants to negotiate your commitment. Paradoxically, a 100 percent commitment is much easier than a 99 percent commitment. If I'm going to avoid eating added sugar 99 percent of the time, I keep asking if today is the day? When you make a commitment, your decision is final.

The word *decide* comes from the Latin term *decire*, which means "to cut." Let's make the decision to cut off other options and enjoy not having to make that decision again.

Did you know the artist Michelangelo chose to portray his famous Statue of David at the moment he made the commitment to fight Goliath? He has a sling over his shoulder, a stone in his hand, and looks ready for battle. Like the great Statue of David, let's envision you making the commitment to truly change your life, to become the best person you are capable of becoming.

CREATE HABITS

One of the most powerful ways to make our actions more consistent is through habits. Habits are behaviors that are repeated on a regular basis, so they become fixed. Our life is ultimately shaped by the daily choices we make, which are repeated over time. Brian Tracy said that "successful people are simply those with successful habits."

Our daily actions are not secure until they become habits, free from contrary inclinations. The beauty of habits is they become automatic. By doing the things we want automatically, we reduce the variability of our behavior. We don't waste our willpower or time thinking about things that are already habits.

One specific type of habit is our routines. For example, most of us have a morning routine where we wake up, take a shower, drink coffee, have breakfast, brush our teeth, etc. Without routines, we would be exhausted mentally and physically from having to make all the daily decisions facing us. Routines give us order, organization, and help conserve our energy.

Of course, the opposite is also true. If you repeat a bad habit, that can lead to damaging and destructive consequences over time. It's like the story of the boiling frog. If you put a frog in boiling water, it will jump out immediately. But, if you slowly turn up the heat just a little bit, the frog will eventually be boiled to death. This is true for your health, your work, and your relationships that are based on bad habits that continue.

Because we can dramatically change our lives by our habits—whether adding a good new habit or stopping an old bad habit—we want to get really good at habit formation. How do we create or stop habits?

The ABC Method of Habit Creation

There are many great books on habits, but my two favorites are *Tiny Habits* by B.J. Fogg and *Atomic Habits* by James Clear. Both authors agree that to establish habits, the most effective way is to follow the same simple steps. They also agree that the inability to form or stick with a habit is not likely caused by weak willpower or some character flaw but more likely by a failure to follow one of the steps.

Dr. Fogg is the Director of the Behavior Design Lab at Stanford University, and he says that new habits can be created by following three simple steps. He calls them the ABCs of habits. "ABC" stands for "Anchor," tiny "Behavior," and "Celebration."

The first step in creating a new habit is to have an anchor. Something that is open and obvious that reminds us to engage in a certain behavior. You are anchoring or tying some reminder to a new behavior.

I wanted to start a new routine of drinking a glass of water when I first wake up in the morning. So, I got a big bright cup and put it prominently on my bathroom counter right next to the sink. It's the first thing I see when I enter the bathroom. The cup is the anchor or cue for me to drink my water. Done!

The key to the Anchor is to make it really obvious. Make your anchor stand out. Dr. Fogg explains, "The concept is pretty simple. If there is a habit you want, find the right Anchor within your current routine to serve as your prompt, your routine."

If you want to stop a bad habit, the first step is just the opposite. Instead of making the anchor obvious, the key to stopping a habit is to make the anchor invisible.

I'm particularly vulnerable to cookies. If I walk into the kitchen and there is a plate of cookies on the counter, I am inclined to eat them—all of them—even if I didn't go into the kitchen to get cookies in the first place. If the cookies are not visible, then I won't eat them. This shows the importance of designing your environment to help delete unwanted habits.

I hear many people say they spend too much time on social media. This is particularly difficult because of the addictive dopamine released in your brain when on your cellphone. One effective method is to put your phone away, so it is not always on your person. I have one friend who plugs his phone upstairs in his bathroom, so he must walk upstairs every time he wants to use his phone. If that doesn't work, you can always lock your phone up, create a no-phone zone, give it to your spouse to hold, or delete the tempting apps altogether.

The second step to habit formation is called "tiny behaviors." The key is to make the behavior so small that it is virtually impossible to fail. In other words, make your action so tiny that it is super easy to do.

If you want to create a new habit of walking daily, start by going outside for sixty seconds. That's it. Nothing more than get outside. If you want to start meditating, consider sitting down for just one breath. Done. You have meditated. You want to start being nicer at work? Then just say "hello" to one person. Done.

The goal is to "master the decisive moment." This creates the momentum necessary to fully establish the habit over time. Don't make the habit so big that it won't stick. As an example, I had a friend who really wanted to start going to the gym. He had good intentions, so he went to the gym every day for a week and worked out for ninety minutes. He was so sore that he quit after just five days. It took him years before he wanted to work out again.

When we want to remove a bad habit, we do the reverse of step two: Make it difficult. We take some action or make some commitment that the undesired behavior becomes practically impossible to do. For instance, if you spend too much time on your phone with games and social media, then delete them.

The final step in establishing or deleting a habit is "celebration." When we engage in a desired behavior, we take a quick moment to positively acknowledge our achievement. Studies show even a little mental recognition goes a long way. We do this celebration immediately after engaging in the tiny behavior.

This step is rooted in the scientific notion of positive reinforcement. Actions which have desirable results will recur. We are likely to repeat what makes us happy or provides a reward. If you devoted a deep time block to getting a project complete, celebrate the progress you made. Positive self-talk is an excellent form of celebration. "That's like me!" Or "Way to go!" When I finish my morning workout, I am not only getting stronger and more energetic, but I also experience the emotional high of that accomplishment.

While your mind is wired to pursue behavior that is satisfying, the opposite is also true. When something creates pain, distress, or dissatisfaction, we are not likely to do it again. As James Clear states, "What is rewarded is repeated. What is punished is avoided."

B.J. Fogg says, "If there is one concept from my book I hope you embrace, it's this: People change best by feeling good, not by feeling bad." In fact, the third step of celebration is so important that Dr. Fogg states: "Celebration will one day be ranked alongside mindfulness and gratitude as daily practices that contribute most to our overall happiness and well-being."

Do it Daily!

Once we have the three steps of habit formation in place, our goal is to repeat that behavior consistently until it becomes cemented as a habit. "Repetition is the mother of learning." This oft-quoted saying is embedded in our physiology. Every time we repeat a behavior, we groove it into our brain, specifically, our basal ganglia. So, if we want to form new habits, we must repeat them over and over.

It is debated as to how long it takes to becomes a habit. The psychologist William James postulated it takes twenty-one consecutive days for a habit to form. However, recent studies say the average time for habit formation is typically about sixty days. This is why we make the habit so small we can't fail.

The famous comedian Jerry Seinfeld had the habit of writing one joke every single day. He kept his streak alive for years. It didn't matter how good or bad the joke was. He was committed to the habit. When he finished writing his joke, he would put a big red X in his calendar. He found the more he engaged in the habit, the easier it got.

Once you have formed a habit, you now have a new way of doing things. Keep your habit firmly established by following the ABC method regularly. The great Buddhist monk, Thich Nhat Hahn, tells us to water the positive seeds we want to grow. It is important to regularly water your habits every single day. We consistently show up as the best version of ourselves in our health, work, and love. When the habits that are best for us are also the things we most enjoy, we know we are on the right track.

INSTALL ALGORITHMS

In his book *A Brief History of Tomorrow*, Professor Yuval Harari says that algorithms are "arguably the single most important concept in our world." That's a bold statement from an intelligent man. "An algorithm is a methodical set of steps that can be used to make calculations, resolve problems and reach decisions." It's the basis of artificial intelligence and machine learning. Computers, self-driving cars, and robots all run on algorithms.

A simple example of an algorithm is your air conditioner. An algorithm is written so that if the thermometer reaches a certain temperature, then the AC turns on. I set the AC thermostat at seventy-five degrees. If it's seventy-five degrees, then the AC turns on.

Humans can benefit tremendously from using algorithms. You can learn to program your own brain to run more effectively using algorithms. I use algorithms regularly in my own life, and they have worked exceptionally well for establishing habits.

How do we create an algorithm for our own life? It involves a simple three step process:

First, you start with a specific goal. You need to know what you want.

Second, you need to know what behavior is necessary to achieve that goal.

Third, turn that behavior into an "if/then" statement. The "if/then" statement is the algorithm. Here are a few examples:

Work— "If I'm working on my motion, then I won't check my phone."

Relationships— "If I see a new person at work, then I'll smile and say hello."

Sleep— "If it's 9:00 p.m., then I turn my lights off in bed."

Think of algorithms as a trigger for making decisions. Every time we are prompted by the trigger, we have a pre-determined response or action. It's a process or system for implementing actions. We can create algorithms in almost all aspects of our lives.

In Chapter 7, we discussed how I coached a lawyer, Patricia, on getting healthier. Recall her biggest concern was her health and weight, so she was able to install a few healthy behaviors into algorithms. She particularly needed to move around more during the day. So, we installed an algorithm: "If I sit down at work, I'll set my timer for 30 minutes to get up and move around." If her timer goes off, then she takes a few minutes to move.

Patricia started to add algorithms for her eating. The beauty of this was that changing her eating didn't have to add any more hours or time to her already busy schedule. In fact, by running on algorithms, it saved her time and was more effective.

Patricia happened to select the vegan diet, but the algorithms are the same if you select a different diet, just tailored to that particular diet. Here are her algorithms:

- If I eat, then I follow a vegetarian diet,
- If it's breakfast, then I have a vegan protein shake,
- If it's lunch, then I make sure I have adequate protein from eggs, beans, or dairy,

- If it's dinner, then I have a protein and a vegetable, and
- If it's snack time, I have some nuts, seeds, or fruit.
- Every time I eat, I only eat moderate amounts—one serving /one portion only.

Over the course of the year, Patricia lost twenty-five pounds and, more importantly, feels great. She told me she can't believe what a huge impact the algorithms have made in her life.

I have found algorithms to be great for relationships as well. One friend wanted to connect with her spouse when they both got home from work. Her algorithm was, "When I walk in the door from work, then the first thing I'll do is greet and talk with my husband."

One of the more helpful algorithms that I use is for emotional resilience. I have used an algorithm that "if" something happens that is beyond my control, "then" I will act with emotional control. In other words, I have committed to pre-resilience, knowing I'm going to get knocked off my game on a regular basis. Recently, I drove to a specialty butcher to buy baby back ribs that I was going to grill. After I parked, I realized I forgot my wallet at home, twenty-five minutes away. I immediately realized this was beyond my control, and there was nothing I could do. I didn't stress, but drove back home, and during the drive, had a nice phone call with my daughter. Remember there was no reason to have a negative emotional reaction; in fact, I celebrated my positive response.

We can also create all types of algorithms for our own legal practice or workplace.

"If I'm at work, then I begin each day by planning out my most important priorities."

"If I'm not in court that day, then I'll start with deep-work time blocks."

"If I schedule deep-work time blocks, then I'll do that work before checking emails or other less important tasks."

When I was in trial, I used algorithms to create good habits. They freed me up to focus on the real issues in the case and not on how to act in court. Here are a few examples:

"If the other side asks an objectionable question, then I'll stand and say, 'Objection' and state the legal ground."

"If I'm cross-examining a witness, then I'll ask leading questions."

"If I wish to approach a witness in court, then I will ask, 'Your Honor, may I please approach the witness?"

Just start with one at a time—you can do just one until it becomes automatic—then move to the next algorithm. Over time, you will have established a number of effective algorithms in your life. Algorithms are great energy savers. By reducing decision fatigue, you have much more willpower to devote to important things. I no longer must constantly think about many of the decisions I face each day.

At this point in the book, you will have gained some clarity on what the best version of yourself looks like. Your algorithms should be consistent with that optimal version of yourself.

So much of your life can be improved by running it on algorithms.

KNOW YOUR MOTIVATION

When I was an undergraduate in college, I had a deep desire to get into law school. When I injured my back playing soccer, I was seriously passionate about my recovery in order to get back onto the field. And, when one of my children was seriously ill, I powerfully yearned for his health to return.

Understanding our motivation is our final tool for taking effective action. As Dr. B.J. Fogg states: "You can change your life by changing your behaviors ... But what you may not know is that only three variables drive those behaviors ... Behavior happens when Motivation & Ability & Prompt converge at the same moment."

In other words, our actions or behaviors at any given moment are the result of three factors. These three factors or variables can be presented in a simple formula: Behavior = Motivation + Ability + Prompt. B = MAP. If you want to change your behavior, then change one of these variables.

In this chapter, we have already discussed the "Ability" variable by using such practices as micro-wins, focus, and habits. We have also discussed the "Prompts" variable by using tools such as anchors, cues, and algorithms. As Dr. Fogg says: "Ability is your capacity to do the behavior. And prompt is your cue to do the behavior."

Now, we turn to the third and final variable—Motivation. Motivation provides the reason for our behavior. "Motivation is your desire to do the behavior," writes Dr. Fogg. It is our "why?" Although motivation is listed first in the MAP equation, I'm finishing with motivation, because if you are still having problems getting motivated to take action, I wanted you to get super clear on that now. If your motivation is lacking, you will not likely engage in the behavior.

In the examples from my life at the beginning of this section, my motivation to get into law school, to recover from an injury, and to help my child get better were profound and intense. Finding a strong motivation is like transforming hot water into steam. At 211 degrees, water can be made into a cup of hot coffee. But, if our motivation is strong, then we can raise the temperature just one more degree to 212, and we'll have boiling water and steam, which can propel a train or a ship. Getting clear on your motivation is like boiling water. It creates the momentum to make a real change in our lives.

There are two primary types of motivation—extrinsic and intrinsic. Both can be effective. Although there are other types of motivation, we are going to focus on those big two. Often, we can have multiple motives (both intrinsic and extrinsic) for taking a certain action.

Extrinsic motivation comes from outside factors or the outside world. It's the carrot and the stick approach. Dangle the carrot to pursue a reward. Do something, and you'll benefit or profit in some material way. Alternatively, there is the stick. You better not do something or there might be some type of penalty or negative consequence. Earn rewards and avoid punishments.

Most people are extrinsically motivated, in part, by some kind of reward. For our work, we want and need to get paid money to buy clothes, put food on the table, provide for housing, take a vacation, and so on. For students, it might be earning that scholarship or a coveted job. You go to the gym to get those ripped abs and take selfies.

In contrast, intrinsic motivation comes from inside the person. People are intrinsically motivated because they enjoy the activity or the internal benefit. We do the work because it brings us great satisfaction or growth. We perform that workout because it gives us great energy. This type of motivation often improves your well-being and self-esteem.

Intrinsic motivation can also derive from negative experiences or knowing that we don't want to behave in a certain way. We want to be different parents to our children than our parents were to us, to not struggle financially, to stop smoking, to take better care of ourselves after a health scare, or to stop wasting time.

While extrinsic motivation can be powerful, those who desire mastery, autonomy, and purpose typically draw on their intrinsic motivation. As leading researcher and author, Dan Pink, noted in his book, *Drive*, people who are intrinsically motivated outperform those who are extrinsically motivated in almost every facet. Pink writes:

"When it comes to motivation, there's a gap between what science knows and what business does. Our current business operating system—which is built around external, carrot-and-stick motivators—doesn't work and often does harm. We need an upgrade. And the science shows the way. This new approach has three essential elements: (a) *Autonomy*—the desire to direct our own lives; (2) *Mastery*—the urge to get better and better at something that matters; and (3) *Purpose*—the yearning to do what we do in the service of something larger than ourselves."[11]

In order to make this highly practical, you will want to identify your spark. Your spark will typically come from your ambitions, desires, or expectations. You want to get really clear on what you want.

As one of the foremost experts in motivation, Brendon Burchard, said in his book, *The Motivation Manifesto*, if we are both clear and committed in our motivation, our action level will be high. And the opposite is true: If we are unclear or uncommitted in our motivation, the intensity level of our actions will be lower.

Not only do we require motivation, but we also need to sustain it. When life gets tough, which it will, we need the motivation to get out of bed every day and then go after our goals, love others, as well as become the best versions of ourselves. We remind ourselves of our motivation consistently. We tap into our strong "why" daily. This empowers us to take effective action toward our most meaningful goals.

Chapter Summary:

You can take effective action toward our goals by:
- Having a single-minded focus on one goal at a time,
- Being fully present and without distractions or interruptions,
- Pursuing one micro-win after another,
- Creating habits and installing algorithms, so your behavior runs on autopilot, and
- Understanding your motivation for your behaviors.

SIDEBAR _____

Let me talk about a different kind of "presence." It's important to have your clients "present" at trial. You want to humanize your client and give a face to the trial. This is easy when your client's life is in shambles or has been injured, but there have been numerous times in trial with corporate and governmental parties where no person appeared at the trial. The entity's attorney asked the jury to show up every day to hear its case, but he or she didn't seem to care enough to send a personal representative to be present. That's a big mistake.

The Third Pillar of Flourishing

VIRTUE: Have High Standards

CHAPTER 15

CHARACTER AND VIRTUE

• • •

"You're never wrong to do the right thing."
— MARK TWAIN

I f you had to pick just one thing that has had the most significant impact in your adult life, what would it be? Aside from the critical decisions of marriage, kids, and career, if I had to choose just one, it would be the book group that I started with one of my best friends, Scott. We were both business majors who had recently graduated and were just starting out in our professional careers. We were making decent money and doing well in our jobs.

At the same time, we both felt there was something missing. We shared a deep curiosity about life but weren't sure where to go or what to do to discover that missing void. So, we agreed to start reading some books to see if they could give us some guidance on our quest. In doing some research, I came across a book program called the Great Books, which consisted of the preeminent classics of Western Civilization.

We read the first book in the program called *Rothschild's Fiddle* by the Russian playwright Anton Chekhov and were immediately hooked. We then read *Apology* by Plato and discovered what he called "that dear delight" of philosophy. We met once a month, devoured the books, and delved deeply into life's great questions. Most of what we learn in school and work is knowledge, but these books provided wisdom.

About a year into our book group, we read Plato's *Republic*. In that book, there is a famous story known as the Allegory of the Cave. Although there are multiple meanings, the Allegory essentially involves people who were shackled in a dark cave since birth. The only thing they could see were shadows on a wall from a fire behind them in the cave. They are then freed and exposed to light, which is a metaphor for wisdom.

When they eventually leave the cave, they are at first blinded by the light. But as their eyes adjusted to the light, they began to see colors, shapes, and depth. As it is with wisdom, the more we become enlightened, the more we can understand the world and our own lives. The Allegory describes how an insightful education can profoundly transform a person.

Based on that Allegory, we named our book group, "Plato's Cave." We have been meeting monthly for over 30 years. This study has been, as Elizabeth Browning said, "my meat and drink." For every book read, we tried to distill the essence of the book down to one key principle. Here is a short sample from our journaling about these books:

Apology by Plato
You are wise if you know that you do not know everything and that you continue to search for the truth. "The unexamined life is not worth living."

The Lessons of History by Will and Ariel Durant
The first lesson of history: Life is competition.

The Heart of the Buddha's Teaching by Thich Nhat Hanh
Buddha teaches us to recognize and be aware of our own suffering. We can transform our suffering into peace and joy.

Nicomachean Ethics by Aristotle
Happiness is the chief good in life (the summum bonum).

Willpower by Roy Baumeister
Willpower is like a muscle; it can be exhausted by overuse or depleted by a lack energy, but it also can be strengthened thru mental exercise, rest, and nutrition.

Let the Trumpet Sound: A Life of Martin Luther King, Jr. by Stephen B. Oates
King used love and non-violent action to fight racism. "Darkness cannot drive out darkness; only light can do that. Hate cannot drive out hate; only love can do that."

The Social Contract by Jean-Jacques Rosseau

Legitimate political authority comes only from a social contract agreed upon by all citizens for their mutual preservation. "Man is born free but everywhere in chains."

Win Forever by Pete Carroll

Always compete, not with others, but yourself to maximize your own potential. Strive every day to become the very best version of you.

Mindset by Carol Dweck

Having a growth mindset is essential for your success in life. Habitually ask: "What can I learn from this? What will I do next time I'm in this situation?"

Plato's Cave has afforded us the great privilege of spending quality time with some of the greatest thinkers throughout history. As the members of our book group have faced our own unique joys and challenges—the ups and downs of life—we have drawn on the wisdom of those esteemed authors.

Based on all those great books, our many deep discussions, and my own personal experience, it has become crystal clear to me that *living with character is key to the good life*. The ancients called it virtue, but in modern times we more often refer to it as character. Many people are good at making goals and taking action (our first and second pillars). But, what most of us (and society) need more of is living with good character. That's why our third and final Pillar for Flourishing is Virtue.

WHAT IS VIRTUE?

I previously discussed in the goals section of this book that John Wooden is considered one of the greatest coaches ever. It wasn't just that his teams won ten national championships in college basketball, including seven in a row. It was *how* he did it, with great character and leadership.

Wooden taught his players to always do things the right way. In fact, at his first practice of each new season, the first thing he did was teach his players how to put on their socks correctly. There is a right way and a wrong way. Once you put on your socks properly, then your shoes fit ideally; you're less likely to get blisters and more likely to perform better. Your feet are the foundation for athletic performance.[1]

Wooden created his famous Pyramid of Success, which served as a roadmap for individual and team excellence. Interestingly, the Pyramid was devoid of any reference to basketball. Instead, the Pyramid consisted of character strengths, such as industriousness, friendship, loyalty, cooperation, and enthusiasm.

The terms "virtue" and "character" will be used interchangeably here. The dictionary defines "virtue" as conforming to a standard of right conduct or moral excellence. Similarly, "character" is defined as moral excellence and firmness.

There are two essential qualities of virtue and character: moral conduct and excellence. It's doing the right thing *and* doing it with excellence. Aristotle said it is doing the right thing rightly. This chapter will examine the first quality of virtues and character, and the next chapter will discuss excellence.

Interestingly, the word *virtue* comes from the Latin word *virtu*, which means "strength" or "prowess." Did you know that virtue gives you strength? Many individuals today think virtue sounds soft or weak. "Oh, he is virtuous like some timid choir boy," or "she is virtuous like some shy flower." Nothing could be farther from the truth.

I prefer to think of individuals who possess virtue as our modern-day heroes, our real-life Marvel or DC Superheroes. We should bring our virtuous strengths to all our challenges and actions.

Equally fascinating is the word *character*, which comes from a Greek word meaning "to be chiseled." Of course, a chisel is a sharp steel tool used for making a sculpture out of a hard material, like marble. Our character is chiseled over time, by acting with either virtue or vice. Everything that happens to you, good or bad, is an opportunity for building your character.

Virtue and character deal with your inner life. Your central core. The essence of who you are. If you read all the wisdom literature throughout history, you would find universal agreement that the good life starts with a good inner life. It's about playing your game well from the inside out.

VIRTUE IS NOT JUST IMPORTANT
BUT ESSENTIAL

I love the Harry Potter books for many reasons, and one of them is their dramatic depiction of Harry attempting to face his challenges with virtue. Harry's headmaster at the Hogwarts school is Dumbledore, who is a model for Aristotle's virtues. Dumbledore's wisdom empowers Harry to act with courage.

In the second Harry Potter movie, *Harry Potter and the Chamber of Secrets*, Harry is concerned his powers are like those of the evil Voldemort. Dispelling those concerns, the sage Dumbledore tells Harry he will not become evil because Harry's character is the foundation of his actions, not his capabilities. Dumbledore states: "It is our choices ... that show what we truly are, far more than our abilities."

Whether it is Harry versus Voldemort, Luke Skywalker versus Darth Vader in *Star Wars*, or Atticus Finch versus Bob Ewell in *To Kill a Mockingbird*, the difference in their behaviors is striking, and what separates them is virtue.

You simply cannot flourish without acting with virtue. If you want to live your best life, you must live with good character. Period. As we discussed earlier in this book, Aristotle made this clear 2,500 years ago, when he stated: "But what is happiness? ... we find that **happiness** is **virtuous** activity of the soul" (emphasis added). Happiness and virtue are inextricably intertwined. No virtue, no flourishing.

The maxim that virtuous activity is essential for flourishing has never wavered across cultures and time. Contemporaneously, when modern positive psychologists comprehensively studied this very issue, they concluded that virtue is absolutely necessary to flourish. Science has shown it is the true foundation for the good life.

At the same time, the world has lost its moral compass. Lawyers' reputations for being virtuous and having character are at an all-time low. We need virtue and character more now than ever before.

In the first year of law school, my Civil Procedure professor, Erwin Chemerinsky, loved to intersperse crucial ethics lessons into his law school lectures. In one hypothetical, he posed an ethical dilemma facing a young lawyer, who had just landed a big new client, a Hollywood star who was starting a major winery. This new client would virtually guarantee the lawyer would make partner. Shortly after retaining the lawyer, however, the client contacted the lawyer to give her bad news. The client had discovered the wine contained trace amounts of a chemical which were potentially injurious, even fatal, to a small segment of the population. If the wine had to be recalled, however, the company would go under.

Most students argued the lawyer owed a duty of loyalty to the client, which compelled her to find a way to sell the wine. A few brave souls, however, said the company could not sell the contaminated wine, even if it meant the company would have to go bankrupt. Professor Chemerinsky concluded his discussion of the hypothetical with the axiom that lawyers must always act ethically first and foremost. He said, "Lawyers who act unethically are worse than prostitutes, because while prostitutes sell their bodies, unethical lawyers sell their souls."

If I could advise lawyers that if they could only have one trait, the most important would be having a strong character. There is simply nothing more important than a lawyer's character and reputation. Once it is gone, it is very difficult to recapture.

Both ancient and modern thinkers agree one of the most important virtues you can possess is courage. We will discuss courage in more detail below, but in essence, I define it as the ability to act virtuously in the face of either fear or greed. Yes, we often think of courage in dealing with our fears, such as flying in an airplane or giving a speech in front of a large crowd. But often, what you are going to face in life and the law is having character in the face of greed. It's very important to get clear on this because you are frequently going to have to make these decisions by yourself. Lawyers will hear that little voice asking, "Can I get away with this?" I'll just fudge the proof of service or make a representation that is not entirely true. It's so easy to justify such behaviors.

Just as in the previous wine hypothetical, the lawyer is so close to making partner. So, she justifies to herself that it may only harm a few people. She further rationalizes that the victims will never know that the wine caused the illness and that recalling the wine would be financially devastating to the client, the company (and herself personally). That's why we must always have the courage to do the right thing.

Yes, lawyers can attain some material success without character, but in the long run, almost all unethical individuals will falter. The problem is that self-interested desires usually prevail over disinterested virtue. The person without virtue will not flourish, find true peace, or attain lasting happiness. A good life must be built on a solid foundation of virtues.

THE SPECIFIC VIRTUES

When Benjamin Franklin was twenty-seven years old, he felt a great need to improve his life and decided to identify the most universal of all truths. He identified thirteen essential virtues: temperance, silence, order, resolution, frugality, industry, sincerity, justice, moderation, cleanliness, tranquility, chastity, and humility.[2]

Franklin's list is excellent but hardly comprehensive. There is no one set of agreed upon virtues for all people across all time. For instance, in Buddhism, although there are numerous schools of thought, one popular list of virtues includes kindness, compassion, joy, generosity, proper conduct, wisdom, energy, patience, honesty, determination, good will, and equanimity.

Likewise, Christian virtues as stated in the Bible include love, joy, peace, patience, kindness, goodness, faithfulness, gentleness, and self-control. According to the Hindu scholar, Manusamhita, Hinduism has essentially five main virtues: non-violence, self-restraint, non-covetousness/non-stealing, inner purity, and truthfulness.

The ancient Greek philosophers, including Socrates and the Stoics, said there are four cardinal virtues: wisdom, justice, courage, and temperance.

Recently, Martin Seligman and Christopher Peterson undertook a comprehensive three-year study to catalog all the virtues around the globe, including different cultures, countries, and religions over the span of three millennia. They identified twenty-four universal character strengths, all of which fell under six main virtues:

1. Wisdom,
2. Courage,
3. Justice,
4. Humanity,
5. Temperance, and
6. Transcendence.

Drs. Seligman and Peterson noted just how much similarity and congruence there is when it comes to virtues and character.[3] All the great cultures, religions, and philosophies, essentially share the same virtues. The bottom line from this detailed survey on virtues is there is substantial agreement across all cultures and all times on what makes a virtuous person and what constitutes character strengths.

JUDGE PFAHLER'S TOP 10 VIRTUES

Most of the ancient lists of virtues are based on moral virtues, but they lack joy and positive emotions. Many of the modern lists of virtues include positive virtues, but they often forget the moral virtues.

As Stephen Covey observed in the *7 Habits of Highly Effective People*, most of the success literature for the first 150 years of the United States' existence focused on virtues of character, such as integrity, fairness, justice, courage, and love. After World War I, the prevailing view shifted to a personality ethic, such as positive attitude, people skills, enthusiasm, and so on.

Personality strengths alone, without moral virtues, is like a house built on sand. It may look nice, but it's not going to hold up to life's challenges. Virtues need to have a moral character to them to be complete and strong. At the same time, the modern emphasis on positive character strengths is an important addition to our overall happiness and well-being. It's the synergistic impact of all essential virtues that leads to flourishing.

With this understanding, I compiled what I believe to be a comprehensive set of humanistic virtues. These essential virtues will allow us to live the good life, overcome setbacks, do the right thing, and develop strength of character.

While all these virtues are vital, the two master virtues in life are love and wisdom. These two virtues are absolutely the cornerstones for the good life. Interestingly, when you combine these two virtues together, do you know what results? The Greek word for love is *philo*, and the Greek word for wisdom is *sophia*. Thus, a combination of love and wisdom is, as you can now guess, "philosophy." The lover of wisdom. As we incorporate virtue into our lives, let's approach it as a practical philosopher with love and wisdom.

Without further ado, here are my Top 10 Virtues.

1. Love

Love is the most powerful force in the universe. Love provides the ultimate super-power. We can love God, ourselves, others, our work, the world, and our passions. In fact, all our priorities are rooted in love. Live by the Golden Rule—perhaps the greatest rule of all time—which implores us to love others as ourselves. An entire constellation of key character strengths emanates out of love: kindness, caring, service, generosity, warmth, gentleness, tenderness, compassion, empathy, loyalty, and gratitude.

While all these character strengths are essential, gratitude seems to have the most studies correlated with happiness. Gratitude includes a love and appreciation for all that you have in life and all those that have made your life so blessed. Gratitude is often considered the key to a happy life.

Remember that love also includes loving ourselves. Don't be harder on yourself than on others. Love for yourself includes all the character strengths mentioned above.

2. Wisdom

Wisdom is defined as guidance for living. It entails both knowledge and action. Neither knowledge nor education alone is wisdom. Most people define wisdom as what you know, but it is *applying* what you know to a specific task. Knowledge is a noun, but wisdom is a verb. It's actively doing something with the knowledge.

The key character strengths arising out of wisdom include rationality, discernment, perception, curiosity, and learning. Through wisdom, we know what is truly important in life and what virtue to apply in any given situation. Wisdom serves as the bridge between knowledge and application.

We have already discussed the critical importance of being rational, especially in determining what we can and cannot control. Now, I want to briefly discuss two other crucial character strengths related to wisdom—curiosity and self-awareness.

Curiosity. Curiosity is the starting point of wisdom. Socrates noted, "The unexamined life is not worth living." Curiosity is the desire to know something; it is the love of learning. Curiosity precedes wisdom. It tells us what needs work and what is working well. Curiosity allows us to evaluate our life, evolve, and spiral upwards.

Curiosity is about approaching life as our classroom and looking at every moment as an opportunity to learn, to get better, to gather data. The opposite of curiosity is apathy. It's not surprising that "[t]he cure for boredom is curiosity. There is no cure for curiosity."[4] Curiosity is a sign your soul is alive. I have some friends who do not possess curiosity. They are good people who are content with their lives. Sometimes such a life is envious, as it can be tiring to always be curious. But then, I realize that if the purpose of life is to progress and to maximize our potential, you simply cannot flourish without a degree of curiosity.

Self-Awareness. In ancient Greece, the very first maxim carved into the stone entrance of the Temple of Apollo is "Know thyself." My mentor called this maxim the two most important words in the English language. Knowing yourself is synonymous with self-awareness. You know who you are, understand your values and beliefs, and are aware of your thoughts and emotions. It's seeing your inner self clearly and objectively. It's not lying or deceiving yourself.

Knowing yourself becomes a superpower. Once you have that superpower, you no longer need to be uncertain or ashamed about who you are and what is important to you. Maslow characterizes such self-awareness as being "post-ambivalent," where you have so completely accepted yourself that you can truly let go of the opinions of others and connect with what truly makes you alive. Shakespeare said, similarly, "To thine own self be true." From ancient to modern—from Socrates to Seligman—self-awareness is key to growth, inner peace, and flourishing.

3. Courage

Courage is the ability to act in the face of fear or the temptation of greed. Courage does not mean eliminating the fear altogether. It means you do what needs to be done even despite your fear. Yes, it's the soldier running toward gun fire, the firefighter running into a burning building, and Rosa Parks refusing to give up her seat on the bus simply because she was Black. But fear and greed also involve the everyday decisions to move toward risk or to simply say "no." It's taking a chance with a new job, not being afraid to be your authentic self, or having a difficult conversation with a spouse.

Also, as discussed previously in this chapter about the law school hypothetical involving the contaminated wine, you maintain your courage even in the face of greed, even if it may harm you in the short run.

Courage comes from the root of the Latin word "*cor*," meaning heart. Aristotle noted that courage is considered a pivotal virtue because, like the heart that pumps blood throughout the body, it vitalizes all the other virtues. It's certainly one of the most important moral virtues because it inspires right actions and is necessary for a flourishing life. The character strengths of courage include bravery, fortitude, valor, and self-confidence.

4. Self-Control

Self-control is the ability to govern, temper, and restrain one's actions, emotions, and desires. Some of the character strengths of self-control include self-discipline, temperance, willpower, moderation, prudence, patience, and frugality. The essence of self-control is self-regulation. The ability to govern oneself and stay on the middle path.

Repeated research has scientifically confirmed that nearly all aspects of your life can be improved by self-control. In his great book, *Willpower*, Roy Baumeister shows there are two scientifically validated predictors for success in life: IQ and willpower. While IQ is mostly fixed, willpower is not. Baumeister says many of the major problems we face in life—such as a lack of exercise, poor eating, overspending, overconsuming alcohol, taking drugs, procrastination, anger management, and overall underachievement—emanate from a lack of self-control.

5. Zest

Zest refers to great energy and enthusiasm. If we want to succeed at work and thrive in our relationships, we need to have the energy to bring to those all-important priorities. If you have zest, you are actively engaged, alive, and full of vitality in your work and love. In fact, zest is so important that positive psychologists believe it is the number one, character strength most affiliated with happiness.

Some of the character strengths of zest include initiative, focus, diligence, goal-oriented, resourcefulness, intensity, zeal, and enthusiasm. Ben Franklin referred to the energy he brought to his activities as "Industry." Good old-fashioned hard work. There is no way around it. Great leaders, thinkers, athletes, and professionals succeed in large part because of the energy and hard work they bring to their endeavors. The great basketball coach, John Wooden, emphatically declared: "I challenge you to show me one single solitary individual who achieved his or her personal greatness without lots of hard work."[5]

6. Justice

Justice is one of the four cardinal virtues of the ancient Greeks and one of the six cornerstone virtues identified by Martin Seligman and his team. Justice concerns how we interact with other people. It instructs us to respect the rights and dignity of all persons. However, it's much more than simply abiding by laws. It is first and foremost a positive virtue. Justice provides positive guidance for living in groups, communities, nation, and the world.

Justice includes the character strengths of fairness, equality, respect, civility, tolerance, goodness, citizenship, impartiality, and responsibility. It teaches us to be good citizens in this world and to aim for a just society. Justice means you are acting for the common good.

Victor Frankl said there are only two races of people—the decent and the indecent. Justice does not tolerate racism, sexism, illegal discrimination, or prejudice of any kind. Justice demands all people are treated equally under the law. We stand up against injustice and confront racial, gender, and other improper biases.

7. Honesty

We all know honesty means telling the truth. We are straightforward in what we say and how we act. We keep our word. The character strengths of honesty include truthfulness, authenticity, sincerity, and integrity. And the vices are ones we all recognize—dishonesty, fraud, fake, insincere, deceit, cheating, stealing, deception, and misrepresentation.

When I attended college, I loved studying in the philosophy library, which was designed after a medieval monastery. At the entrance to the building, there was a Statue of Diogenes, the famous Cynic philosopher with lantern in hand, still looking for the first honest man. What an unfortunate commentary that honesty is such a difficult virtue to attain.

We would be well served to model our veracity after "Honest Abe." In 1850, when Abraham Lincoln was a lawyer, he gave a speech discussing the key qualities of a lawyer. He implored: "[R]esolve to be honest at all events; and if in your own judgment you cannot be an honest lawyer, resolve to be honest without being a lawyer."[6]

8. Joy

Having a sense of inner joy and a positive attitude is essential for well-being and flourishing. My primary criticism of the four cardinal virtues is they lack joy and happiness. Modern positive psychology is premised on having a sense of well-being and lists "positive emotions" as the first attribute of flourishing. In fact, it is so important that psychologists named their entire field "positive" psychology.

The character strengths of joy include positivity, optimism, hope, confidence, playfulness, and a sense of humor. I would assert that joy is a moral virtue. A negative attitude can cause worry, stress, and anxiety on yourself and others. Negativity and despair often place a genuine burden on others. On the other hand, a positive attitude can be a real strength to yourself and the people around you. People with a genuine sense of joy tend to act more graciously and civilly.

One of the greatest "aha" moments in my life came when I truly understood that happiness and joy are an inside job. Most people think joy and happiness are based on external circumstances. If my health or weight is good, I'm happy. If my career is going well or I won that case, I'm joyful. If my relationship is not having problems, I'll be positive. No! And do not equate happiness with success or money. They are both good but never a condition for happiness. As Lincoln famously said, "Most people are about as happy as they make up their minds to be." Our attitudes are always within our own control.

9. Perseverance

Because we face constant obstacles and challenges, we must be able to keep going. When we get knocked down, perseverance picks us back up and finishes the race. The character strengths of perseverance include endurance, grit, patience, and resilience.

My mother was one of nine children. Tragically, six of the nine children (including my mother) were afflicted with the deadly polio virus before a vaccination existed. They stayed strong, persevered, and eventually beat the disease. In overcoming her hardship, my mother inspired me by example to have a strong sense of resolve.

"When the going gets tough, the tough get going." It gives you that inner strength to finish, to push through challenges, to remain resilient. Katherine Dunham said: "Go within every day and find your inner strength so that the world will not blow your candle out."[7] "Perseverance must finish its work."[8]

10. Humility

My tenth indispensable virtue is humility. It is often defined as a state of being humble or modest. However, humility is not a virtue of weakness. To the contrary, it is a virtue of great strength. Strong people don't need the spotlight. They don't crave attention or need to be seen as someone special. They do the work that needs to be done without expecting any applause. Humility gives us the power to be free from certain traits, such as arrogance, conceit, egotism, assumption, superiority, pride, and pretension. Without humility, we don't see our own shortcomings, and they are often concealed by our own ego or pride.

With humility, you also become aware that you are not perfect and never will be. That you don't know everything and never will. That you are not always right. That you don't have all the answers. With humility, you can learn, grow, and become better. If you want to be wise, then be humble. As the Jewish proverb says, "With humility comes wisdom."

OPERATIONALIZING VIRTUE

Most of us are aware that virtues exist but either find them too vague and imprecise to be helpful, or they don't apply them to their lives. Yet, the more I have studied virtues, the more I have come to the emphatic conclusion they are both sufficiently clear and extremely essential to each of our lives.

In fact, the more we study, live, and practice developing our character, the stronger our character becomes. Almost everything can be done with virtue. Because virtues are so far-reaching and important, we want to excel at applying them to our lives. It's what Rosa Chun called "operationalizing virtue." This is playing the virtue game well. Let me offer three of the most effective practices to implement virtuous living: the golden mean, integrity, and daily practice.

The Golden Mean

One of the most practical ways to live with virtue is to use the "golden mean." This term was coined by Aristotle, who said each virtue has two vices on either side of it. One is the vice of deficiency, and the other is the vice of excess. In between the two is the sweet spot – the golden mean. (The term "mean" is the middle point.)

For example, take the virtue of courage. You can have too much or too little courage. The vice of deficiency of courage is cowardice. To not face your fears but to run away or avoid them altogether. The vice of excess is rashness. To do something completely foolhardy, such as trying to run across a busy freeway. That is not courage but stupidity. But courage is the willingness to confront our challenges and act in the face of fear.

Buddha called this the "middle way." The path between two extremes. Aristotle said that virtue "is incompatible with excess or deficiency." One of the most effective ways to think about the golden mean is an Inverted-U curve. The top of the curve represents the maximum benefit.

It is possible to have too much of a good thing.

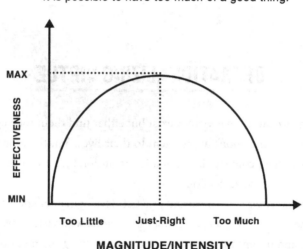

The inverted or upside down "U" shows at one end the vice of deficiency or too little of something. At the other end, is the vice of excess or too much. At the top is just right… the golden mean.

The golden mean can apply to virtually all aspects in our life. Take your finances for instance. You don't want to spend more money than you have, so that you are in debt. Nor do you want to spend so little that you are a miser. The middle ground is temperance and moderation.

We can examine and apply any of our virtues and character strengths through the lens of the golden mean. Take exercise as another example. Some people tend to do little to nothing in terms of exercise. Others, including me, are often guilty of doing too much. But finding that right amount of exercise will lead to optimal health and vitality.

Of course, what constitutes the golden mean will be unique to every individual. A person who is a well-trained, competitive distance runner is going to have a different sweet spot for exercise than a sedentary person who has never exercised before. While virtues are universal, applying the golden mean is flexible and personal to each person.

Integrity

Unlike many of the concepts in this book—such as goal setting, daily planning, AM and PM bookends—living with virtue is not easily quantifiable. Instead of an objective standard, we seek to live our virtues with integrity. Integrity means an alignment between your virtues and values, on the one hand, and your actions, on the other. Integrity derives from the Latin word, *integer*, meaning completeness or wholeness. It's walking your talk. Keeping your promises to yourself and others.

The opposite of integrity is often self-deception and justification. When we take actions inconsistent with our virtues, we then try to justify or explain away our misbehavior. We make excuses, such as "Yeah, I should help my spouse but …" or "I 'have' to do this … so I can't finish my important project."

Stephen Covey powerfully describes the importance of integrity in his book, *The 7 Habits of Highly Effective People*: "I believe that a life of integrity is the most fundamental source of personal worth. I do not agree with the popular success literature that says that self-esteem is primarily a matter of mindset, of attitude—that you can psych yourself into peace of mind. Peace of mind comes when your life is in harmony with true principles and values and in no other way."

When I was in my second year of law school, I was dating a few people but no one seriously. I then went on a date with an attractive young woman, Jolie. She was special! We had a few more amazing dates, and I knew there was long-term potential. However, shortly before our first date, another girl I was dating invited me to an Elton John concert, and I accepted.

The night after my third date with Jolie, she came over and asked me if I wanted to go to the Elton John concert—the same concert I was already going to with another girl. I said, "Thank you very much, but I can't, as I already have other plans that night." Jolie said no problem, as she had other friends who would love to go.

My mind immediately started thinking. What are the odds that I run into Jolie at the concert while I'm on date with this other girl? I could just picture it: "Oh, hi Jolie, this is Mary.

She invited me to Elton John before you did. Sorry I didn't tell you." More importantly, my conscience told me that I was not being completely candid with Jolie. It didn't feel right.

The next day, I told Jolie the truth. I stated that I had previously accepted another invite to the Elton John concert, but the reality was I really wanted to go with her. I jokingly said, "I would be happy to meet you somewhere at intermission!" I realized that my heart and mind were with Jolie, and I told her so. Very maturely, she said, "No," and to have fun at the concert.

That concert was the last time I dated anyone other than Jolie. She is now my wife and has told me she appreciates my integrity. I have thought about how my decision to live in alignment with my values of being open and honest paved the way for marrying my beautiful wife. I also thought about how I could have ruined our relationship before it got off the ground. We may not have gotten married and had our three amazing children.

Whether it is in your relationships, health, or work, you should always strive for integrity. How's your own integrity? Are you living in alignment with your virtues and values? If you want to flourish, this is the key: to be virtuous. Not just to put on an act. The Latin phrase *esse quam videri* means "to be rather than to seem." Let's not just seem to be virtuous; let's *be* virtuous. Let's strive for integrity daily.

Virtue Practice

While virtue is technically a noun, but if must be acted upon. I think of virtue as a verb. It's only effective as an action word. It's measured by our deeds. Virtue without action is meaningless. Because we strive to attach *all* our actions to virtues, it is essential we have a deliberate daily practice. I'm absolutely convinced that the most effective way to live with virtue is to remind ourselves—nay, immerse ourselves—every day in our virtues and then consciously and intentionally act with virtue, so it becomes habitual.

Why do we need a daily practice? The answer is simple. Because we want to live with virtue *always*. That's right. If somebody asks: When should we live with virtue? The answer is "always". Virtuous action is valuable under all circumstances. It helps you deal with the good times and the bad. Whether we are lucky or unlucky, our character is constant.

But what if someone doesn't deserve our virtuous actions? Aren't there certain conditions under which we don't act with virtue? The answer is unequivocally "No." You remain virtuous even if others are not. Just because someone acts inappropriately, unethically, or impolitely should never give you an excuse to do the same. For most people, when they are wronged, the natural thing is to get angry, seek revenge, or do something spiteful in return. However, we want to turn that type of "natural" behavior upside down. Virtue calls us to live in a radically different way.

So, we live with virtue unconditionally because of who we are, not because of what the other person has done. Your virtue is unconditional because of your own character. You take the high road, because it is the right thing to do, whether the other person deserves it or not. Character is not conditional.

The first step in our daily practice is to review and remind ourselves of our virtues. Character is not inborn. It does not happen automatically. In fact, the opposite is true. Without parenting, education, and practice, people will lack strong character. We need to take deliberate and careful effort toward cultivating our character through education and habitual repetition.

In his book, *Staring Down the Wolf,* former Navy SEAL Mark Divine drives home the point of the need for a daily virtues practice, using a Native American parable:

On a beautiful, starlit evening, a Cherokee grandfather told his grandson about a battle that goes on inside of people.

The battle is between two wolves inside each of us.

One wolf is named vice. That wolf is filled with greed, anger, fear, hate, lust, dishonesty, envy, arrogance, regret, superiority, and ego.

The other wolf is named virtue. This wolf demonstrates love, wisdom, joy, serenity, hope, courage, loyalty, trust, justice, kindness, generosity, truth, and humility.

Pondering the grandfather's words, the grandson asks: "Which wolf wins?"

The wise grandfather simply responds: "The one you feed."[9]

Just like we need to feed ourselves food every day, I would assert that if you want to forge strong character, you must feed your mind daily with virtue. I do this daily in my Masterpeace Day Plan, where I identify the key virtues that I most want to embody. I also journal in the evenings, where my primary focus is on the virtues identified that day. So, I begin and end each day with virtues.

After reminding ourselves of the virtues we want to embody, then, most importantly, we need to practice them. Put your virtues in action. In his autobiography, Ben Franklin discussed how he strove daily for moral perfection by trying to live his life according to the thirteen virtues. Near the end of his life, Franklin reflected on this pursuit:

"Tho I never arrived at the perfection of them that I had been so ambitious of obtaining but fell far short of it, yet I was by the endeavor, a better and happier man than I otherwise should have been if I had not attempted it at all."[10]

Franklin devised a specific plan for his endeavor. He focused on one virtue at a time. He kept a journal of how he did each day. Each time Franklin thought he had mastered a virtue, he was reminded of the thirteenth virtue—humility. Franklin's ultimate aim was to have virtue so baked into his character that they became habits.

Let's follow Ben Franklin's example and practice our virtues every day. It is the persistent practice and application of virtue that forms a habit, which becomes your character. Each day, ask how you can act with virtue at this very moment? This is where it all comes together: We are living a purpose-driven life, taking actions toward that purpose, and doing it with virtue. This is flourishing—where your goals, actions, and virtues are all aligned.

You wake up in the morning and summon your *zest* and tap into your *wisdom* to guide you throughout the day. You start your exercise and seize on your *self-discipline* and *persistence*. When it's time to eat, and you are offered a donut or that sugary cereal is staring at you from the pantry, then you can call upon your *self-control*. You get to work and are *industrious, focused, and courageous*. You arrive home from work and spend time *in joy* and *presence* with your family. Throughout your day, you live out these virtues.

It's time to set a new standard for ourselves, one built on a solid foundation of character. Remember the ultimate game we are playing is flourishing, and this life can only be attained through living with virtue. Starting today, be that radiantly virtuous self.

....

Chapter Summary:

- **Virtue and character describe your ideal behaviors.**
- **You should act with character and virtue always, as they are essential for flourishing.**
- **Determine what virtues and character strengths are most important for you.**
- **Strive for integrity by aligning your virtues and your actions.**

SIDEBAR _____

Always take the high road. Treat opposing counsel with respect, even if he or she does not do the same. Being civil, courteous, and considerate to others is not only better for your personal well-being, but it also makes you a much more effective lawyer.

CHAPTER 16

EXCELLENCE AND MASTERY

• • •

"If it's not worth doing excellently,
it's not worth doing at all."

—JOHN W. GARDENER

It was the first day of trial and Terry awoke at 5:00 a.m. after a good night's sleep to finish her opening statement. It was "go time." Terry loved trial, and she was a skilled trial lawyer. She had practiced her opening statement for the past week, and now it was almost perfect.

Terry didn't just wake up at 5:00 a.m. for her trial. She woke up at 5:00 a.m. every weekday to go to work. She was up before dawn to do her deep work before the busyness of the day started. Every day, Terry practiced her craft of being a great lawyer and of taking care of her energy through good sleep and an exercise routine. And it showed. Her success rate was phenomenal; she had more business than she knew what to do with and was in good health.

This is what excellent professionals do. They practice their profession every day with the intent to be great. In his book, *Raise Your Game*, Alan Stein Jr., tells the story about asking the late, great basketball player Kobe Bryant if he could watch him practice. Kobe said sure and that it starts at 4 o'clock. Stein inquired, "4:00 p.m.?" Kobe smiled, saying, "No, 4:00 a.m."

At the 4:00 a.m. practice session, Kobe worked on the most fundamental of skills, including basic dribbling, footwork, and layups, doing so with incredible focus. Blown away by the elementary nature of Kobe's practice, Stein asked, "Why does the greatest player in the game need to practice such basic moves?" Kobe again responded with a big smile "Well, how do you think I became the best player in the game?"[1]

Kobe—like Terry—understood that excellence and greatness begin with disciplined practice and focused intensity on the fundamentals. Greatness is built brick by brick. You don't necessarily have to wake up at 4:00 a.m., but how are you doing on the fundamentals we have discussed in this book, such as healthy eating, moving, sleeping, daily planning, deep work blocks, and AM/PM bookends? Are you aiming for excellence? Are you taking the steps necessary to be great?

As you may recall, when the ancient Greeks discussed virtue—which they called "arête"—it consisted of two concepts. One was moral virtue, which we discussed in the previous chapter. The second was excellence, which we will discuss here. Virtue is doing the right thing; excellence is doing it the right way. Doing the right thing in the right way is arête. Let's turn to excellence.

WHATEVER YOU DO, DO WITH EXCELLENCE

Excellence is defined as being superior or extremely good at something. When aiming for excellence, we try to reach our full potential. Striving for excellence is the vehicle by which we close the gap between where we currently are and where we want to be. Each of us has a genuine desire to reach our highest potential.

Excellence involves setting clear high standards for ourselves. Excellence always falls outside of our comfort zone. By aiming for targets outside of our comfort zone, we are, by definition, moving toward growth and excellence.

We can't be excellent at everything. Lots of people are mediocre at many things. Because we have limited time and because it takes a concerted effort to be excellent at something, we want to be careful to choose those things that are most vital to our lives. At a minimum, we will want to pursue excellence in the prioritized, life categories of health, work, and relationships.

What does excellent health look like for you? Are you sleeping, moving, and eating excellently? Drill down even more—are you an excellent sleeper by making it a priority to get eight hours of sleep? What can you specifically do in exercise and regular movement to be in excellent physical shape? What can you do nutrition-wise that would allow you to eat excellently?

Are you excellent at your job? It doesn't matter what you do for your work or life's calling, do it with excellence. As a lawyer, think in terms of your main roles, whether it is a litigator, transactional lawyer, or leader. You should have a sense of what excellence looks like in your job and what you can do to strive for it.

If you have seen the inspiring movie, *Erin Brockovich*, based on the true story of an environmental activist, who was not even a lawyer, then you understand what I mean by approaching your job with excellence. Brockovich worked as a file clerk in a law office when she was handed several boxes of documents involving the sale of a resident's home to Pacific Gas & Electric (known as PG&E). It was a standard real estate deal.

Curious as to why there were medical records in a real estate file, Brockovich on her own initiative decided to visit the seller. Brockovich learned the seller had several tumors, and her husband had Hodgkin's lymphoma. She also discovered PG&E had dumped toxic chemicals into the ground water, causing all types of serious injuries, including cancer, to the residents of the town, where the home was located. A lawsuit was filed, and the case (spoiler alert) ultimately settled for $333 million, which at the time was the highest settlement ever of its kind.

When discussing health, work, or relationships, I hear many people say that those aspects of their life are "good enough." For things that are unimportant, the "good enough" standard is fine. Take the orderliness of my home, "good enough" certainly applies. Remember, we cannot be excellent at everything in our life because we don't have unlimited time.

For our highest priorities, however, I would not use "good enough" as the standard. In fact, good is often the enemy of great. We get satisfied with being good, so we fail to strive to be great. Let's make a conscious choice on our vital priorities to have "excellence" as our new standard.

Excellence is Not Perfection

When we strive for excellence, we are not trying to be perfect. For many individuals—and this applies particularly to the legal profession, including me—they are often overachievers and seek perfection. However, it's important to understand that no person is perfect. Because there are no perfect individuals, perfection is not attainable. This is so important; please read the previous sentence again.

Fully accept and, in fact, welcome that it's okay not to be perfect. We must not get caught in the trap of feeling like we failed because we weren't perfect. Nobody is going to do everything flawlessly. Everybody is going to make mistakes. Everybody is going to face criticism, defeats, and difficulties.

Since you are not going to be the world's first perfect human being, you can stop beating yourself up and begin to focus on excellence. We strive for excellence. It is good to have very high standards and see "perfect" only as a guiding star. Instead of being a perfectionist, let's strive to be an optimalist. An optimalist pursues excellence.

ACHIEVE MASTERY (BY PURSUINIG EXCELLENCE)

I love the story of Tom Seaver, which illustrates how anyone can improve and flourish by pursuing excellence. Tom was not born with natural, athletic talent. He wasn't the biggest, the fastest, or the strongest. In fact, he failed to make his high school baseball team until his senior year. But he loved baseball and was incredibly committed to being a great pitcher. When he graduated from high school, he went to a community college, where he was a good—but not a great—pitcher. When he transferred to the University of Southern California, he continued to pursue his pitching with excellence and finally developed into an outstanding pitcher.

Tom's hard work paid off when he was drafted into professional baseball and played for the New York Mets. The rest is history. He won the Rookie of the Year Award; he became one of the most dominant pitchers in baseball history; and he led the 1969 "Miracle Mets" to winning the World Series. He also won the National League Cy Young Award that year as baseball's top pitcher, and his accolades continued throughout his career.

When Seaver retired, he was voted into the Baseball Hall of Fame by 98.8 percent of the first ballots cast, the highest percentage of votes ever received—even higher than the percentage of votes for Babe Ruth. The secret to Seaver's success was that he pursued excellence every day until he became a master.[2]

Excellence precedes mastery. You can only become a true master at something when you consistently pursue excellence over a long period of time. It's why the famous historian, Will Durant, said: "We are what we repeatedly do. Excellence, then, is not an act, but a habit."[3] These consistent habits of excellence eventually lead to mastery.

What Is Mastery?

Mastery means you possess great skill or knowledge at an endeavor. You have command over a subject or skill. You become an expert in something. You achieve *greatness*. Think of the great masters in different fields—in athletics, like Tom Seaver or Michael Jordan, in science, like Thomas Edison or Albert Einstein, in writing, like Jane Austen and J.K. Rowling.

You may not know yet what subject or skill you want to master, and that's perfectly OK. Let me reiterate: Start with the top priorities of health, work, and relationships. Watch yourself grow over time, and you will gain clarity over what else you want to master. With enough self-reflection, you will be intrinsically drawn to your true north. You will begin to know your one thing.

The opposite of mastery is mediocrity. The etymology of "mediocre" is being stuck in the middle. Don't let that happen. If you try to become an expert at something that doesn't really matter to you, it is unlikely you will stick with it long enough to become a master. You will be just a dabbler. Trying things until you either get bored, frustrated, or lose interest. However, if it is truly important to you—if deep down, with all your heart, you want it badly—then you will overcome the inevitable failures, pain, and grind necessary to become a master.

As we strive for mastery, we will hit inevitable plateaus. Our growth will not be a straight line up. That's impossible. Life will undoubtedly offer long stretches of unexciting highways. There will be times when you are feeling unsatisfied or just not feeling it. We will have periods where we are incubating, restoring, learning, and building a firm foundation, but then we finally break free and have a spurt of real progress in our lives.

When you eventually emerge from the plateau, you will be ready to move to the next level of development. In martial arts, they track progress toward mastery through different belt levels. A martial arts student starts as a white belt, denoting beginner. Different arts use different color belts as they progress, but all culminate in a black belt, which demonstrates mastery. Likewise, for lawyers, many states offer certifications of specialization as do several national board certifications. For example, the American Bar Association's National Board of Trial Advocacy certifies lawyers in civil trial advocacy, criminal trial advocacy, and family law.

In life, there are no such belts or certifications to mark your progress. Yet, for those of us who are intentionally trying to improve as individuals, we can set our own distinct benchmarks or stages of development. Masters become radiant exemplars in all facets of their lives, physically, mentally, emotionally, relationally, and professionally.

So how do you become a master? Numerous studies and personal stories have identified the four key principles necessary for mastery. These are (1) deliberate practice over a long duration of time, (2) grit, (3) a growth mindset, and (4) asymptotic striving. Let's take a deeper look at each of these four principles.

MASTERY IS A MARATHON

In 2011, Keiko Fukuda was awarded a 10th degree black belt in Judo, which is the highest level that can be achieved. It's an amazing feat for any person. The fact that Fukuda earned it at the age of ninety-eight and became the first woman in history to do so is even more remarkable.

Fukuda served as a judo instructor, where she was referred to as "sensei," which means "master" in Japanese. But the term "sensei" is deeper than that. It's a symbol of honor to show respect for somebody who has achieved the highest level of mastery.

Fukuda stood less than five feet tall, weighed fewer than 100 pounds, and did not have great physical strength. However, the diminutive Fukuda obtained mastery through great consistency and passion over many years. She started at age twenty-one in 1935. Sixteen years later, she became a fifth degree blackbelt. Then for almost 30 years, she remained a fifth degree blackbelt. Fukuda reached something of a master's plateau, but she also faced gender discrimination too. Fukuda said the authorizing board "just decided that women didn't need any ranks over fifth degree." She continued to dedicate her life's work to judo and eventually broke through the gender barrier.[4]

The first principle of achieving mastery is intentional and consistent practice over a long duration of time. There is no shortcut. You need to perform a skill repeatedly. You need to learn what works and what doesn't work. This takes time.

In his excellent book, *Outliers*, Malcom Gladwell showed it takes a minimum of 10,000 hours of deliberate practice to obtain mastery. The 10,000-hour rule is based on scientific research by K. Anders Ericsson, who discovered it took about 10,000 hours to truly excel at something like golf, chess, or music. A person's ability in a specific endeavor correlated closely with the amount of time he or she practiced the craft or skill: 8,000 hours to become good, 10,000 hours to be great.

While talent can be an important factor, alone it is never enough. In any event, our inborn talent is fixed. So, the question is how do we maximize our own individual potential? For most of us, mastery will only come as a result of hard work. Geoff Colvin, in his book *Talent Is Overrated*, writes:

"The phenomenon seems nearly universal. In a famous study of chess players, Nobel Prize winner Herbert Simon and William Chase proposed 'the ten-year rule,' based on their observation that no one seemed to reach the top ranks of chess players without a decade or so of intensive study, and some required much more time. Even Bobby Fischer was not an exception; when he became a grand master at age sixteen, he had been studying chess intensively for nine years. Subsequent research in a wide range of fields has substantiated the ten-year rule everywhere the researchers have looked. In math, science, musical composition, swimming, X-ray diagnosis, tennis, literature—no one, not even the most 'talented' performers, became great without at least ten years of very hard preparation."

As a lawyer, this means having a deliberate education plan in all the key aspects of your legal practice, gaining experience through repetition, continuing to hone your craft. Over time, you, too, can become an expert in your field, a true master lawyer. I found my own legal career really started to take off after about seven years, and by the tenth year, I believe I was beginning to approach mastery. I was confident in my skills and abilities, possessed a solid understanding of the law, and had strong practice management and marketing plans. My own professional trajectory was consistent with the ten-year rule.

Equally important as the amount of time is "how" you practice. Ericsson noted the person seeking mastery must engage in *deliberate or purposeful practice* with the aim of getting better.[5] If you want to master an instrument, you don't just casually play once in a while. You purposefully try to progress. If you want to excel as a marathoner, you're not just going out for an easy jog. The casual musician and jogger are perfectly fine. But, if you want to be a great musician or great runner, it takes intentionally pushing yourself just outside of your comfort zone.

Famous martial artist Bruce Lee said: "I fear not the man who has practiced 10,000 kicks once." Instead, "I fear the man who has practiced one kick ten thousand times." You must consistently and intentionally focus on your one metaphorical kick.

There are few skills more difficult to master in lawyering than cross-examining a witness. That's the way lawyer and judge, Irving Younger, focused on the science of it and came up with his well-known Ten Commandments of Cross-Examination. Younger said it took a minimum of twenty-five jury trials, as well as consistently and deliberately applying these commandments, before a lawyer moved from a technician to an artist.

While it takes persistent practice to become great at your craft, it's not just any kind of practice—it's the kind of practice that hurts, that stretches and grows you, and that pushes you out of your comfort zone to achieve new heights. But this is not where the practice ends; it's just where it begins. In other words, you don't clock in 10,000 hours and instantly become an expert. So, let's turn to the next principle of mastery, having grit.

GRIT

I mentioned previously one of my best friends, Rick. When Rick attended college, he joined ROTC. After graduating, he went straight into Army boot camp.

Knowing Rick, I was not surprised he wanted to become an Army Ranger. The Rangers are an elite infantry force that is part of the Army Special Operations Command. The training is beyond rigorous, akin to the Navy SEALs. The training is grueling physically, mentally, and emotionally. I remember Rick writing me immediately after the training that he had lost twenty-five pounds and had been eating insects for food.

Once Rick had committed to becoming an Army Ranger, I knew he was going to finish it. He told me there were many times he wanted to quit. He was in pain, tired, starving, emotionally and mentally drained, and physically exhausted. But Rick was driven, with a deep purpose and a fierce persistence.

Only one problem: Rick hated—or should I say feared—jumping out of airplanes. He needed a kick in the butt, or more like a shove out of the plane. And Airborne school was a requirement before becoming a Ranger.

However, Rick had made a commitment to finish Ranger School. When Rick said he was either going to finish Ranger school or they were going to have kill him, that included jumping out of an airplane which, of course, he did. He graduated as a Ranger with flying colors, served our country with distinction, and is now a super-successful businessman.

University of Pennsylvania Professor Angela Duckworth conducted a thorough study of why some Navy SEALs candidates graduate while others don't. The candidates who enter Navy SEALs boot camp are the best of the best. They are among the most physically fit in the world, including triathletes and former Olympians. Yet, after just the first eight weeks of training, an average of 80 percent of the candidates drop out.

Duckworth found the one characteristic that separated the candidates who suc-ceeded was "mental toughness." Duckworth called it "grit" or "passion and perseverance for very long-term goals."[6] In her best-selling book, *Grit*, she found the single biggest predictor for those who succeed in difficult challenges is persistent effort. The SEALs candidates who survived the continual cold, wet, sandy, and tormenting ocean had re-markable tenacity. They were relentless.

The second principle of mastery is grit. It's never quitting. Staying in the game. Not giving up. It's like the movie Rocky; you might get knocked down, but you get back up every time. How's your own perseverance for the thing you want to master?

I think of law school and the bar exam as good examples of grit. Finishing the three years of law school is an arduous grind. The saying goes: In the first year, they scare you to death; the second year, they work you to death, and the third year, they bore you to death. Immediately after graduating, you begin studying day and night for the bar exam. I thought I studied hard in law school, but the bar exam took it to another level. You can't practice law unless you pass the bar exam, and some states, such as California, have passage rates of less than 50 percent. It takes grit to successfully navigate the bar exam.

Don't let anybody ever tell you becoming a master is easy. I guarantee you; it's not. Because mastery involves pain and suffering, you must have grit to fight through and overcome those obstacles. The chronology of mastery is often "U"-shaped in that you start out on fire and then slowly move through the challenging, difficult phases, eventu-ally to re-emerge as a master.

Purpose plus perseverance, fire, and ferocity. A powerful drive plus a deep resolve produce grit. You know and expect challenges and problems. You approach each chal-lenge as an opportunity to overcome and get better. You get knocked down, and you get up again. That's the grit necessary to achieve mastery.

A MINDSET FOR GROWTH

A growth mindset is the third principle necessary for mastery. A "mindset" is a way of believing and seeing the world. The growth comes from learning from every experience in your life. As shown in the diagram below, virtually all growth follows the same process: try, fail, learn, try a different way.

Do you have a growth or a fixed mindset?

The "growth mindset" was conceived by Stanford psychologist, Carol Dweck, who found that people can progress over time by learning from their efforts.[7] The opposite of a growth mindset is a "fixed mindset." A fixed mindset incorrectly assumes challenges and failures are due to our limited abilities. The fixed mindset believes you are born with your own fixed sets of talents and abilities. You either have it or you don't. There's nothing you can do about it.

In contrast, a growth mindset sees failure and challenges as opportunities to learn and grow. In her website, Dweck explains the distinction: "In a fixed mindset, people believe their basic qualities, like their intelligence or talent, are simply fixed traits. They spend their time documenting their intelligence or talent instead of developing them. They also believe that talent alone creates success—without effort. They're wrong."

Dweck continues, "In a growth mindset, people believe that their most basic abilities can be developed through dedication and hard work—brains and talent are just the starting point. This view creates a love of learning and a resilience that is essential for great accomplishment. Virtually all great people have had these qualities."

Do you bring a hammer or lantern to your own problems? If you consistently respond to a mistake or failure with "that's like me," "there's nothing I can do," or "I'm really bad at this," then you're likely taking a hammer to your problems by beating yourself up with a fixed mindset approach. However, if you look at everything as "information" or "data" and that you can learn from every situation, then you have a lantern approach by illuminating the challenge with a growth mindset. It's knowing you're "not there yet."

One great illustration of the growth mindset is Elon Musk and his inspiring, some might say crazy, vision of space exploration and taking humans to Mars. He has an exuberant sense of what is possible. When he first created his company SpaceX, he began in humble quarters. He set bold and ambitious goals for building cutting-edge rocket engines.

After years of experimenting, Musk was finally ready for his first commercial launch. It was a dramatic moment when the rocket left the launch pad. But after just twenty-five seconds, the rocket failed, spinning uncontrollably and landing almost directly on the launch pad. It destroyed most of the infrastructure on the ground as well as smashing its satellite cargo.

But Musk learned a great deal from that failure. He built a better and bigger rocket called the Falcon 1. He believed he finally got it right. That launch also failed with the Falcon 1 exploding. After years of dedicated work, Musk's employees were heartbroken. However, Musk immediately spoke to them, telling them not to get discouraged, and they were going to continue to learn from their failures.

Still, one rocket after another exploded or crashed. Other problems persisted with avionics, software, and launch systems. When others wanted to give up, Musk was at his best during those trying times. With each failure, he continued learning. He analyzed why the engines failed, improved them, and tested them again and again.

Space X has now successfully launched many rockets into space. It is prospering with hundreds of millions of dollars' worth of orders. The rockets not only successfully completed their missions but self-landed, as opposed to plunging into the ocean. Musk is an incredible portrait of the growth mindset in action. Given this, I believe Musk will one day succeed in landing humans on Mars.

With a growth mindset, we are a student all the time. *We don't win or lose; we win or learn*. We can do this in our own lives. At the end of the day, a master asks three questions:

1. What did I do well?
2. What did I learn?
3. What can I do better next time?

Let's put on our lab coats daily and act like scientists. With a growth mindset, we always ask ourselves, "How can I learn from that experience?" We are collecting data. We don't get emotional from challenges; we get better. As Ralph Waldo Emerson said, "All life is an experiment. The more experiments, the better."

Learn From Mistakes, Challenges, and Negative Thoughts

As we discussed in the chapter on antifragile growth, challenges and obstacles are how we grow. Losing, falling short, and making mistakes are often our greatest teachers. In the *Star Wars* saga, when Luke Skywalker is training to become a Jedi Master, he often got frustrated when he failed at a task. His teacher, the wise Yoda, focused on having a growth mindset. In one scene, Master Yoda says to Luke: "Heeded my words not, did you? Pass on what you have learned. Strength, mastery. But weakness, folly, failure also. Yes, failure most of all. The greatest teacher, failure is."

If you didn't sleep well last night ... no problem ... hopefully you learned how to sleep better the next time. When you get criticized at work ... no worries ... what did you learn and what can you do better next time? When your spouse gets under your skin or you react improperly, you simply say—after apologizing, if appropriate— "Thank you, Stoic gods, for giving me the opportunity to learn to be a better spouse next time."

Each new experience allows us to learn, as it is all data. Each time we learn, we are a different person. When the great philosopher-king, Marcus Aurelius, said we can never step in the same river twice, he was encouraging us to grow. We cannot content ourselves with first impressions or encounters, we must constantly revisit everything. Now that you have, hopefully, made changes in your life, I encourage you to revisit the pages of books you have previously read and the insights you have overlooked.

One way I measure my own growth mindset is by the "road rage test." I used to get upset when someone cut me off, drove too slowly, or wouldn't let me merge onto the freeway, but now I just shrug it off. It's not a concern anymore. I used to get visibly angry but then progressed to no longer displaying anger (but still kept it inside of me), to now proactively letting the other person just go ahead. Paradoxically, I actually feel good when it happens because I acknowledge that it no longer affects me.

This is a small example, but the greater the challenge, the greater the opportunity to grow ... and the greater the reward. The extent of the challenge creates the extent of the benefit. This was the formula for one of the world's wealthiest and most influential men, Ray Dalio. He set extremely bold goals (i.e., big challenges), failed, and learned.

This ability to learn, grow, and get better from each challenge or opportunity is what Ray Dalio called the "mistake learner's high." He loved learning and improving. And that he did. But it's also true in other aspects of your life. "If you are not failing," says Ray Dalio, "you are not pushing your limits, and if you are not pushing your limits, you're not maximizing your potential. This becomes the fun part."[8]

Be Proactive in Pursuing Growth

Of course, we don't wait for problems and challenges before growing. To the contrary, we ought to make education and training one of our greatest aims. Be motivated to constantly grow and pursue intellectual development in all the key domains in your life. This entire book is premised on the notion that we need to educate ourselves—to grow—in how to live the good life.

We do this by acquiring knowledge, wisely practicing and applying that knowledge, learning from our setbacks, and eventually mastering the subject at hand. A growth mindset applies to all these steps. We grow in our knowledge. If our knowledge is not working for us, we need to replace it with better, superior knowledge. If we are not practicing our principles, living what we know to be the good life, then we can't have a growth mindset and figure out how to bring our actions in alignment with our values.

One of the best ways to be proactive with your growth mindset is having a systematic plan for education, such as daily reading. I have three letters staring at me in my office that spell—R.E.D.—which stands for "read every day." Even if you are not a big reader, there are so many alternative ways to learn from audio books, podcasts, blogs, and the internet. Like healthy food, I aim to feed my mind with daily wisdom.

We can proactively educate ourselves by spending time with the "great teachers" throughout civilization. Curious what Buddha thinks about suffering in this world? Want to know what Jesus thought about love? How did Socrates examine life? How did Abraham Lincoln stay the course with a country being torn apart by civil war? How did Martin Luther King, Jr. pursue change through peaceful means? Through reading, you can spend time with all these monumental life changers.

Another suggestion for growth is to set up a "mind gym." While you go to an exercise gym for your body, you can also go to a mental gymnasium where the great thinkers help and guide you. If you are not sure how to handle a particular situation, crisis, or challenge, you can have your own personal mind gym of advisors or your own board of directors and ask them what to do. This is akin to the popular idea, "What would Jesus do?"

Your personal board of directors could include whomever you want, such as inspirational individuals like the Dalai Lama or Amelia Earhart; great political leaders like Lincoln, MLK, or Cesar Chavez; great famous lawyers like Ruth Bader Ginsberg, Thurgood Marshall, or Johnnie Cochran; or great servants like Gandhi or Mother Teresa. Maybe there's a great mom or dad you want to emulate? Or some athlete or fit person? Invite them to join your board and then imagine how they would guide you.

In any given moment, you can choose to move forward into growth or backwards away from becoming the best version of yourself. Are you going to grow toward mastery or stay where you are? A growth mindset is essential for mastery.

ASYMPTOTE

The fourth and final principle of mastery is an "asymptote." You may be asking, "What is an 'asymptote'?" Sounds like something bad. Like, "He's such an asymptote!" Or "She's not feeling well; she has an asymptote." Well, an asymptote is a mathematical model showing a curve that approaches a line but never actually reaches it, all the way to infinity. It doesn't matter how far the curve extends; it will never reach the end line. Ever. That's like the pursuit of mastery. You will never get there—ever. Daniel Pink in his book, *Drive*, writes: "You can approach it. You can get really, really close to it. But... you can never touch it. Mastery is impossible to realize fully." Thus, mastery requires asymptotic striving.

But wait, if we will never get to the destination—never truly arrive at perfect mastery— then what's the point? Why would we ever strive for something unattainable? Ah, but that's the key to success, the necessary ingredient of the master: to always strive, to keep learning, to never be satisfied, to know that perfection is unattainable. That's the amazing paradox, always seeking to advance, but there is no "there."

The Mastery Asymptote

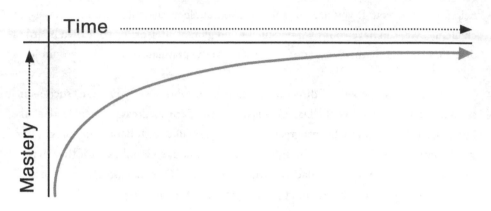

While this might discourage some people, it is also a great attraction. For the master, the fact that it will always elude you provides a wonderful, never-ending pursuit. Dan Pink poignantly states: "The joy is in the pursuit more than the realization. In the end, mastery attracts precisely because mastery eludes."

In Japan, they refer to this constant pursuit of improvement by the term, "Kaizen" ("Kai" means "change," and "Zen" means "good.") The concept of Kaizen was actually created in the U.S. during World War II. Without a huge war budget and short on time, the U.S. was unable to build new, state-of-the art factories. Instead, the factories had to focus on how they could make small improvements on all the different aspects of their manufacturing.

This concept was then brought to Japan after the war to help them re-build their economy. Using Kaizen, Japan's companies strove for incessant, incremental improvements, and it gained popularity when Japan's Toyota passed General Motors as the world's largest auto manufacturer. Toyota's philosophy was built around Kaizen, and soon the idea grew.

You can apply the principle of asymptotic striving to literally everything—sleeping, eating, exercising, writing, oral advocacy skills, communicating, listening. Get in the habit of constantly asking yourself how you can improve 1 percent in a certain area. Today, how can I improve just 1 percent at work? Today, how can I improve just 1 percent in my exercise? How can I improve my relationships by 1 percent or, in being more present with my family?

Perhaps the most famous example in sports of this 1 percent never-ending pursuit for perfection is the British Cycling team—which went from irrelevancy to repeat world champions through ruthlessly examining everything it did—from its uniforms to bike maintenance, to sleeping, to staying healthy. They didn't make major overhauls to their approach but made constant minor changes to keep improving.

The Navy SEALs' motto is "Earn Your Trident Every Day." Imagine the day when a Navy SEALs candidate survives. I mean, graduates from basic training. He or she has literally made it through hell on earth. It's an amazing accomplishment. Yet, one of the first things the Commanding Officer tells those graduates is, "Today is day one." That's right, their graduation is just the beginning of their training, their journey. They are now on their own asymptotic road toward SEALs mastery.

A life of mastery—indeed, the good life—is one quest, one adventure after another. Then, you realize flourishing is not just a destination but also a journey. It's both. Every day you get back on the path. As one day does not make a master, neither does, as Aristotle said, "One swallow makes a summer." Mastery, like flourishing, is measured over a lifetime.

The most important message in this chapter is that all of us have the potential to become masters. We all have the power to accomplish the extraordinary. When we pursue excellence and mastery in what we do—especially in our health, love, and work—we begin to flourish in our lives like never before.

Every day, you get to begin fresh—a new beginning and as a beginner. Mind wide open, excited, and ready to go. You start with an eye on the finish line, but now, with a master's mindset, you realize you will never reach it. You will never be exonerated. But how fun! Enjoy the pursuit, and let's see how close you can get to flourishing!

Chapter Summary:

- Strive for excellence every day.
- As we strive for daily excellence, we begin to make progress toward mastery.
- The four principles of mastery are 10,000 hours of deliberate effort, grit, a growth mindset, and asymptotic striving.

SIDEBAR _____

Show unfailing courtesy to all—to opposing counsel, the parties, the witnesses, the jurors, the clerk, court staff, and the court. The words "civil" and "litigator" are not oxymorons. I believe the courts and jurors have a more favorable impression to the lawyers who are polite and respectful.

CONCLUSION

THE FINAL VERDICT
AND THE NEXT CASE

• • •

"This is our predicament.
Over and over again, we lose sight of what's
important and what isn't."
— EPICTETUS

YOUR CLOSING ARGUMENT

In my opinion, the closing argument is the single most important event in a trial. Sure, there are exceptions, and yes, other parts of the trial are crucial too. But it is the closing argument that can ultimately make or break the case.

We have now come to the close of your case. The end of the book. Recall in the very first chapter where I posed a hypothetical trial involving the ideal version of you against the current version of you. My sincere and strong hope is that after reading this book, you will have a much better understanding of what it means to realize your full potential.

When advising lawyers on preparing closing arguments, I recommend they start with one of the most effective communication strategies: the rule of three. From a neuroscience perspective, people remember information more readily when it is grouped in threes. Think of your area code, ABC, 123, the *Three Little Pigs*, the Holy Trinity, the beginning, middle, and end, and the three inalienable rights of life, liberty, and the pursuit of happiness from the Declaration of Independence. The Romans had a maxim for the rule of three: "*omne trium perfectum*," meaning "everything that comes in threes is perfect."

Fortunately, as we have discussed in this book, the quintessence of flourishing has three aspects. Every principle in this book centers around one of these Three Pillars of Flourishing:

1. Vision
2. Action
3. Virtue

We move from knowledge (our purpose/vision) to practice (our process/actions) to mastery (our character and virtues).

My hope is that you have taken the information from this book and started to put it into practice. If you have, I believe you will begin to flourish. I also believe that, if you were trying your hypothetical case again, you would organize your closing argument—and your life—around these Three Pillars.

The new and improved current version of you starts with the first Pillar: Vision. You demonstrate improved clarity on your purpose. You begin with a vision for yourself—your personal well-being—because you can only give away what you have. The better you make yourself and the more energy you have, the more you can give away to others in service and love. Then focus on how to have a successful, rewarding career and positive, meaningful relationships. And you ensure you take some time for balance, renewal, recreation, and play.

Next, you move to the second Pillar: Action. In your closing, you demonstrate a straightforward process for achieving your purpose. Your process starts by identifying your vital priorities, planning a masterpeace day, and taking strong action on that plan. Realizing life can only be lived in the present moment, you focus your energy and effort on what's important now, going after one micro-win after another. A series of successful days culminates in a successful life.

Then, you turn to the third Pillar: Virtue. Proudly proclaim your commitment to doing the right thing in the right way. When? Always. You live with character and integrity such as wisdom, kindness, courage, and honesty. If it's worth doing, strive to do it with excellence. Over time, your habitual excellence turns to mastery. Eventually, you become a master in your personal well-being, your relationships, and your work.

And now fully engaged with these Three Pillars, you apply them to your life regardless of your circumstances and time. They will serve you especially well in our dramatically changing world. They will act as constellations to guide you during your journey in life.

Conclude your newly inspired closing argument by thanking the court and/or the jury, smiling confidently, and sitting down. You have done your best, and that's all you can control.

The good life requires the synergy of all Three Pillars. It requires your living with the whole truth. Your goals in life are important. But, without action, you are just living a dream. Your actions are important, but without the right destination, you may end up in the wrong place. And if you have good goals and a strong work ethic, but you don't live with character and ethics, you may end up sacrificing everything, including your soul.

That's the chief message of this book. That a flourishing life is to be lived as a whole person. Understanding that all your vital priorities are interconnected and interdependent. The concept is simple to understand but not easy to execute.

The best closing arguments show and explain the verdict form. They will tell the jury how they should answer each of the questions on the verdict form. Similarly, in your life, you can track and celebrate your progress through your own personal verdict form. At the end of each day, you can ask yourself the following three penultimate questions:

1. How well did you fulfill your purpose?
2. How well did you love others and yourself?
3. How well did you serve others?

The more you can answer those questions in a positive manner, the more your life will flourish.

THE FINAL VERDICT

After your closing argument is finished, the bailiff escorts the jury to the jury deliberation room to render a final verdict in this new trial. After several days of deliberation, the jury signals the bailiff that it has reached a verdict. The jury then returns from the sequestered deliberation room into the courtroom. As they enter the courtroom, there is a hush.

The judge asks the jury foreperson if the jury has reached a verdict. "Yes, we have, your Honor." The bailiff takes the verdict form and walks it over to the judge. No other words are spoken. The judge carefully examines the verdict form to make sure it has been properly completed.

The Court then hands the verdict form to the clerk. At this point, you can hear a pin drop as the anticipation has built to a crescendo. "Will the defendant please rise and face the jury? In the case of *The Optimal You v. The Actual You*, the jury finds the defendant ..."

Oh, I forgot to tell you that in this second, imaginary lawsuit in which the ideal version of yourself sued the current version of yourself, you are also the jury. You get to make the decision of how you are doing. The jury finds in favor of the defendant—the actual You—because if you have followed the principles in this book, you have begun to close the gap between where you are now and where you will be at your full potential. The reason this second trial is with a jury is because you will now need to serve as your own jury in your own life every day: asking yourself what went well and what needs work.

Undoubtedly, the single most dramatic moment in a trial is the reading of the verdict. After all the hard work, there is a final decision. This brings the case to an ending.

Like every trial, this book too is coming to a close. As does your life. Each will have an ending. Your case has a beginning: the filing of a complaint—and an end: the verdict. So does your life—birth and death.

It is fitting to finish with a final truth—and I do mean, "final"—which is we must always remember and accept there is an end. An end to every case. An end to our work. An end to our lives.

Although Steve Jobs wasn't a lawyer, he shared many similar traits with our profession. The founder and chief evangelical officer of Apple was obsessed with his work. He had a brilliant mind, unimaginable creativity, and a charismatic personality, but he was also characterized as fiery, insulting, and manipulative. His temper tantrums were legendary. However, his life profoundly changed after he was diagnosed with cancer.

Two years after his diagnosis, Jobs gave a commencement speech at Stanford University that is often considered one of the greatest graduation speeches of all time. During that speech, he didn't talk about his obsession with work or his latest Apple innovation. He talked about the life-changing message of death. Jobs said:

"Remembering that I'll be dead soon is the most important tool I've ever encountered to help me make the big choices in life. Because almost everything—all external expectations, all pride, all fear of embarrassment or failure—these things just fall away in the face of death, leaving only what is truly important.

"Remembering that you are going to die is the best way I know to avoid the trap of thinking you have something to lose. You are already naked. There is no reason not to follow your heart.

"Death is very likely the single best invention of Life. It is Life's change agent. It clears out the old to make way for the new.

"Sorry to be so dramatic, but it is quite true.

"Your time is limited, so don't waste it living someone else's life.

"And most important, have the courage to follow your heart and intuition. They somehow already know what you truly want to become. Everything else is secondary."[1]

Jobs' cancer diagnosis was indeed a wake-up call. But only six years later, he died at the young age of fifty-six. The most powerful and influential man on the planet. He could have almost anything he wanted. He controlled an empire but didn't have ultimate control over what was most important—his life.

This book more than anything else is how about we spend our time. What do we do with the limited time we are here on Earth? Death is why we don't want to waste time. We must know we are going to die. It's guaranteed. It reminds us to make the big choices in life. To focus on our health, loving others, and serving in our work and community. And it gives us the courage to follow our heart and realize our unique potential.

For many of us, the concept of death is vague and distant. "Sure, it will happen; I get it. But I'm too busy living my life to think about dying." OK, if you want to make it real, look at the actuarial life tables on the internet. There you can actually make it real. It will tell you, statistically, how many years you have left. Or, if you really want to get clear, go to *www.death-clock.org*. It will give you the specific date of your expected death.

This is not meant to be morbid or dark. To the contrary, as Steve Jobs said, it's *"the most important tool"* you can possess for living a great life.[2] It's why the Stoics constantly reminded themselves of *"memento mori."* By "remembering death," they could live their best lives in the present.

In *Rothschild's Fiddle,* the very first book I read in my book group, author Anton Chekov said the fact that there is death makes life significant. That was a transformative idea for me. A true revelation. It no longer became a dark thought but enlightenment. If we lived forever, our time would not be valued. Now it became significant. Our time is limited, so it is our most precious gift.[3]

With the true end in mind, let's move forward boldly and deliberately with how we spend our time. Let's not waste a minute with things that are useless, irrelevant, or unimportant. Let's use our most precious commodity—time—to become the best person we can, to demonstrate our love in words and actions, and to give our greatest gifts in service to making the world a better place.

CALLING YOUR NEXT CASE

The jury has rendered its verdict and been excused. The case is over. What now? It's time to move on to your next case. Your next project. Your next day. Every single day is a new beginning. Remember, you cannot live in the past or the future; there is only the now. So, you start again. Each day. Hopefully, a little wiser, a little improved. But nonetheless, every day presents a new opportunity to live fully.

That's why Epictetus's quote at the top of this chapter is so important. We often lose sight of and forget what's most important now. Every day, we need to connect with our vital priorities and take energized action toward those priorities. A single day at a time.

Recall the opening of this book when I forgot my pants at my very first court appearance? While I haven't repeated that, I have made many more mistakes since then. I have faced many more difficult challenges, fallen repeatedly, and failed often. However, I have learned to fail intelligently. To learn from each mistake. To grow stronger from my challenges. Now, when I move to my next case, my next project, my new health goal, my significant relationships, I am better prepared.

In that way, life becomes a series of continuous adventures. Through each adventure, you learn lessons that are used on your next adventure. Each quest prepares you for the following one. As we continue to make progress, our path eventually leads toward mastery. Yet, we wisely understand the paradox that we will never fully arrive at true mastery. It's a never-ending pursuit. In short, flourishing is the continual life experience of climbing toward the metaphorical mountain peak and enjoying the views along the way. I call this the journey to Mount Happiness.

As you live out the principles in this book, you will begin to ascend to a higher plane of living, an elevated level of intelligence. You will move from one mountain to another higher peak. But it's a different mountain. You will see life from a different perspective. You become more mindful and joyful, have calm confidence, possess emotional intelligence, look for opportunities to love, act with virtue, and contribute to the betterment of others. Your life will be filled with a strong purpose and vital energy. You will be transformed and will contribute to transforming the world.

As we continue our journey through life, let us never forget the importance of the whole truths contained in this book. As we live those truths, may this ever-growing wisdom serve as our guiding light, so we don't just live, but live well and flourish.[4]

The beginning!

FINAL SIDEBAR _____

Dress appropriately. The courtroom is a dignified setting, so you, your clients, and your witnesses should all wear business attire. And most importantly, don't forget your pants!

APPENDIX 1

A CHECKLIST FOR SUCCEEDING IN COURT

. . .

O ver the years, while on the bench, I have kept a list of what I believe are the most important tips for succeeding in court. I have compiled all those tips in this appendix, including the ones previously mentioned in the Sidebars at the end of each chapter, so you can have them all in one place. I believe you will find them incredibly useful in your practice.

Before You Go to Court:

Just like we need to know the rules of life, we must also know the procedural rules of the specific court in which you are practicing. In addition, make sure you read and understand the local or general court rules that keep our courts running smoothly and efficiently. It's amazing how many gems are contained in the local rules.

Think like a judge. Ask yourself: What does the judge need to know at today's hearing? If it's a status conference, the judge will want to know the most current procedural posture, what the parties are doing to resolve the matter, and when the parties will be ready for trial. If it's a hearing, the judge will need to know the governing law and the relevant facts to rule in your favor.

Don't get caught up in irrelevant minutiae. Whether in oral argument or in your legal briefs, lawyers should focus on their strongest arguments rather than argue the picayune. There's an old saying in card games like bridge: Lead through strength.

Be overly prepared. Certainly, know the facts and the law of your case better than the judge. The law does not "cast a sympathetic eye on the unprepared."

Dress appropriately. The courtroom is a dignified setting, so you, your clients, and your witnesses should all wear business attire.

Respect others' time. Plan to arrive at least ten minutes early to court and always check in with the staff to let them know you are present. If you are going to be late, notify the court and opposing counsel in advance. This means you should have the phone number for both.

Communicating in Court:

When you are in court, know how to address individuals appropriately. Always refer to the judge as "Your Honor," not "Sir" or "Judge." Refer to the clerk, as "Madam or Mister Clerk." Refer to the court reporter as "Madam or Mister Reporter." When examining witnesses, don't use first names; rather refer to them by their last name, "Sir," or "Ma'am." If referring to opposing counsel, either use their last name or simply, "Opposing Counsel." These references are not only out of respect for the institution and the individuals but for the solemnity of the proceedings.

Oral Argument:

Keep your oral argument concise and to the point. When arguing a motion, don't repeat what you already said in your papers. If the court's tentative is not in your favor, be respectful of that tentative and then respectfully show the court how the decision can better comport to the law and facts. If the tentative is in your favor, respond to any material arguments by the other side and remind the court why its well-reasoned tentative is correct.

Don't speak directly to opposing counsel in court, and never interrupt opposing counsel when they are speaking to the judge. Let them finish, and then you can address the court.

Don't make negative personal comments or inappropriate facial expressions such as rolling your eyes.

At the Final Status Conference or Trial Readiness Conference:

Know your way around the courtroom at trial. Ask the judge how he or she prefers you to move around the courtroom for jury selection, opening statement, examining witnesses, and closing argument.

Make sure your technology works well. Before your court appearance, double check connections, lighting, and microphone. Remember, a virtual appearance is the same as a court appearance.

Trial—Jury Selection:

Always rise when the jury enters the room.

If you pass for cause, simply state: "Your Honor, the plaintiff/defendant passes for cause."

When exercising a peremptory challenge, state: "Your Honor, the plaintiff/defendant thanks and asks the court to please excuse juror no. __." Don't excuse the juror yourself.

When you are agreeable to the jury panel, state: "Your Honor, the plaintiff/defendant accepts the panel as presently constituted."

Trial—Examining Witnesses:

It's important to have your clients present at trial. You want to humanize your client and give a face to the trial. This is easy when your client's life is in shambles or has been injured, but there have been numerous times in trial with corporate and governmental parties where no person appeared at the trial. The party asked the jury to show up every day to hear its case, but it didn't seem to care enough to send a personal representative to be present. That's a big mistake.

Ask the judge for permission before approaching a witness, by inquiring, "Your Honor, may I please approach the witness?"

When you are done examining a witness, state, "Your Honor, I have no further questions of this witness at this time."

Use sidebars sparingly and appropriately. Only ask the court for a sidebar when it is a true emergency that can't wait for a break. Remember, side bars during trial interrupt the flow of trial and waste the jurors' time. If it's a true emergency, always make a formal request by asking, "Your Honor, may we please approach the bench?" Then wait for the judge to grant your request before approaching.

Trial—Exhibits:

When you are first using an exhibit, state: "Your Honor, I am holding (very briefly describe the exhibit). It has been previously shown to counsel and has been marked as plaintiff's Exhibit 1 / defendant's Exhibit A."

When first showing a witness an exhibit, state: "Showing you plaintiff's Exhibit 1, do you recognize this?"

If you don't already have an agreed-upon method with the court for moving exhibits into evidence, state: "Your honor, the defendant moves Exhibits A through Z into evidence."

Trial—Objections:

If a question is objectionable, simply state: "Objection, Your Honor, (and state the grounds, e.g., compound)."

If a witness statement is objectionable, state: "Objection, Your Honor, move to strike, (state the grounds, e.g., hearsay)."

Trial—Closing Your Case-In-Chief:

If you have concluded calling all your witnesses and moved all your exhibits into evidence, state: "Your Honor, with the introduction of the plaintiff's exhibits into evidence, the plaintiff rests."

Trial—Opening and Closing:

For opening statements, tell them like a story and make them flow. For closing, use charts—help the jury understand the law and the facts, and take them through the verdict form.

Resolving Disputes:

Don't be afraid to be pragmatic. Don't fight over every little thing. Be solution oriented. Your cases, your judge, and your clients will appreciate the time and cost-savings by not taking unnecessary positions or filing scorched-earth motions. Use your discretion and be reasonable when appropriate.

Civility and Respect:

Always take the high road. Treat opposing counsel with respect, even if he or she does not do the same. Being courteous and considerate to others is not only better for your personal well-being, but it also makes you a much more effective lawyer.

Show unfailing courtesy to all—to opposing counsel, the parties, the witnesses, the jurors, the clerk, court staff, and the court. The words "civil" and "litigator" are not oxymorons. I believe the courts and jurors have a more favorable impression towards the lawyers who are polite and respectful.

Honesty and civility are the two cornerstones for a long-term successful practice. Always, always tell the truth. Be civil to all persons involved in the case, especially opposing counsel. Pick up the phone and speak to the other side. Good relations will only help your client's case.

When Mistakes Happen:

Don't be afraid to apologize to the court if you have made a mistake. Courts are typically much more forgiving when counsel or a party accepts responsibility rather than makes excuses or blames others.

PLATO'S CAVE 4-YEAR READING PLAN

• • •

T hank you for reading this book. Much of my life's work and this book have been shaped by my love for reading in general and specifically by the books I read in my book club, Plato's Cave. As such, I wanted to offer you my recommended reading plan for your continued personal development. Although this book provides you with all the information you need to flourish, the reading plan is for you to take a deeper dive. In coming up with this reading plan, I was not able to include many incredible books, so my apologies to the many great authors that easily could have made the list.

Since I modeled this book after my "Dream Class," I designed this reading plan like a four-year college program, assuming you read one book a month. That's twelve books per year or forty-eight books in total. Upon completion, you would earn an honorary degree in The Art and Science of Flourishing. I will update and add to this reading list on my website at StephenPfahler.com.

Without further ado, here is my four-year reading plan:

Freshman Year:
Philosophy, Psychology, and Virtues
Apology by Plato
Man's Search for Meaning by Viktor Frankl
Self-Reliance by Ralph Waldo Emerson
Antifragile by Nassim Taleb
Harry Potter and the Sorcerer's Stone by J.K. Rowling

Health and Well-Being
Why We Sleep by Mathew Walker
Willpower by Roy Baumeister

Work
The Autobiography of Benjamin Franklin by Benjamin Franklin
The 7 Habits of Highly Effective People by Stephen Covey
The Elements of Style by William Strunk, Jr.

Relationships (Yourself, Others, and the World)
How to Win Friends and Influence People by Dale Carnegie
Love by Leo Buscaglia

Sophomore Year:
Philosophy, Psychology, and Virtues
Nicomachean Ethics by Aristotle
Flourish by Martin Seligman
Mindset by Carol Dweck
Diary of a Young Girl by Anne Frank
Heart of Darkness by Joseph Conrad

Health and Well-Being
Atomic Habits by James Clear
Eat, Move, Sleep by Tom Rath

Work
See You at the Top by Zig Ziglar
Deep Work by Cal Newport
Getting Things Done by David Allen

Relationships (Yourself, Others, and the World)
Love 2.0 by Barbara Fredrickson
To Kill a Mockingbird by Harper Lee

APPENDIX

Junior Year:
Philosophy, Psychology, and Values
The Power of Now by Eckhart Tolle
The Enchiridion (The Handbook) by Epictetus
Don Quixote by Miguel de Cervantes
Walden by Henry David Thoreau
Grit by Angela Duckworth

Health and Well-Being
Starting Strength by Mark Rippetoe
Food Fix by Dr. Mark Hyman

Work
Start with Why Action by Simon Sinek
Principles by Ray Dalio
Tomorrow's Lawyers by Richard Susskind

Relationships (Yourself, Others, and the World)
Pride and Prejudice by Jane Austen
Daring Greatly by Brené Brown

Senior Year:
Philosophy, Psychology, and Values
Meditations by Marcus Aurelius
Happier by Tal Ben-Shahar
Zorba The Greek by Nikos Kazantzakis
The Lessons of History by Will and Ariel Durant
The Republic by Plato

Health and Well-Being
It Starts with Food by Dallas and Melissa Hartwig
Play by Stuart Brown

Work

Spiritual Economics by Eric Butterworth

How to Start & Build a Law Practice by Jay Foonberg,

The Total Money Makeover by Dave Ramsey

Relationships (Yourself, Others, and the World)

The Five Love Languages by Dr. Gary Chapman

Silent Spring by Rachel Carlson

ACKNOWLEDGMENTS

• • •

Let me begin by thanking you, the reader, for taking the time to read this book. With your daily to-do lists and unending choices, I sincerely appreciate your spending some of your valuable time with me in our collective journey to live our best lives.

Next, I want to thank my great friend and co-founder of Plato's Cave, Scott Ehrlich, who was my daily Yoda in writing this book. Thanks for being my fellow philosopher and swim buddy throughout this process.

To Dan Strull, my other swim buddy in life, thank you for constantly championing me and my book. Your friendship is priceless.

I was profoundly influenced by my coach, Brian Johnson, who is founder and CEO of Optimize by Heroic and the Heroic App. His ability to turn theory into practice and to operationalize virtue was transformational in my life. If you have enjoyed this book, I highly recommend that you visit the Heroic App.

Thank you to my editor, Virginia Bhashkar, who expertly guided me through the various stages of writing this book. Her wisdom and insight as well as her kindness and thoroughness helped this book evolve from a crude first draft into a polished manuscript.

I also would like to thank the individuals who read my draft manuscript and provided input, including Lauren Anderson, Erwin Chemerinsky, Mark Divine, Sylvia Dsouza, Michelle Hiepler, Brian Johnson, Sean Johnson, Richard Lopez, Michael Moreland, Diane Pfahler, Chalak Richards, Boyd Rutherford, Kim Shapira, and Hayden Zacky. Your own life experience and expertise were more valuable and appreciated than you can know.

Thank you to Rob Price and Aimee Jenkins at Gatekeeper Press for your great help and guidance throughout the publishing process. Thanks to Duane Faitel and Gary Hewitt for all your technological expertise and assistance.

I am also grateful to my many friends and colleagues who asked about my book and provided words of encouragement. Every day you provided energy and motivation to get me to the finish line.

If I inadvertently left out any person, please accept my apology. I am keeping an on-going list of those who have impacted my life, book, and thinking in meaningful ways.

Last, but certainly not least, I want to thank my wife and family. I have an incredibly loving, caring, and wonderfully supportive wife, Jolie, who has continually encouraged me to pursue my dream of writing this book. She read, critiqued, and offered helpful suggestions for the book. Thank you for being my wife, my best friend, my support, my challenger, and the most amazing mother to our children.

I am beyond grateful to my three incredible kids—Ali, Justin, and Ryan—who have served as my inspiration and taught me so much about life. Thank you for your constant encouragement and love. Being your dad is the greatest gift in my life. A special thanks to Ryan for creating the inspirational book cover, to Ali for her expert guidance with social media, and to Justin for his wise feedback on the book.

To my mom, Pati, thank you for gifting me with your love, optimism, hope, and zest for life. To my dad, Steve, thank you for teaching and showing me what it means to be loyal, self-disciplined, and responsible, as well as how to live with integrity. To my "other mother," Diane, thank you for your love, care, and guidance, as well as for inspiring to me to pursue my passion of the English language. To my three parents and my brother, Erik, you have all been great role models and supporters, and I am the person I am today in large part because of who you are. Thank you.

To Ken and Lynn, my in-laws, thank you for being radiant exemplars of living your values and for your never-ending love, wisdom, and support.

I love my all family dearly, and this book is dedicated to you.

My greatest hope for all of you is that you flourish throughout your life!

NOTES AND REFERENCES

• • •

INTRODUCTION – THE DAY I FORGOT MY PANTS

1. ALM Intelligence: *Mental Health and Substance Abuse Survey,* May 2021.
2. *National Association of Law Placement*, Foundation Study, 2005.
3. Brown, Brené, *The Power of Vulnerability*, TEDx Houston, 2010.

THE WHOLE TRUTH

4. Dalio, Ray, *Principles: Life and Work* (Simon & Schuster 2017), p. 1.
5. Rousseau, Jean-Jacques, *The Social Contract*, 1895.
6. Gandhi, Mahatma, Speech delivered in Sewan in Hindi on 1-16-1927.

CHAPTER 1 – THE ULTIMATE OBJECTIVE OF LIFE

1. Hamilton, Alexander, *Federalist Papers #51*, 1788.
2. De Tocqueville, Alexis, *Democracy in America*, 1838.
3. *Gamet v. Blanchard*, 91 Cal.App.4th 1276, 1283, 2001.
4. Sinek, Simon, *Start with Why: How Great Leaders Inspire Everyone to Take Action,* (Portfolio 2009).
5. *Nicomachean Ethics*, 340 BC, 1097a 30-34.
6. "Happy." See Etymonline.com.
7. Maslow, Abraham, *Motivation and Personality*, Second Ed. (Harper & Row 1970).
8. Seligman, Martin, *Flourish, A Visionary New Understanding of Happiness and Well-Being* (Free Press 2011), p. 1.
9. Seligman, Martin, *Flourish, supra,* p. 13.

10. Frankl, Viktor, *Man's Search for Meaning (Beacon Press 2006)*.

11. Vujicic, Nick, *Life without Limits: Inspiration for a Ridiculously Good* Life (Double-day 2010).

CHAPTER 2 – THE RULES FOR ACHIEVING YOUR ULTIMATE PURPOSE

1. Suits, Bernard, *Ethics* Journal, Vol. 77, No. 3 (1967), p. 209.

2. Carbon sequestration means that plants draw down carbon through photosynthesis, which is then stored in the soil. This lowers the overall amount of carbon in the atmosphere, thereby reducing global climate change. See Carbon Farming: *Sequestering Carbon in Plants and Soil*, Waddington, Elizabeth, June 4, 2020, ethical.net.

3. Fredrickson, Barbara, Losada, Marcial, *Positive Affect and Complex Dynamics of Human Flourishing*, American Psychologist, 2005.

4. Aristotle, *Nicomachean Ethics*, Book 1, Chapter 7.

5. There are alternative ways to label the Flourishing Formula, including Purpose + Process + Principles. In Greek, it's Telos + Energia + Arête.

6. Aurelius, Marcus, *Meditations* 3.13.

7. Waterfield, Robin, Plato, *Phaedrus (Oxford World's Classics 2002)*.

8. Ben-Shahar, Tal, *Happier: Learn the Secrets to Daily Joy and Lasting Fulfillment* (McGraw Hill 2007).

CHAPTER 3 – APPLYING THE RULES TO LIVE OUT YOUR PURPOSE

1. *Palsgraf v. Long Island Railroad Co.*, 1928 248 N.Y. 339.

2. Frankl, Viktor, *Man's Search for Meaning, supra*.

3. Fogel, Hon. Jeremy D., *Mindfulness and Judging* (Duke Law School 2016), p. 2.

CHAPTER 4 – THE RIGHT FOUNDATION

1. *Bible*, Book of Matthew, 5:25, ENGLISH STANDARD VERSION.

CHAPTER 5 – A PURPOSE-DRIVEN LIFE

1. Covey, Stephen, *The 7 Habits of Highly Effective People* (Simon & Schuster 2013), p. 98.

2. Thompson, Nicholas, *The New Yorker, Who Shared the Electric Car?* June 13, 2014.

3. Dalio, Ray, *Principles, supra*.

4. Covey, Stephen, *The 7 Habits of Highly Effective People*, supra.

5. Herman, Tom, *Alter Ego Effect* (Harper Business 2019), p. 120.

6. Herman, Tom, *Alter Ego Effect, supra*.

7. Clear, James, *Atomic Habits: An Easy & Proven Way to Build Good Habits & Break Bad Ones* (Avery 2018).

8. Jung, Carl, *Modern Man in Search of a Soul* (Harcourt, Brace 1933).

CHAPTER 6 – THE FREEDOM TO CHOOSE

1. Frankl, Viktor, *Man's Search for Meaning, supra.*

2. Aurelius, Marcus, *Meditations*, AD 161-180.

3. Covey, Stephen, *The 7 Habits of Highly Effective People, supra.*

4. *Marbury v. Madison* 5 U.S. 137, 1803.

5. Epictetus, *The Discourses of Epictetus*, circa 108 A.D, 2.5 - 4.5.

6. Covey, Stephen, *The 7 Habits, supra.*

7. Covey, Stephen, *The 7 Habits, supra.*

8. Willink, Jocko and Babin, Leif, *Extreme Ownership: How U.S. Navy SEALs Lead and Win* (St. Martin's Press 2017).

9. Peterson, Jordan B., *12 Rules for Life: An Antidote to Chaos* (Random House 2018).

CHAPTER 7 – HAPPINESS IS A PURSUIT

1. Seligman, Martin, *Why Lawyers Are Unhappy*, 23 Cardozo Law Review 33, 52, 2001.

2. *New International Version, Bible*, James 3:2.

3. Taleb, Nassim, *Antifragile: Things That Gain from Disorder* (Random House 2012).

4. Megginson, Leon, *Lessons from Europe for American* Business, Southwestern Social Science Quarterly (1963), p. 4.

5. Peck, M. Scott, *The Road Less Traveled* (Walker 1978), *p. 1.*

6. *Brown v. Board of Education*, 347 U.S. 483, 1954.

7. Thompson, Charles, *Harlan's Great Dissent*, Brandeis School of Law Library.

8. I was particularly inspired by Stasi Eldredge's blog, "Choose Your Hard," WildAtHeart.org, July 10, 2015.

9. Dalio, Ray, *Principles, supra*, 2017.

10. Young, Sarah, *Jesus Calling*, 2004.

CHAPTER 8 – PERSONAL WELL-BEING

1. Rath, Tom, *Eat, Move, Sleep: How Small Choices Lead to Big Changes* (Mission Day 2013).

2. Graham, Tyler and Ramsey, Drew, *The Happiness Diet: A Nutritional Prescription for a Sharp Brain, Balanced Mood, and Lean, Energized Body*, 2011.

3. Ashwell, Margaret & Gibson, Sigrid, BMC Medicine, A proposal for a primary screening tool: Keep your waist circumference to less than half your weight, November 7, 2014.

4. Pollan, Michael, *Food Rules: An Eater's Manual* (2011).

5. cdc.gov/physicalactivity, 2022.

6. Rippetoe, Mark, *Starting Strength, Basic Barbell Training*, 2011 (I recommend this if you are interested in learning about weightlifting.)

7. Vernikos, Dr. Joan, *Sitting Kills, Moving Heals: How Everyday Movement Will Prevent Pain, Illness, and early Death* (Quill Driver Books 2011).

8. Walker, Matthew, *Why We Sleep: Unlocking the Power of Sleep and Dreams* (Scribner 2017).

9. Hays, Gregory, *Meditations: A New Translation, Introduction* (2003).

10. Ellis, Albert, *How to Control Your Anxiety Before It Controls You* (Citadel *2016*).

11. Marcus Aurelius Quotes, (n.d.) Goodreads. Retrieved April 15, 2022, from goodreads.com/author/quotes.

12. Etymonline.com/word/resilience, retried on April 15, 2022.

13. Hillenbrand, Lauren, *Unbroken: A World War II Story of Survival, Resilience and Redemption* (Random House 2010).

14. Definitions.net/definition/equanimity, Retrieved on April 15, 2022.

15. Quotecatalog.com/quote/nelson-mandela, Retrieved on April 15, 2022.

16. Seligman, Martin, *Why Lawyers are Unhappy*, 23 Cardozo Law Rev. 33, 40, 2001.

17. Seligman, Martin, *Flourish*, supra, p. 16.

18. Goggins, David, *Can't Hurt Me: Master Your Mind and Defy the Odds* (Lioncrest Publishing 2018).

19. Goodreads.com/quotes/82838, Retrieved April 15, 2022.

20. Daily Stoic.com/trust-yourself, retrieved on April 20, 2022, quoting from Seneca's essay on tranquility.

21. Das, Ratan, *The Global Vision of Mahatma Gandhi*, p. 192.

22. Quotefancy.com/quote/22401/Mother-Teresa, Retrieved on April 20, 2022.

CHAPTER 9 – WORK

1. Gibran, Kahlil, *The Prophet* (Penguin Classics 2019).

2. Goodreads.com/quotes/21405, by Martin Luther King, Jr., Retrieved on April 20, 2022.

3. Gibran, Kahlil, *The Prophet, supra.*

4. Collins, Jim, *Good to Great: Why Some Companies Make the Leap and Others Don't* (2011).

5. King, Jr., Martin Luther, *Where Do We Go from Here?,* Aug. 16, 1967.

6. For an excellent discussion of this quote and concept, see Cal Newport's book, *So Good They Can't Ignore You,* 2012.

7. Newport, Cal, *So Good They Can't Ignore You: Why Skills Trump Passion in the Quest for Work You Love* (Grand Central Publishing 2012).

8. Gerber, Michael, *The E-Myth Attorney: Why Most Legal Practices Don't Work and What to Do About It,* (2010), p. 40.

9. Deutschle, Susan, *Law Firm Retention Strategies,* Columbus Business First, 2007.

10. Stein, Ben, *Capitalist Code: It Can Save Your Life and Make You Very Rich* (2017).

11. Robin, Vicki, Dominguez, Joe, *Your Money or Your Life: 9 Steps to Transforming Your Relationship with Money and Achieving Financial Independence* (Penguin Books 2008).

CHAPTER 10 – RELATIONSHIPS WITH OTHERS

1. Brown, Brené, *Daring Greatly: How the Courage to be Vulnerable Transforms the Way We Live, Love, Parent, and Lead* (Avery 2012).

2. Fredrickson, Barbara, *Love 2.0: Finding Happiness and Health in Moments of Connection* (2013).

3. Brown, Brené, *The Gifts of Imperfectionism: Let Go of Who You Think You're Supposed to Be, supra.*

4. Inc.com article, Curtin, Melanie, *This 75-Year Harvard Study Found the 1 Secret to Leading a Fulfilling Life.*

5. Brown, Brené, *Daring Greatly: How the Courage to be Vulnerable, supra.*

6. Branden, Nathaniel, *The Six Pillars of Self-Esteem* (1995).

7. Brown, Brené, *The Gifts of Imperfection: Let Go of Who You Think You're Supposed to Be, supra.*

8. Millman, Dan, *Body Mind Mastery: Training for Sport and Life: Creating Success in Sports and Life* (1999).

9. Gottman, John, *The Seven Principles for Making Marriage Work* (2015).

10. Sears, William and Sears, Martha, *Everything You Need to Know About Your Baby from Birth to Age Two* (2013).

11. Gregston, Mark, *Tough Guys and Drama Queens: How Not to Get Blindsided by Your Child's Teen Years* (2012).

12. Gregston, Mark, *Tough Guys and Drama Queens, supra.*

13. Rogers, Fred, *Many Ways to Say I Love You* (2006).

14. Aristotle, *Nicomachean Ethics*, 1156b07-08.

15. Smith-Lovin, Flynn, Wilson, Robert, *Social Isolation in America: Changes in Core Discussion Networks Over Two Decades*, American Sociological Review, 2006.

16. Carnegie, Dale, *How to Win Friends and Influence People* (1936).

17. Buscaglia, Leo, *Love: What Life is All About* (1996).

18. Fredrickson, Barbara, *Love 2.0: Finding Happiness, supra.*

19. Pope Francis, *Ten Rules to Live Long*, 2014.

20. Carnegie, Dale, *How to Win Friends, supra.*

CHAPTER 11 – RE-CREATE

1. Covey, Stephen, *The 7 Habits of Highly Effective People, supra.*

2. *European Heart Journal*, May 12, 2010.

3. Sciencedaily.com, citing *World Related stress a risk factor for type 2 diabetes*, German Research Centre for Environmental Health, 2014.

4. Silva, Jose, Godman, Burt, *Silva Mind Control Method of Mental Dynamics* (Gallery Books 2022).

5. Stulberg, Brad, Magness, Steve, *Peak Performance: Elevate Your Game, Avoid Burnout, and Thrive with the New Science of Success* (2017).

6. von Oech, Roger, *A Whack on the Side of the Head: How You can be More Creative* (1998).

7. Brown, Stuart, *Play: How it Shapes the Brain, Opens the Imagination, and Invigorates the Soul* (2009).

8. Gray, Peter, *Free to Learn: Why Unleashing the Instinct to Play will Make Our Children Happier, More Self-Reliant, and Better Students for Life* (2013).

CHAPTER 12 – PRIORITIZE

1. Kiev, Ari, *A Strategy for Daily Living* (Free Press 2008).

2. Forbes.com, *How to Set Goals (And Why You Should Write Them Down*, by Annabel Acton, Nov. 3, 2017.

3. The Wilmington Patch, *103-Year-Old South Shore Woman Shares Secret to Long Life*, 11/18/19.

4. Collins, Jim, *Built to Last: Successful Habits of Visionary Companies* (1994).

5. Koch, Richard, *The 80 /20 Principle: The Secret to Achieving More with Less* (1999).

6. Ferriss, Timothy, *The 4-Hour Workweek* (Harmony 2009).

CHAPTER 13 – PLAN

1. Adams, Scott, *How to Fail at Almost Everything and Still Win Big* (Portfolio 2013).

2. Hardy, Darren, *Compound Effect* (2021).

3. Newport, Cal, *Deep Work: Rules for Focused Success in a Distracted World* (Grand Central Publishing 2016).

4. Sciencedaily.com, National Sleep Foundation, *Sleepy Connected Americans*, March 11, 2011.

5. Divine, Mark, *The Way of the SEAL: Think Like an Elite Warrior to Lead and Succeed* (Trusted Media Brands 2013).

6. Morath, E., *The 5-Hour Workday Gets Put to the Test*, Wall Street Journal, 10/24/19.

7. Keller, Gary, *The One Thing: The Surprisingly Simple Truth About Extraordinary Results* (2013).

8. Keller, Gary, *The One Thing, supra*, p. 201.

9. Siegel, Dan, *Mindsight: The New Science of Personal Transformation* (2010).

10. Morris, Tom, *The Art of Achievement* (2013).

CHAPTER 14 – TAKE ACTION

1. Wikipedia, Alabama Crimson Tide Football under Nick Saban 2022.

2. Bassham, Lanny, *Winning in Mind: The Mental Management System* (Bookpartners 2012).

3. Star Wars Movie, Episode I, *The Phantom Menace*, 1999.

4. Tolle, Eckhart, *The Power of Now: A Guide to Spiritual Enlightenment* (2010), p. 35.

5. Tolle, Eckhart, *The Power of Now, supra*, p. 59.

6. Kazantzakis, Nikos, *Zorba the Greek* (1965).

7. Kazantzakis, Nikos, *Zorba, supra*.

8. Keane, Bill, *Family Circus*, 8/31/1994.

9. Cohen, Judi, *Warrior One*, 2020.

10. Seligman, Martin, *Flourishing, supra*, p. 11.

11. Pink, Daniel, *Drive: The Surprising Truth About What Motivates Us* (2011).

CHAPTER 15 – CHARACTER AND VIRTUE

1. Wooden, John, *Wooden: A Lifetime of Observations and Reflections On and Off the Court*, (Contemporary Books 1997).
2. Franklin, Benjamin, *The Autobiography of Benjamin Franklin* (1791).
3. Peterson, Christopher, Seligman, Martin, *Character Strengths and Virtues: A Handbook and Classification* (2004).
4. Parr, Ellen, *Reader's Digest*, December 1980.
5. Heroic.us/optimize/quotes/john-wooden, retrieved April 26, 2022.
6. Goodreads.com/quotes/392581, retrieved April 26, 2022.
7. Library.cod.edu/BHM/daily/Katherine-Dunham, retrieved on April 26, 2022.
8. Book of James 1:4, New International Version.
9. Divine, Mark, *Staring Down the Wolf* (St. Martin's Press 2020).
10. Franklin, Ben, *The Autobiography of Benjamin Franklin, supra*.

CHAPTER 16 – EXCELLENCE AND MASTERY

1. Stein, Jr., Alan, *Raise Your Game: High Performance Secrets from the Best of the Best* (Center Street 2020).
2. Sports Illustrated, *Tom Seaver and the Enduring Hope of the 1969 Mets*, by Tom Verducci, October 23, 2019.
3. DailyStoic.com/we-are-what-we-repeatedly-do, Retrieved April 26, 2022.
4. Dailymail.co.uk/news/article-2025064, *Don't Mess with Keiko! 98-year-old Judo master becomes first woman to earn highest-level black belt*, August 12, 2011.
5. Ericsson, Anders and Pool, Robert, *Peak: Secrets from the New Science of Expertise* (2016).
6. Duckworth, Angela, *Grit: The Power of Passion and Perseverance* (Scribner 2016).
7. Dweck, Carol, *Mindset: The New Psychology of Success* (Random House 2006).
8. Dalio, Ray, *Principles, supra*, 2017.

CONCLUSION – THE FINAL VERDICT AND THE NEXT CASE

1. Jobs, Steve, *Stanford Commencement Speech*, 2005.
2. Jobs, Steve, *Stanford Commencement Speech, supra*.
3. Chekov, Anton, *Rothschild's Fiddle* (The Great Books Foundation 1985).
4. This last paragraph is how we essentially close every meeting of our Plato's Cave book group: "As we continue our journey in life, let us never forget the lessons we learn in Plato's Cave. May this ever-growing wisdom serve as our guiding light, so we don't just live, but live well and flourish."

ABOUT

• • •

Stephen Pfahler has served as a Superior Court Judge for the State of California for the past sixteen years. As a judge, he has primarily handled civil and criminal cases in Los Angeles County, the largest county court system in the world. Prior to that, he practiced law for over sixteen years and was recognized as a Super Lawyer.

Judge Pfahler served for six years as Police Commissioner for the City of Calabasas. He also currently teaches Public Policy and the Law as an adjunct professor at the University of Southern California.

Combining his love for the law with his other passion for helping people optimize their lives, Pfahler became a certified life coach, studied Positive Psychology from the University of Pennsylvania, and strongly advocates for lawyer well-being. He also serves on the Mindfulness and Wellness Committee for the California Judges Association.

Pfahler lives in Los Angeles, California, with his wife, three kids, and dog.

CPSIA information can be obtained
at www.ICGtesting.com
Printed in the USA
LVHW080646230822
726585LV00006B/248